RIVER OF NO REPRIEVE

Descending Siberia's Waterway
of Exile, Death, and Destiny

JEFFREY TAYLER

HOUGHTON MIFFLIN COMPANY

Boston · New York · 2006

For information about permission to reproduce selections from this book, write to Permissions, Houghton Mifflin Company, 215 Park Avenue South, New York, New York 10003.

Visit our Web site: www.houghtonmifflinbooks.com.

Library of Congress Cataloging-in-Publication Data
Tayler, Jeffrey.
River of no reprieve : descending Siberia's waterway of exile, death, and destiny / Jeffrey Tayler.
    p. cm.
ISBN-13: 978-0-618-53909-3
ISBN-10: 0-618-53909-3
1. Siberia (Russia) — Description and travel. 2. Tayler, Jeffrey — Travel — Russia (Federation) — Siberia. I. Title.
DK756.2.T39 2006
915.704'86 — dc22   2005024728

Book design by Melissa Lotfy

Printed in the United States of America

MP 10 9 8 7 6 5 4 3 2 1

NOTE: Certain names and minor identifying characteristics have been changed to protect the privacy of people described in this book. Specifically, the names Alina and Sasha in Chapter 1; Luka in Chapter 3; Olga, Katya, and Vera in Chapter 14; Vova, Eduard, and Sanya in Chapter 18; Petrov in Chapter 19; and Klara in Chapter 20 are pseudonyms.

TO MY FATHER

A Note on Transliteration

When transliterating Russian place names and nouns without accepted English spellings, I have used an apostrophe to indicate the Russian letter *myagkiy znak* (soft sign), which palatizes the preceding consonant and for which there is no English equivalent.

The names of most Russian rulers and other famous people from the past are conventionally anglicized, and I have preferred these forms to the Russian. Hence, when referring to tsars, I write Basil III for Vasily III and Michael for Mikhail. However, for lesser-known or more contemporary figures, I have retained the Russian, as is now customary in the press. By this convention, the first name of the former president Gorbachev is Mikhail, not Michael.

I ask the reader's indulgence for any inconsistencies that may occur.

The Cossacks created Russia.

Tout notre raisonnement se réduit à céder au sentiment.

Al pasar bajo del arco de la eternidad, en la suprema comprensión de nuestra vida mortal, está el premio y está el castigo.

Black raven, why do you spread your claws above my head?
Black raven, you won't get me!

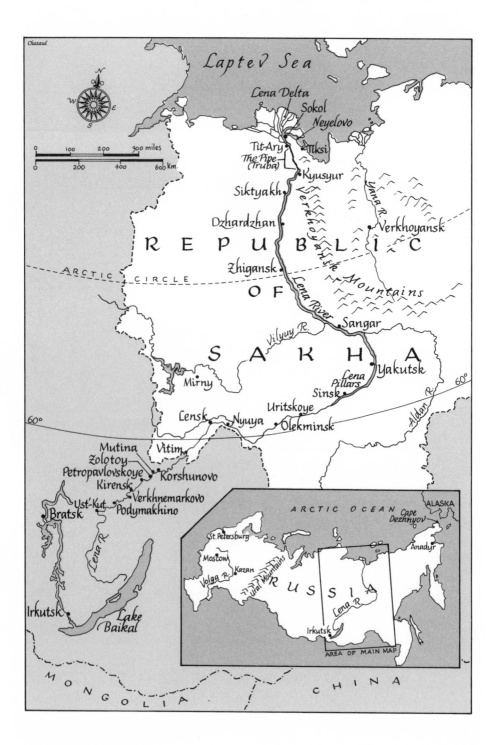

PROLOGUE

Birth of an Empire. The Midnight Lands and
the Great River. Destiny Manifest, Destiny Personal.

THE TYRANT WAS DERANGED, and, like other idolized monarchs to come in his country's history, a mass murderer of his own subjects. Beginning in 1565, Ivan the Terrible, the first ruler crowned Tsar of All Russia, dispatched the *oprichniki*, his private army of six thousand assassins, garbed in black capes and mounted on black horses, throughout his kingdom to slaughter his opponents, real or imagined, and seize their estates. Potentially rivalrous relatives and nobles, peasants and tradesmen and townsmen, even priests and archbishops and the Metropolitan of Russia, all perished at the *oprichniki*'s swords. During five weeks in 1570, in Novgorod alone, till then Russia's star democratic city-state (its northern location allowed it to escape the ravages of Tatar-Mongolian invaders), the *oprichniki*, with Ivan's personal participation, hacked apart, drowned, boiled alive, or strangled three thousand Russians in savage public orgies of bloodshed and mayhem. Others, the luckiest, were forced through show trials, pronounced guilty, and imprisoned or banished. Yet after the butchery, Ivan repented lavishly at the altar, begging God to show mercy on his victims' souls. Possibly he knew he was mad, unbalanced as a child by a regency during which palace nobles demeaned and humiliated him, schemed to usurp his power, and may have poisoned his mother, but historians still debate the motives for his atrocities. One thing is certain, though: Ivan the Terrible united under the Kremlin's control a Russia that Tatar-Mongolian warriors had occupied, divided, and dominated since the mid-1300s.

In 1581 Ivan swung his staff in a fit of rage and felled his son (and heir to the throne). Three years later the tsar died, gaunt and hairless, broken by grief and madness, possibly poisoned. Although his massacres left once thriving stretches of Russia "vacant and desolate without any inhabitant" (in the words of a contemporary British traveler), Ivan believed himself to be exercising a divinely sanctioned absolutism; by murdering his subjects and consolidating his power, he was carrying out God's will in accordance with the doctrine of caesaropapism that he had inherited from his father, Basil III (who himself had imported it from the Byzantine Greeks). The changes he wrought on Russia proved manifold and lasting. By destroying autonomous nobles, replacing proud princes with cringing loyalists, making land ownership depend on fealty to the crown, and subjugating the church, he founded autocratic traditions of governance that persist in Russia to this day. He pressed the gentry into the military and reformed the army. He promulgated a new code of laws, and, most significantly for the greater part of his population (and subsequent centuries of Russian history), he entrenched serfdom throughout his domain, ensuring that, until emancipation came in 1861, most Russians would live and die as slaves, either to nobles (themselves lackeys to the tsars) or to state enterprises of one sort or another.

Nevertheless, for casting off the Tatar-Mongolian yoke, a majority of Russians of the time, as far as we know, adored Ivan the Terrible as much as they feared him. The horrific methods by which he ruled — mass executions, mass deportations, mass expropriation, mass enslavement, and the totalitarian regulation of public life — would also distinguish the reigns of Russia's other most redoubtable yet revered despots, Peter the Great and Joseph Stalin.

Yet it was Ivan's launching of costly expansionist wars (requiring more subjects to tax, new lands to exploit) that would truly transform Russia and ultimately define its role in history, its place among nations. In the sixteenth century Russia was poised to shed its identity as Rus', a European state of Eastern Slavs, and become Russia, a country that would be ruled by a majority Russian population but comprise more than one hundred ethnic groups on two continents, practicing not only Orthodox Christianity but also Judaism, Islam, Shamanism, and Buddhism. Muscovy and other north Russian principalities, most notably that of Novgorod, had already penetrated the European Arctic, taking advantage of the isolation that distance and cold afforded them from Tatar-Mongolian overlords, whose presence was strongest in the warmer and more fertile regions of the south, in what today is Ukraine. Basil III had beaten back the Poles and Lithuanians to push Russia's European border to the west. Ivan, however, set his people marching east toward a Russian version of Manifest Destiny, using, in 1552, his newly formed units of *strel'tsy* (musketeers) to crush the Muslim Tatar khanate of Kazan, on the Volga, and open up a land route east to the Urals.

As far back as the eleventh century, a few intrepid Russians had trekked over the far northern foothills of the Urals to settle and trade, but they lacked a practicable southern route to follow into the greater part of what they called, owing to the latitude's hibernal polar nights, the *polunochnyye strany,* or "midnight lands" east of the mountains. Russians already suspected that these lands abounded in "soft gold" (furs), as well as precious walrus tusk (*rybiy zub,* or "fish tooth"), the ivory of that era. Enter the Stroganovs, a merchant family operating just west of the Urals. In the 1580s the Stroganovs, with the support of Ivan the Terrible, marshaled forces and smashed through the last Muslim kingdom blocking the way east of the Urals, the khanate of Sibir' — Siberia, or "sleeping land" in the Mongol-Altaic language and, thenceforth, in Russian.

With the defeat of the khanate of Sibir', the Kremlin's annexation of Siberia commenced in earnest. Russia's Manifest Destiny would consist of the slogging progress of *zemleprokhodtsy* ("traversers of land," the equivalent of America's settlers) across a boundless, mostly flat realm of boreal forest, bog, tundra, and Arctic desert covering 8.7 million square miles — the greatest contiguous land mass on earth, the pristine abode of the bear and the wolf, the reindeer and the wolverine. Siberia's pervasive ice, cold, and blizzards would shape the Russian character; and among the *zemleprokhodtsy* numbered the towering heroes who would come to embody the best and, at times, the worst of Russia, the Cossacks.

Most of Siberia is so inhospitable that few, at least initially, would move there readily. But the serfdom and misery that Ivan the Terrible spread incited mass migration south and east, into terrain where his oppressive state could hardly reach. The Stroganovs' soldiers, and Siberia's foremost explorers, would be the Cossacks, originally equestrian warriors of Russia's lawless southern steppes. A spirited people of Slavic and Scythian blood, augmented by growing numbers of renegade serfs and refugees from the Kremlin's despotism, the Cossacks accepted the tsars' grant of autonomy (they elected their own leaders in rowdy popular assemblies) in return for military service protecting Russian borderlands from the raids of Tatars, Turks, and other nomads now long vanished. The Cossacks' courage, discipline, and military prowess became legend, as did their fanatical devotion to Orthodox Christianity, and, eventually, to the tsars. They strove to bring ever more Siberian lands under their sovereign's control, and fill his coffers with *yasak* (a tax in furs) extracted from the region's few native peoples.

By 1587 the Cossacks had reached the Irtysh River, in central Siberia, and built Tobolsk on its reedy banks. Soon thereafter they made it to the Yenisey. Then, in 1619, the first Romanov tsar, Michael (a descendant of Ivan the Terrible), outlawed sailing along Siberia's northern coast, fearing that Cossack mariners might inadvertently alert Russia's commercial competitors, Holland and England, to a sea route from the Occident to the Orient. After that, to explore Siberia beyond the Yenisey, the Cossacks would have to sail its multitudinous rivers. As guides to the maze of waterways the Cossacks relied often on sparse, basically peaceful populations of indigenous Yakuts and Evenks — Asiatic, seminomadic reindeer herders and breeders of cattle.

Lured by rumors of forests rich in sable and ermine along a giant river called, in Yakut, Ölyüne ("Lena," in Russian), the Cossack chieftain Panteley Pyanda departed Yeniseysk in 1619, leading a band of forty adventurers, heading east. Four years later they reached the Lena, eastern Siberia's largest waterway. The Lena originates in a spring-nourished mountain pond just west of Lake Baikal and flows 2,734 miles north to debouch into the Laptev Sea on the Arctic Ocean. The river's bounty in "soft gold" astonished its discoverers, and Russians would come to refer to it as *Velikaya Reka Lena,* or the Great Lena River. More Cossacks, traders, and peasants followed, "as if seized by a fever" in the words of one historian, establishing on the Lena in 1632 an *ostrog* (stockaded town) that they would call Ust'-Kut, almost three thousand miles east of Moscow. Furs collected as Siberian *yasak* eventually totaled half the wealth in the Kremlin's treasury. From new Slavic arrivals in Ust'-Kut Cossacks collected other taxes that, in their array and onerousness, reflected the mercantile spirit firing Russia's eastward spread.

Amazingly, once encamped in Ust'-Kut, the Cossacks found that they still had a lot of Siberian territory left to explore, annex, and put in the service of their tsar. In search of more *yasak* and "fish tooth," Cossacks ventured down the Lena and its tributaries out into the Arctic and Pacific oceans, sailed through the channel dividing Asia from North America, and thereby delineated Russia's easternmost boundaries. Cape Dezhnyov, Russia's easternmost tip (just fifty-three miles from Alaska), bears the surname of the Cossack chieftain Semyon who in 1648 first navigated the strait, preceding by eight decades the Danish explorer Vitus Bering after which it would be (unjustly) named. It is even possible that some of Dezhnyov's men found themselves shipwrecked on Alaska's shores.

By initiating the annexation of Siberia, Ivan the Terrible and the Cossacks facilitated Russia's transformation from a middle-size European state into the largest country on earth, a Eurasian superpower with ports on seven seas covering, during the Soviet days, one-sixth of the planet's land surface. Today, diminished by the loss of its satellite republics, but thanks to Siberia, Russia still stretches some seven thousand miles east to west and almost three thousand miles north to south — enough terrain to accommodate roughly twice the territory of the United States, including Alaska and Hawaii. Siberia, of course, would eventually yield a trove of resources far more precious than "fish tooth" and furs, including gold, diamonds, uranium, and, crucially, now, natural gas (of which it holds one-third of the world's supply) and oil. Beneath Siberia's permafrost lie the bulk of Russia's 72 billion barrels of estimated petroleum reserves (the seventh largest on earth) and fourteen of its seventeen fields of natural gas. Oil alone accounts for 45 percent of modern Russia's export revenues — in 2003 Russia surpassed Saudi Arabia in barrels pumped — and finances 20 percent of its federal budget.

During the century it took for Russia to realize its Manifest Destiny, the Cossacks and the tsars had only an imperfect grasp of Siberia's true bounty, but one thing is certain: the Lena River would serve as the watery highway down which Russia would travel to superpower status.

. . .

When I first saw the Lena in April of 1993, it was under the wheels of the truck taking me across Siberia, covered by an eight-foot-thick layer of ice. (Like many Siberian rivers during the cold months, the Lena freezes thick enough to serve as a *zimnik*, a road passable only in *zima*, or winter.) But the ice was almost as blue as the sky, and I conceived a yearning to travel by ferry from Ust'-Kut to Yakutsk, about halfway down the river, when it would be bare and beautiful, bathed in light that would show it at its best — the soft and delicate light of summer's white nights. I knew that two of the Russian hinterland's main problems, alcoholism and poverty, would make such a cruise less than tranquil — but then, tranquility is not one of Russia's virtues. I finally made that trip in the year 2000, but the many inebriated passengers, to say nothing of the village debauches (entire families, drunken all, bawling on shore during farewells to teenage conscripts leaving for service in the army), diesel fumes, and chugging engine, left me pleased to get off the boat.

Still, the Lena stayed with me, haunting my waking hours and dreams with visions of midnight skies burning red with the sun's falling phaeton, with vistas of mists wafting in staggered skeins across pine-blanketed mountains, with remembrances of silvered currents mirroring a shifting tableau of sugary cloud and lapis lazuli sky. When I chanced to find myself in the woods outside Moscow, I found I could close my eyes and inhale, and, intoxicated by the scent of birch sap on the breeze, almost imagine myself alone on the Lena, a speck of a human amid Siberia's incomparably vast wilds. Those wilds, I sensed, had something to teach me; they proffered a sort of personal liberation, a cleansing of the floss and dross of civilization that accumulates even in the life of a writer who spends six months a year on the road, though mostly in cities and towns.

It might seem ironic to seek liberation along the Lena, considering what had happened to Russia since my first glimpse of its blue ice back in 1993. Then, Russia's grim present seemed to be giving way to a promising albeit chaotic future, when something akin to progress and democracy would occur — *had* to occur. After all, Eastern Europe was transforming itself, so why shouldn't Russia? But in the eleven years that followed my cross-Siberian odyssey, the country had suffered calamity after regression, disaster after debacle: under the glazed eyes of a besotted if probably well-intentioned president, the *mafiya* took over trade; gunfire resolved murky business disputes and luminaries of Russian society fell victim to unsolved murders; the Kremlin shelled the parliament to suppress an insurrection and twice embarked on ruinous wars in Chechnya that did little more than expose the corruption and decline of a once powerful military. Rigged auctions left most of Russia's oil and gas industries in the hands of venal insiders; the economy collapsed in 1998 and the currency devalued. When in 2000 President Vladimir Putin, a former KGB agent, was elected to his first term in office, promising a "dictatorship of the law," masses of Russians rejoiced, but the countrywide spiral downward continued, obscured only by high oil prices that created an atmosphere of stability while little was being built and capital continued to flee. Yet the war in Chechnya dragged on, hostage-takings and bomb blasts shattered Putin's promises of security, and the Kremlin turned on those who would report the truth, strangulating the independent media and lashing out at potential rivals. Putin spoke often of restoring the state, but for Russians, the state, since Ivan the Terrible's days, had always been the problem, never the answer.

Yet, Putin won reelection in 2004. This prompted me to reflect on the worldview I had imbibed during eleven years in Russia. Yes, it is a *worldview,* for Russia is more a world apart than a country, isolated from the West by daunting distances, a history of state-orchestrated violence against its own citizens, a perduring culture of institutionalized injustice and deceit, and an obsession with finding a "Russian" way based on great power status. In Russia one loves family and friends, and distrusts, even fears, one's neighbors and strangers, whom one frequently dismisses as *bydlo* (cattle). Loyalty is primary, connections everything, and family and friends deserve favor above all others. The government is predatory; politicians and bureaucrats are on the take, striving not to serve their country but to keep their *mordy* (snouts) in the *kormushka* (feeding trough). Life is grief, thieves get rich, the honest stay poor. A central authority — once the tsar, later the general secretary of the Communist Party, and now the president — must rule dictatorially to ensure citizens of if not prosperity then at least equality in poverty; communal misery, not individual success, is the unstated but shared desideratum. Order and security flow from autocracy, from the "iron fist" of the ruler, and take precedence over freedom; in fact, the harsher the ruler is with his "herd," the better, and if he commits "excesses" and the innocent suffer, well, as Stalin said, *"Les rubyat, shchepki letyat"* (When you cut down a forest, splinters will fly). Freedom and democracy are shams, or, if real, they function only in the West, not in Russia, where "the rules are different," where human nature has suffered a meltdown and remolding under the blowtorch of a unique history. The Westernizing "reforms" that came after 1991 were an elaborate plot hatched by the West (in particular, the United States) to destroy Russia as a superpower. If Russia is to be saved, the prevailing mood now dictates, a new *Terrible* ruler must emerge, one who will jail the bandits, hunt down the thugs, and rule autocratically but justly.

Grudgingly, I admit that I myself have accepted much of this worldview. Russia is an exacting taskmaster, a bludgeoning educator, and those who suffer under its tutelage here cannot retain their naïveté and illusions — delusions — for long and survive. Yet I cannot imagine my life without Russia, and neither do I want to. If the country has, at times, almost taken my life, it has also made me a writer and given me a wife; its heroes, among them the Cossacks, have provided me with almost superhuman exemplars of fortitude and courage. But as Russia steps back to autocracy, a mode of governance that led it to disaster in the past and could offer it nothing in the future, and, as well-publicized statistical indicators portend a population decline unprecedented in peacetime (Russia, thanks to calamitous birth, mortality, and disease rates, will probably shrink demographically by a third by 2050), I was seized by a desire to find out what had gone wrong. Had I really devoted my life to a doomed land?

To find answers, and suspecting they lay in Russia's parturition from Rus', I knew I would have to leave Moscow, a city-state where 10 million of Russia's 143 million live, where 80 percent of Russia's capital is parked, and where a tiny, Western-oriented elite has pushed for liberal reform, alienated from the masses living beyond the giant muddy highways ringing the city. The contrast between the increasingly affluent lifestyle of Muscovites and the deepening impoverishment of rural Russia continues to grow and buttresses the argument that to understand the country one has to leave the capital and head for the hinterland, among whose inhabitants Putin enjoys his strongest support.

The Lena came to mind. The villagers, settlers, descendants of exiles, and indigenous peoples along its banks represent a distillate of Russia's outback masses. In tsarist Russia, the Lena functioned as a watery highway into an icebound hell of forced labor and exile, shackles and grief, where revolutionaries, Trotsky and the Decembrists among them, passed sentences along remote shores. A ukase issued by Ivan the Terrible in 1582 proclaimed exile a legal form of punishment in Russia, but the 1917 Bolshevik coup led by Lenin ushered in the Lena's most tragic era, when Stalin, especially during the Great Terror of the 1930s, dispatched millions to hard labor and death in Siberia. (During his rule, some 25 million Russians were arrested, and 18.5 million passed through the gulags.) Countless barges carried inmates from Ust'-Kut — once the Soviet Union's busiest inland port — to the five gulags on the river's banks, where they logged larches and firs, mined gold and diamonds, and even fished to feed the military and proletariat back west. In fact, with thirty-six labor camps scattered across northeastern Siberia, the Lena was nothing less than the trunk route of the world's largest natural prison. After Stalin died, Soviet leaders mostly replaced forced-labor schemes with incentive-based plans to exploit the region, but these collapsed with the fall of the Soviet Union in 1991.

I began mulling over the idea of a partial recreation, by small boat, of Cossack exploratory journeys down the Lena, starting in June 2004 at Ust'-Kut, where rapids end and navigation begins, and finishing, I projected, two months later, 2,400 miles to the north, in Tiksi, on the shores of the Laptev Sea. My research uncovered daunting geographic and climatic facts that had barely concerned me when I was taking the ferry downriver in 2000. North of Mongolia and Manchuria, draining an area as large as Spain, France, and all the countries of Eastern Europe combined, and fed by five hundred tributaries, the Lena is the tenth longest river in the world, and the third longest in Russia. It flows down from the Baikal Mountains through the taiga of the Siberian Plateau into the boggy lowlands and tundra of the Republic of Sakha (known as Yakutia until 1991, and one of Russia's main ethnic entities) to empty, through a broad delta, into the stormy Laptev Sea, a bay of the Arctic Ocean, some 450 miles above the Arctic Circle — a course through barrens that even now are largely terra incognita and are usually represented on maps as blank green expanses veined with rivers bearing the obscurest, most inscrutable of appellations, even to

Russians' ears. Neither the Gulf Stream nor the Japan Current warms the region, and nearly ubiquitous permafrost runs as deep as five thousand feet. Six hundred miles east of the Lena's banks lies the coldest inhabited place on the planet, the former Stalinist gulag mining settlement of Oymyakon, where −95.8 degrees is the official record. Four hundred miles east of the river's last northern curve is Verkhoyansk, where the greatest known temperature variations occur; Soviet meteorologists have recorded both −90 and 105 degrees. Sakha, thus, has the severest climate of any permanently inhabited region on earth.

During spring thaws the river floods lethally, rising thirty to sixty feet above winter levels and sweeping away homes and people. Since the upper Lena thaws before its lower reaches, gigantic jams of ice form that at times the Russian government has to break up with explosives. The last 150 miles before the delta have been dubbed the *Truba* (the Pipe); there, sheer cliffs, rushing currents, rough waters, and Arctic squalls were said to make the river too dangerous for anything but barges; and even they have to sit out spells of violent weather or risk being cracked in two by giant waves.

Most of Siberia's oil and gas are in the well-connected west, not in the untrammeled east, where getting around can be perilous and is rendered even tougher by bureaucratic hurdles. I faced a host of paper problems in planning my voyage. After a few years of post-Soviet openness, Moscow and the Republic of Sakha reimposed restrictions on foreigners' access to much of the region. I thus found myself compelled to appeal for help to a well-placed intermediary, my friend and polar adventurer Dmitry Shparo, who wrestled permits for my journey from the authorities of Sakha and a triad of suspicious Russian agencies: the Federal Security Service (the successor to the KGB), the Border Guards, and the Foreign Ministry. Dmitry also found me my guide, a thirty-seven-year-old Muscovite named Vadim Alekseyev. Beefy-shouldered, with a pig-iron grip and the piercing blue-eyed gaze of a fanatic, Vadim, a former dentist, spends six months a year adventuring in the Russian far north, enduring of his own volition the foul meteorological stew of blizzard, ice, rain, and gale that Stalin's victims suffered as punishment. Vadim had never seen the Lena, but Dmitry and I decided that if anyone could get me from Ust'-Kut to Tiksi, he could. Vadim warned me of desperate villagers and hungry bears, corrupt officials, and sudden storms that could capsize us in icy water; above the Arctic Circle, even in the brief six weeks of summer, temperatures could drop below freezing. We did discover one saving aspect to the Lena's remoteness: it is the only major Russian waterway flowing unimpeded by dams or hydroelectric stations; nowhere save at Ust'-Kut does a proper road reach its banks, and the dearth of industry in the region leaves its waters clean enough to drink untreated. I thrilled to this fact, which bespoke the primal liberation I so desired from the journey.

Cossacks plied the Lena in *kochi* — ice-breaking, high-gunwaled ships of pine outfitted with sails of canvas and reindeer hide. We, however, would travel in a modern craft built to Vadim's specifications: an arrow-shaped, seventeen-by-five-foot inflatable raft of canvas and rubber that could carry a ton of freight. We would need this capacity. Gasoline is rare along the river, so half of our 1,500-pound load would consist of fuel; most of the rest of it would be provisions and gear, including Vadim's double-barreled shotgun, always kept loaded. ("You never know who or what might step out of the taiga uninvited," he told me.) A four-horsepower motor (which offered the optimum balance between speed and fuel consumption) would propel us. To be safe, Vadim had equipped the bow and midsection with a tie-down tarp that would hold our supplies aboard if we capsized — possible given the Arctic storms we expected during the trip's second half. Our life jackets would be useful as seat cushions, nothing more. "The cold water and waves," he said with a smirk I found as disturbing as it was, at the time, incomprehensible, "will kill us long before we can make shore."

Clothes, like the weather, could be a matter of life or death for us on the Lena, even in summer, as it was for the Cossacks. (Especially when dowsed in cold water, travelers can die from hypothermia even in temperatures above freezing.) In summer, like most Russian peasants, Cossacks dressed in a loose long-sleeved shirt called a *rubakha* and baggy *sharovary* trousers, held up with a sash, and were shod in basted *lapti*. In winter, to withstand the −90-degree frosts, they would wrap their feet in *onuchi* (lengths of coarse wool) and over them don *valenki* (knee-high felt boots). Atop the *rubakha* and *sharovary,* they would wear an ankle-length *shuba* (fur coat, preferably sable) or a sheepskin *tulup.* A tall, conical sheepskin hat known as a *papakha* or a *kolpak* would keep the head warm, as would an abundant beard. Synthetic materials, waterproof or at least quick-drying, would make our clothing much less cumbersome, and more effective (or so I thought).

In tsarist times, most prisoners were marched in fettered phalanxes east out of Moscow for a year, two years, down the infamous *Kandal'ny Trakt* (Road of Shackles), across the Urals, east, ever east, until the survivors (10 to 15 percent died en route of disease, exhaustion, or trying to escape) reached the Lena and boarded barges for points of exile downriver. Their chains, which bound hands and ankles, weighed five pounds; identifying marks were branded onto their legs and arms with hot irons (some escapees hacked off limbs or doused themselves in acid to rid themselves of the marks); and they suffered repeated beatings by guards. Vadim and I would face no such difficulties in reaching Siberia. We agreed that I would fly to the town of Bratsk (which has the nearest airport to Ust'-Kut) in mid-June, and Vadim would arrive a couple of days later with all our gear aboard the Moscow-Severobaikalsk Express — a cross-country ride providing solitude that, he said, he would relish.

In the weeks before flying to Ust'-Kut, my nerves grew taut and I asked myself all sorts of questions. Throughout the Soviet era people along the Lena saw almost no foreigners — the Kremlin kept the river closed to the outside world, fearing exposure of its labor camps and exiles. Now, suspicious of the West anew and especially of Americans, how would villagers react to me? Had any of the strength I so admired in Russians rubbed off on me? In short, could I hack it on the Lena, camping amid clouds of mosquitoes, enduring the cold and Arctic storms, as the Cossacks did? I felt I *had* to know — or how could I ever understand, let alone be worthy of, the country to which I had devoted my life?

On the last hot June evening before my flight east, I stood in my Moscow apartment and stared into the mirror. My hair was now leavened with gray, and wrinkles were forming around my eyes where there had been none a year or two before. Memento mori! I found inspiration in stanzas by Longfellow that, written in the mid-nineteenth century, hearkened back to the age of exploration in my own country:

> Art is long, and Time is fleeting,
> > And our hearts, though stout and brave,
> Still, like muffled drums, are beating
> > Funeral marches to the grave.

In the world's broad field of battle,
    In the bivouac of life,
Be not like dumb, driven cattle!
    Be a hero in the strife!
Trust no Future, howe'er pleasant!
    Let the dead Past bury its dead!
Act, — act in the living Present!
    Heart within, and God o'erhead!

I do not believe in God. But I do believe in action, in forcing Fate's hand. What better way to do so, and to defy mortality, than to descend the Lena and emulate the deeds of Russia's consummate heroes, soldiers of fortune, and footmen of fate, the Cossacks! The only way to learn the value of life is to risk it.

RIVER OF NO REPRIEVE

1

THE PLANE WAS HALF EMPTY, the air inside muggy and rank, redolent of sweat and latrines. A couple of hours into the all-night flight from Moscow to Bratsk, where I hoped to find a car or truck to take me three hundred miles northeast through the taiga to Ust'-Kut, I wiped away the condensation and peered groggily through the porthole. Below the jetliner, a Soviet-era TU-154 seating some eighty passengers, a darkly verdant carpet of forest laced with silver-gray rivers — Siberia — swept away toward the horizon under a pale sky — midnight on the twentieth of June.

Always an expedition's first hours hit me the hardest, leaving me the nonplussed victim of my own wanderlust and obsessions. My distress began at Domodedovo Airport, in southeastern Moscow, earlier that hot, humid evening. Jostled by red-faced travelers dragging checkered vinyl sacks and plastic-wrapped suitcases for flights to Siberia, I had stood on the dusty linoleum with my wife near security control. Her eyes watering and wide open, she pressed her trembling cheeks to mine. We had been rushed on departure from our apartment and had not managed to sit for a few moments of silence, hands clasped and eyes locked, as Russian custom required for good luck on such a journey. Being Russian, and knowing her country, Tatyana distrusted everything Russian. I knew her fears. She felt she might be touching me for the last time before releasing me into a semibarbarous hinterland beginning just outside Moscow and stretching into infinity, all forest, bog, and low mountain, peopled with drunks and thugs, divided into satrapies ruled by petty tyrants who would love to get their hands on an American. Her fears were exaggerated, I knew, but I no longer argued with her — to make positive predictions before an undertaking in Russia is to tempt fate.

They called my flight. I pulled away from her, shouldering my bag. She stood at the guardrail and watched me pass through security, alarm washing over her face as an airport policeman pointed to my knapsack and asked me to open it. He pulled out my maps of the Lena. Large-scale maps are still viewed as quasi military in Russia. What would a foreigner need them for, if not espionage, he asked? Expedition? What sort of expedition? What exactly was I planning to do in Siberia? And why Siberia, for that matter? During Yeltsin's time, he probably would not have cared about maps or bothered detaining me. Now, with Putin in power, security officers did whatever they wanted and were as suspicious as they often were greedy. How much money was he going to demand to let me go? He questioned me for so long that I began worrying whether I would make the flight. Only mention of my affiliation to Dmitry Shparo won my release.

Finally free, I waved goodbye to Tatyana, jogged to the gate, and just made the bus that took me on a rattling ride over heat-warped tarmac and out to the plane.

Now, gazing through the porthole, I started to doze off. But soon the sky shaded into azure and swords of sunlight from a point on the earth's sharp rim stabbed my eyes. Before I knew it, I was standing in Bratsk's dank terminal barn, swatting mosquitoes, dazed by the lack of sleep and the five-hour time difference, waiting next to a derelict luggage conveyor for my backpack and other gear to appear, with three or four drunken passengers who had also checked bags. (To avoid theft, most in Russia prefer to carry on.) Luggage retrieved, I then found myself haggling outside in the sun with the sole driver on the lot: a shaved-headed, pug-nosed, paunchy man in his late forties. His Russian's aspirated *g*'s indicated Ukrainian provenance. With his crude mug and scarred hands, he looked like a criminal, but then out here driving was serious business; vehicle repairs in Siberian frosts often involved getting your damp bare hands frozen to steel and losing shards of skin. He had a peasant frankness about him that I found reassuring.

His taxi was a gray, listing Volga sedan of a model that I had seen only in old Soviet movies.

"Ust'-Kut?" he said. "Christ, we've had rain and the road's all mucked up. But, well . . . well, okay, hop in."

He introduced himself as Volodya. We drove off the lot, rocking onto a narrow, beat-up highway running like an alley through the forest. I tried in vain to sleep. The violent ascending road, a swerving track of gravel in parts and mud in others, cut through a looming taiga of scraggly larch and majestic spruce, lucent with light flooding through broadly spaced boughs. Now and then logging settlements appeared on the hillsides, above rushing streams blue with the sky, glittering with the sun.

"Look at this mud!" said Volodya, wrestling with his wheel. "They dare call it a 'federal highway'! Just this winter wolves tore a woman to pieces out here." He was smiling with pride. "Siberia!"

"When did you move here from Ukraine?"

"Back in the seventies. I came to work at the dam power station in Bratsk. I'm too old to go home now, and anyway, I like the peace and quiet here. You can't leave Siberia once you learn to live here."

The news came on the radio. I waited for the now customary litany of Putin's daily meetings and wise pronouncements, but they never came. Local events filled the airtime.

"You don't get national news out here?" I asked.

"Hell, we don't care what they do in Moscow," Volodya declared. "Whatever they decide in the capital, whatever wonderful changes they say are coming to us, out here nothing changes. Our local deputies are always fending off some inspector come from Moscow to make trouble. Either that or they're out for themselves. What do I care about Moscow, tell me!"

A minor explosion sounded from the front of the car. A tire had blown out. We stopped. Volodya continued his tirade as he wrestled the spare free from debris in the trunk. "However, all politicians everywhere, even here, are just out for themselves . . . But who cares, and who does anything about it? But let some poor drug addict break into an apartment to get money for his fix. They throw him in jail for stealing a few rubles. Look, I don't need the *materik*" — the "mainland," as Siberians call European Russia. "'A fish rots from the head,' we say. Get it? See why I don't care about hearing Moscow news? Here I have my peace and quiet. No rotten smells."

After we finished changing tires, I stepped away from the road and walked to the edge of the taiga. Here it was all birch, leaves so green they seemed to glow, and trunks gleaming as if painted with fresh coats of white and zebra-slashed with black from base to crown. Bumblebees buzzed around my ankles; a giant horsefly sailed out of the foliage and took to circling me. Soon I was standing in cloud of fat bugs, all swirling slowly as if drunk from the heat and sun.

"Hey, get away from the woods!" Volodya shouted. "You can get a tick in the grass and catch encephalitis! You could be dead in a day out here! Siberia!"

I trotted back to the car and jumped in for the last three hours of jolts and bumps to Ust'-Kut.

For most of Russia's history, nothing more than a mud track, which north of Mongolia and China disappeared into bog and forest, connected Saint Petersburg and Moscow to the Far East. In 1891, however, the tsar ordered the construction of the Trans-Siberian Railway. Once completed twenty-five years later, it would run almost six thousand miles from Saint Petersburg to Vladivostok on the Sea of Japan. Yet even before the Trans-Sib was finished, Russians began suspecting that in wartime the railway, paralleling the Chinese border in places, might be vulnerable to attack. Desiring a more secure and thus more northerly line, in 1911 the government started work on BAM — the Baikal-Amur *Magistral'* (trunk railway). To be built at a strategically sound distance from the frontier, BAM was to carry Siberia's wealth in timber, coal, gold, and other minerals safely back west to the *materik,* while opening up the region north of Lake Baikal to settlement. Plans metamorphosed, waxing and waning with their political expediency (one pre-Soviet scheme even had BAM connecting easternmost Siberia to Alaska) but in any case, over the coming seven decades some two thousand miles of track were laid to branch off the Trans-Sib at Taishet (2,600 miles east of Moscow), reach Ust'-Kut (its northernmost station, another 375 miles east), and wend across the taiga to finish at Sovetskaya Gavan on the Tatar Strait. Crossing through bog and over permafrost, BAM constituted the largest and most complex construction project the Soviet Union ever undertook. To build most of it, the government, as short of cash as ever, initially had to resort to the deployment of troops and gulag prisoners, Japanese POWs and indentured students. Later, in the 1960s and 1970s, Soviet propaganda persuaded tens of thousands of young workers to head east and advance the project. Owing to secretive and shoddy Soviet accounting, BAM's true cost will never be known, and large segments remain incomplete.

Still, in a few decades BAM transformed Ust'-Kut from a village of twelve thousand into a town of seventy thousand, and longtime residents past the age of forty I was to meet sang the joys of being young and strong and full of hope in BAM time, when they were engaged in the great project of putting Siberia's riches at the service of the mighty Soviet state. In Ust'-Kut's heyday two million tons of freight — timber, minerals, and fish shipped by barge up the Lena, and supplies brought from the *materik* by rail for the settlements downriver, as far as Tiksi — passed through the town every year. Now, with the death of Soviet planning and construction projects, scarcely 500,000 tons pass the docks per annum.

After paying Volodya and wishing him Godspeed, I checked in to the Hotel Lena on the poplar-lined square opposite Ust'-Kut's old river station. The station was a teal green Soviet baroque palace of sorts, attesting to pretensions of the past: a transport hub for the Communist taming of Siberia had to project a grandeur in which the proletariat could take pride. Now the building exuded tranquility in homey decay, and I recognized it with a tinge of nostalgia as where I had begun my ferry trip to Yakutsk four years earlier, on a morning cooled by a breeze fragrant with spruce sap and pine needles. If on the plane I had been disoriented and despairing, here, now, I felt I was coming home.

This sensation only increased as I unpacked in my room. My blood began stirring, yet not really in anticipation of the expedition. Rather, every time I leave Moscow to venture into the *glush'* (the "outback"; the noun, the root for the adjective *glukhoy,* or "deaf," conjures up the dreamy tranquility of a Russian birch grove), an inspiring élan steals over me once the shock of departure passes. In the *glush'* life is slow, people earnest, the air fresh, and the nights placid — balm for a Moscow resident's soul.

I would relish my last hours of solitude. My guide, Vadim, wasn't due to arrive until the day after next, so I left my room to find a seat at one of the several cafés on the square. There, in the lambency of a summer's eve, shaggy poplars shed seed puffs over green and red café tarpaulins painted with Heineken and Coca-Cola logos. Clustering near the station on a warped tarmac, amid unkempt grass lots intersected by cracked sidewalks, the tarpaulins looked like the remnants of a circus long gone. Most of the tables stood outside them, in the open air.

I pulled out a chair at one of them and sat down. Beyond the green-walled station, the Lena surged a rippling band of bluish silver, reflecting the sky of the white nights. The river here was a quarter-mile across, narrower and faster than it would be ahead, and it tugged frothily at a buoy in midstream. From radios playing on the opposite bank, in the yards of izbas, or traditional Russian log cabins, old Soviet dance tunes drifted over to us, amplified by the waters. It seemed impossible to imagine now that there had ever been a Stalin, or a time when the town had been the port for gulag land beyond, in a country called the Soviet Union.

A waitress approached, creamy-skinned, cat-eyed, dressed in a frumpy blue cashier's smock and jeans and flip-flops. Her long russet hair was pinned up in a bun, with locks dangling over her pale and fleshy cleavage. She didn't greet me but rather lingered by my table, drawing circles with her index finger on the dust, as if waiting for an indecent proposal. I asked her for a beer. Saying nothing, she sloughed away, rattled around behind the bar, and returned to me smiling, a bottle in hand.

Most of the socializing on the square, I noticed, took place just off the café grounds, where people stood drinking at a nearby kiosk rather than pay for a café seat. Loud young men, their voices hoarse from smoking, their skulls shaved, gathered in threes and fours and guzzled beer from two-liter brown plastic bottles and cursed and laughed. On the sidewalks pretty young women pushed baby carriages, navigating the buckled cement, sipping bottles of beer or sucking on cigarettes, chatting, brushing the poplar puffs from their eyes — pale blue eyes, jade eyes, honey eyes, set in regal faces. In 1848 the tsar had exiled Polish gentry here after the anti-Russian revolts in Poland — surely these women were their descendants.

By a charred brazier near my table, an Armenian kebab-maker stood turning spits of pork chunks roasting over coals, fanning the flames with a sheet of cardboard. Sniffing the meat, I developed a ravenous appetite and ordered some. "Happy Nation" then crackled through the loudspeaker, a song that took me back to my early days in Moscow, halcyon days for me, days of discovery and risk and erotic adventure in the summer of 1993. There was something fitting in this. Though the firebrand revolutionary Leon Trotsky didn't enjoy his time in exile here (the locals never cottoned to the aloof intellectual), Ust'-Kut had been known as a party-hardy haven since the early seventeenth century, when Pyanda's bedraggled Cossacks arrived after years of sailing down whitewater tributaries. Finally, on this beatific spot of land, they could rest and have fun. They named the tributary entering the Lena here "Kut," from *kutit'*, "to carouse"; and carouse they surely did, intermarrying with local Evenk women, peaceable, teepee-dwelling animists. Popular lore has it that the name "Lena" itself came not from Yakut or Evenk but rather, in the spirit of *kutit'*, derived from the verb *polenit'sya*, "to be lazy." If this isn't true, "Lena," by coincidence the diminutive of the Russian "Yelena" (Helen), has a soft feminine ring to it.

Mosquitoes now danced thick against the sky. The cook brought me a plastic plate laden with kebabs, a daub of adzhika hot sauce on the side, and I dug in. Savoring the meat, I gazed away from the river and into town, out onto the crumbling five-story cement apartment blocks built during Ust'-Kut's "boom years." From their midst a black Opel careened toward the square, its sides painted with lizard-tongue flames, Russian rock blaring from within. A gray militia van followed and pulled up alongside. The officers, billy clubs in hand, got out and peered at the young men inside. The Opel peeled out, forcing a young woman to yank her baby carriage out of the road; soon, by the station two teens were scuffling. In Russia, during the evenings, even in the *glush'*, public places are often more unsafe the later it gets: vodka and beer mix to liberate anger and charge the air with tension.

The sun set, tinting rose the gray underbellies of clouds billowing above the fir-covered *sopki* (the low mountains of Siberia) ranging up and down the Lena. A chill settled over the square and the mosquitoes turned in for the night. I decided to do the same.

The day after next dawned hot and humid. At half past seven Vadim arrived on the train from Moscow, and I went to meet him at the station. He jumped down from his carriage's doorway, relaxed from the four-day trip, and shook my hand with his powerful grip. Dressed in loose camouflage pants and sandals, with a white T-shirt stretching over his muscled frame, three days' growth on his cheeks, and his hair cropped short, he looked both at ease and imposing. Straightaway I noticed a blue-flame burn in his eyes, which rarely met mine. For the first time I became aware of his height; he was more than six feet tall.

In Moscow, when I saw him in city clothes, with longer hair, I had not noted his presence, his stature. There he had been talkative; here he was taciturn, almost glowering. I thought, *I hardly know this guy, but I'm about to spend two months at close quarters with him. I'll be putting my life in his hands.* I wondered how we would get along.

We climbed back aboard the carriage and set about unloading our gear. I grabbed at the straps of our packed-up and deflated raft, yanked, and almost threw my shoulder out of joint. It weighed almost two hundred pounds. Vadim silently prompted me to step aside and with one arm slung it over his shoulder, leaped down onto the platform, and hoisted it into our hired van. He then whisked our hundred-pound motor into position beside it. Two other man-size canvas rucksacks, bulky as if loaded with cadavers, contained our staple foodstuffs — sausage, dried beef, flour and buckwheat and macaroni, plus myriad condiments and little things Vadim said we couldn't do without. These sacks he allowed me to help him lug to the van. A dozen twenty-liter plastic jerry cans — still empty, of course — would carry our fuel.

After a morning spent buying perishables, I found myself at loose ends for the afternoon. Relaxed by the fresh river air, and feeling melancholy, as though I had left already and Ust'-Kut was nothing but a memory, I dropped into the town museum. A woman in her late thirties was the only other visitor.

She wore a pleated skirt and fresh white blouse. Her eyes were slanted and set above high cheekbones — features common to Russia's Tatars (who have their own republic on the Volga, with Kazan, as in Ivan the Terrible's day, still its capital). The museum was small, so we ended up staring at the same exhibits. Usually I would have felt uncomfortable starting up a conversation, but here in Ust'-Kut I didn't.

We reached a heated jumpsuit from the 1950s, a wire and felt getup that looked positively dangerous. Wiring often failed in Russian apartment buildings, causing terrible fires; the thought of one's own garb exploding in flames out in negative-seventy-degree frosts was terrifying. I told her this. She had a different take on the suit.

"Oh, the government wouldn't have issued common workers with such high technology. That's just for show. Most people worked out here in whatever they had."

Through the window the river shimmered with sunlight.

"It's peaceful here," I said.

"Oh . . . oh, yes," she answered. "You're new in town?"

I told her why I was here. She said her name was Alina and told me she often came to the museum to relax and ponder the exhibits and "better times." With her thick russet hair and svelte figure, I thought her quite pretty. But there was something sad about her.

"How do you like it here?" she asked.

"I like it very much. People seem friendly and forthright. Much different from Moscow."

"Oh, I agree with you on that. I'm from Tatarstan myself, so I know the difference between the *materik* and Siberia. I ended up here because the state sent me here to do obligatory service after university. I married a local and ended up staying. I'm a trader by nature; the market is in my blood. Even in Soviet days I could manage to sell anything. Now and then I've had to go to Moscow on business. I hate it."

"Why?"

"They see people like me, from the provinces, and don't give me the time of day. They're deceitful."

"Unlike here."

"Well . . . maybe."

"Are you working in sales now?"

She began trembling. Ever so slightly, but she was trembling.

"I . . . well, I'm taking a break from my work. An indefinite break." She looked down. I noticed lines on her neck, careworn skin around her eyes.

"Is something wrong?"

"You like it here. I should too. But my son . . . he finished high school with the highest marks. That and my family's financial situation meant that he qualified for a free spot at the engineering institute. He applied and we began making plans for his move. Well, he was refused. They said he'd have to pay."

"Why?"

"I went to see the institute's director in his office. He listened to me tell about my son and how he should have won a free spot. I started crying, and he laughed. 'You're naïve enough to believe that free spots go to the *poor?* Wise up, honey: I give them out to the children of influential people here, people who can do me favors. What can *you* do for *me?*' I was trembling with rage! He had ruined my son's future and he was laughing at me!" She paused, and when she began again her voice quivered. "Well, it was then that I began suffering tremors and other problems. I couldn't calm down anymore, I couldn't sleep. The doctor told me I was suffering from something called chronic fatigue syndrome and that I needed a break from my job. So, now I spend a lot of time in my apartment, which looks out onto the Lena. Seeing the river gives me peace."

Ust'-Kut, of course, was still Russia. The élan I felt on arrival began to dissipate.

After we said goodbye, I walked out to the Lena. The sun was gone, and thunderclouds were now rolling in from the northeast, where we were about to head. All at once I remembered the thousands of miles of river between us and the Arctic Ocean; I foresaw, with a shudder, storms and snows and our raft pitching on the Laptev Sea. And then I remembered the blue flame in Vadim's gaze. He knew what we faced, and I had to be ready.

I returned to my room to pack, passing youths in suits and girls in gowns. It was graduation day at the local high school, and that evening there would be a ball.

The rain fell in warm torrents that night, and with it came blasts of thunder, tridents of lightning, and gales that tore awnings from stores, branches from trees. Now and then through this meteorological anarchy sounded the hollering of boys, the squeals of girls, the smashing of bottles — graduates in revelry.

At six in the morning, when the storm ceased, just as I managed to doze off, my alarm buzzed. Looking out the window at the milky weeping sky of dawn, I dressed and then went to the next floor to rouse Vadim.

In silence we loaded the Gazel' minivan, waiting by the lobby doors, that we had hired to take us down to the river. As we labored, a dense fog settled over the town, which was strewn with leaves and broken branches from the storm and with spent champagne and vodka bottles and soggy corsages.

Our driver was Sasha, a chain smoker in his forties with sleep-mussed hair, a phlegm-clogged voice, and a scrunched-up face. He drove us out of the town center, talking nonstop about how rotten life had been here since the Soviet Union collapsed. ("Everything here's breaking down, falling apart — there's no life.") After filling our jerry cans at a gas station with enough fuel to last to Yakutsk, we crossed a bridge and turned off the road onto a dirt track that led down to a secluded spot on the river. Vadim and I agreed that, for security reasons, no one should see us leaving.

Frost-scarred concrete tenements rose above the Lena's southern bank, their windows still dark, their entranceways empty, junk-scattered muddy fields out front. We would not manage to depart unnoticed: teenage boys sporting crewcuts and rumpled brown suits and rouged girls in strapless gowns staggered along the gravel road ahead of our minivan, laughing and shouting and bumping into one another, clutching giant brown plastic bottles of beer, heading home to the tenements from graduation festivities petering out only now. Among graduates in Russia it is traditional to "greet the sunrise" of the first postschool day — a custom symbolizing hope and a fresh start. That morning the sun had not risen, but the kids had gathered on the riverbank all the same.

"Things can't be that bad here if these kids have preserved this tradition," I said to Sasha.

He snorted and smirked, the cigarette in the corner of his mouth dropping ash. The van hit bumps, and he coughed acrid smoke, his lungs wheezing, but he took fresh, deep drags. Ahead of us, an apple-cheeked girl tottered giddily on high heels, her hair in permed loops. He honked to scare her out of the road. As if hit by gunfire she contorted herself violently and stumbled toward the side of the road.

"Screw your mother!" Sasha muttered. "Whore! Just look at these kids, still drunk and now guzzling beer to kill the dry mouth! And this neighborhood is *banditsky!* Don't take your eyes off your gear or those punks will snatch it!"

"They don't look like punks to me," I said.

"I mean *those* kids." He grimaced toward a pair of skinheaded brutes with low, bony brows farther on. Past us bounced an ancient motorcycle. It crisscrossed the road ahead of us, its young male driver so drunk he couldn't steer. Sasha honked again. The cyclist veered off the road and slowed so much that he toppled over into the mud. He did not get up.

Soon thereafter we left the road and clanked down rutted clay swells to a gravelly spot by the river's edge. Sasha cut the motor. The water — panes of liquid silver speckled with raindrops — coursed lazily away into the fog-shrouded forest and hills to the northeast.

Vadim and I could hardly contain our enthusiasm, Sasha, his misgivings.

"Look," he said, "Ust'-Kut used to send a boat or a helicopter to airlift villagers to hospital if they got sick. But since the Soviet Union fell apart, everything's rotted away. These days we don't even a first-aid team, let alone a boat or a helicopter. People've been thrown to the mercy of fate out there. They're trapped in their villages for months on end, with no roads. Up ahead, for a while, you've got Russians. After Vitim, you've got Yakuts. A drunken people, nasty and violent. You won't have it sweet. No sir, not sweet at *all*."

"*Da ladno!*" said Vadim. "We'll manage."

"I think we can handle it," I added.

"Oh, you do! A good number of our young in the villages are idle these days. You think they're polite. Well, you're right. They come up to you and politely say, 'Uncle, please give me a light!' before they bash in your skull. You don't know what you're up against out there."

I really couldn't take him too seriously. Pontificating about their country's flaws is a favorite pastime among Russians, who surely must be the most self-deprecating people on earth.

We started unloading our gear: jerry cans of fuel, provisions, a kit of spare parts for the motor, our rucksacks filled with foul-weather suits, insulated underwear, everything we would need to survive Siberia's climate until we reached Tiksi . . . Tiksi, on the Arctic Ocean! How impossibly distant!

Vadim last pulled out his double-barreled shotgun and a box of ammo. He handed me the gun. "Be careful," he warned. "It's loaded."

Not paid to lift, Sasha stood by and hacked smoke in our direction. He cleared his throat and spat onto the gravel, wiping raindrops from his brow. "What'll you be eating out there? A lot of canned crap, I bet."

Vadim grabbed a trunk and plopped it down onto the gravel. "Oh, no. We're going to fish. I've got nets. We'll hunt if we can."

"Huh." Sasha hawked up phlegm and spat. "My brother likes fish. I always tell that son of a bitch, my favorite fish is *pork!* You'll get mighty sick of fish out there."

We set about assembling our raft, spreading it on the bank, straightening it out, pumping it up, and attaching the motor to the wooden panel at the stern. After we launched it, I climbed in, noting the bouncy pontoons, the hard bench just behind our tarp-covered load just in front of the wooden crossbeam. We didn't tarry. Within an hour the raft was loaded, the motor chugging. Sasha delivered an expletive-laden valediction, and we shoved off into the drizzle and fog.

The tenements soon ended, but beneath rising and falling *sopki*, here green with spruce, through hanging patches of mist, lay ruined barges and wrecked tugboats; crumbling cement docks and rickety cranes; ancient heaps of scrap metal rusting to dust — the very grave-yard of Russian civilization, I thought.

Two hours later, the skies cleared. We passed under a rusted bridge and out of the wasteland of barges, gliding atop burbling currents dappled with the fresh turquoise of the sky, the green of the conifers, and the rippling black and white serrations of birches.

I was spellbound by the boreal beauty of the land. Vadim wasn't.

"This isn't the north yet," he said. Ust'-Kut, he pointed out, was "only" at the latitude of Juneau, Alaska. *His* beloved north began at the sixtieth parallel — on a geographical par with Greenland — where hardy larches stood beneath summits too wind-battered for anything else to take root. Such a severe landscape was impossible for me to conjure up on the first heady day of our expedition.

2

AS WE CRUISED AHEAD over green waters, gliding from eddy to swirl, I faced the sun and inhaled the warm, now piney breeze, noting how the Lena zigzagged between *sopki* — ancient bulges of forested earth two or three thousand feet high covering the Leno-Angarskoye Plateau. One hand holding a waterproof plastic folder containing a segment of map, Vadim with the other unbuttoned a vest pocket and extracted a black plastic gadget (a GPS module) attached to his neck by a cord and flicked it on, looking at the readout and checking it against the map.

"Our altitude is nine hundred and thirty-one feet and falling. We'll be at half that or less by the time we make the bogs of Yakutia. [Like most Russians he used the old Russian name for Sakha.] The current will weaken, but our speed will pick up as our load lessens, as we use fuel and eat our staples."

He relished the logistical aspects of our expedition, and reminded me now, as he would often later, that our success depended on his mastery of them. I nodded and jotted down our altitude in my notebook. Heading for the Arctic under a vaulting blue sky, with our motor gently chugging, with the sun bronzing my cheeks and drying my drizzle-damp clothes, I felt free, drunk on fresh air, on the novelty of this adventure.

In most languages "Siberia" evokes shattered lives and exile. For Russians it means these things and more, much more — somnolent taiga, revivifying wilderness, peace and escape from the trials that humans afflict on one another. After serving their sentences, many of those banished here from European Russia in tsarist and Soviet times chose never to return to the *materik*.

I glanced back at Vadim. He constantly shifted in his seat and examined the shore through his binoculars, comparing what he saw to the squiggles on his map; he checked and rechecked his GPS; he commented on the curving banks, the deepening waters, the circling hawks and heavy-winged ravens, as if seeing them all for the first time. Had he, like the exiles who had stayed on, suffered some trauma back in "civilization" that drove him to spend half the year in the north, where he could immerse himself in nature and forget about humankind? I wondered. I didn't yet know him well enough to ask.

In midafternoon we pulled up to a high, level stretch of grassy bank where the *sopki* retreated from the river. An old cattle fence ran along the ridge atop the bank, and the gabled roofs of a few cabins peeked above it. According to the map, this was the village of Podymakhino.

"You really want to stop here?" Vadim asked. "Remember how wild people can be in these parts."

"I know what they say. But please stop."

Podymakhino was the first village on our route, and I was eager to take a look. The director of the museum in Ust'-Kut had suggested that I drop in on the schoolteachers here. They would appreciate the company, and they could show me a collection of tsarist-era artifacts they had been assembling.

We coasted ashore beneath where a path cut gravelly white down the verdant bank, here some twenty feet high, and I jumped out. I climbed the path into the breeze and sunlight. Once at the top I saw a spread of izbas built along untrammeled dirt roads, most painted dark green or pale blue, others abandoned, their walls abraded into gray by snows and rains. Collapsing wooden fences ran higgledy-piggledy around farm plots and untended pasture. There was a lot of fence and few cattle. Not a soul was about.

But as faraway peals of thunder rang out from beyond the *sopki* opposite the village and wind stirred the grass, shifting its green to silver, I heard, or thought I heard, the laughter of children. Oddly apprehensive, wondering if the wind wasn't playing some sort of auditory trick on me, I set out to find them.

After cutting through a cluster of boarded-up houses and ducking under fence beams, following loudening laughter and squeals of delight, I spotted, with some relief, a two-story brick schoolhouse with twenty or twenty-five ten- to fifteen-year-olds playing tag in a daisy-dotted field out front. Sitting on a bench by the school door was a short, plump woman in her thirties, with a potato nose and mousy brown hair, her arms crossed over her belly. Her face was tanned; like so many Siberians, she probably spent every sunny summer hour she could outdoors.

Feeling like an intruder, I walked up to her.

"*Zdrasst'ye!*" I said.

"*Zdrasst'ye, zdrasst'ye,*" she intoned, not really removing her eyes from the children, whom she was supervising. "What can I do for you?" she asked absentmindedly, seeming unfazed by the sudden appearance of a stranger in her village.

"I'm American, and I'm traveling the Lena. I heard you have a museum here."

She turned and glanced down at my rolled-up trousers, wet on the bottom, and muddy sandals. Her eyes widened and she smiled. "Oh! Oh, really! Why, welcome! Come upstairs and I'll show you around."

Rising from her bench, she introduced herself as Olga and asked my name, mispronouncing it several times before giving up. As we entered the building we met another teacher, Svetlana, coming out. Younger and fair-complexioned, with a mane of henna-tinted curly hair, Svetlana wore a white sundress that clung to her comfortable curves. With no ceremony, as if she had been expecting me, she offered to show me the museum, which just happened to be one floor up.

We climbed the stairs to a yellow classroom decorated with a mural showing mighty, bearded Cossacks in caftans and baggy trousers and knee-high boots, the Lena's blue course looping northward, and various key dates in Podymakhino's history. The Cossack Ivashko Timofeyevich Podymakha founded the village in 1699, the text said, and bequeathed it his name. Sergei Radishchev, the author of *From Saint Petersburg to Moscow,* the 1796 travelogue that would become Russia's first revolutionary treatise, passed through here on his way to exile downriver. Though the mural looked to have been painted recently, it covered in detail the Soviet era and the operations of its sawmill and state farm.

"So you have a sawmill and farm here," I remarked.

"Our sawmill closed down after perestroika," replied Olga. "Our farm went to seed. Everything fell apart. People started leaving for Ust'-Kut and Irkutsk [the regional capital]. We once had four hundred students here; now we've got a hundred and fifty, and for a long time women didn't have babies."

Svetlana cut in, her voice singsong. "What man could afford a family out here these days, with the way things have fallen apart in our country?"

Olga continued. "Lately an old Communist has been reviving our state farm. We now train our young men to be tractor drivers. So they have a reason to stay in the village. Our women, in the past couple of years, *have* started having babies again." A broad smile creased her plain face. "Children — they're all I live for! With their energy, you forget everything, even whether you've eaten or not! Children are such a joy!"

"Oh, let me show him our collection!" said Svetlana. She grabbed my hand and pulled me over to a narrow side room with crooked wall shelves from floor to ceiling — the museum. The shelves brimmed with wooden knickknacks and metallic bric-a-brac, covered with dust and all jumbled together.

Svetlana shoved a rusted hunk of iron with a handle into my hands; it must have weighed fifteen pounds. "Look at this iron from old Russia," she said. "It's an authentic *Russian* iron, coal powered! You see, they opened this lid in the top and put in the hot coals." She grabbed it from me and made an ironing motion in the air. "Our women back in tsarist days had to be *strong* to use it — they were *much* stronger than we are today! Look, come over here." She rifled through the debris and out came a torrent of excited words. "Here are baskets made from birch bark: the bark has a sap that's a natural antiseptic, so berries and meat stayed fresh for a long time. Our old-time villagers knew everything. And take a look at this bottle." She handed me a heavy green vial with an elaborate herald rippling the glass near the neck. "See the name of the pharmacist here? Think of the *pride* people took in their work back then, even in a bottle! Everything was so *personal* for them. When they worked for themselves, they *cared* about what they did. Our Soviet people now don't care about anything."

"Really?" I asked. "Even with private property now?"

"It's too late. Our civilization and traditions are dying. Out here, anyway. We don't even . . . oh, excuse me, this is our local history buff, Alexander. He can tell you more about Podymakhino than I can."

A stern, fit middle-aged man in dark-rimmed glasses came up and shook my hand. "You're the American? Ah-ha, uh-huh. Well, Svetlana's showing you the past, but the sad thing is, it's also our future. Everything is breaking down. Soon we'll have no electricity, no phones, no doctor. We already have no kindergarten. Everyone is fleeing to Irkutsk."

"We get our drinking water from the river, the way our grandparents did," said Svetlana, her tone hinting at pride Russians often take in showing foreigners that no one, but no one, could live worse than they. I still haven't found an adequate way to respond to this.

"I myself *have* plumbing," said Olga. "But the water comes out all brown and rusty. It's better to drink from the river."

Svetlana continued, "To wash, we have to heat our bath water on wood stoves. Imagine, this is the twenty-first century! You saw all the boarded-up houses on the way here? Podymakhino is dying. The rumor is that they're going to cut off the heating for our school, and that'll be the end of us. We'll *have* to leave then. It's frightening."

Alexander cut in. "Borisovo, three hundred years old, dying. Tayura, founded in 1663, and Kazarki, 1652, they're dying too. All these villages were established by Cossacks and had their traditions, their history. But the state just lets them die. I've seen a report by the state statistical office that said we already have something like *fourteen thousand* dead villages in Russia."

"Why are they dying?" I asked.

"The best and most cultured of us are leaving the villages," Svetlana said. "Can you blame them? What future is there out here? But where we can we go, where can we find work? No one needs us on the *materik*."

"We did just fine until Gorbachev," said Alexander. "He told us, 'You're so isolated and far away that you're expensive to maintain! Move to the cities!' We didn't go, so they started closing down schools to get us out of here."

They were speaking to me of decay and the death of their village, but the school in which we stood was clean, solid, and serviceably furnished. They were healthy, as far as I could tell, and the children in the yard looked happy. I felt like objecting, pointing out that not everything was that bad out here; urban Russia hardly offered better and in fact could be much worse. But I kept quiet: I felt I had no right to tell them about their country, and I hardly knew anything about their lives.

After chatting some more, we stepped outside so that they could show me the World War II monument in which Alexander took great pride. By the edge of the riverbank, beneath a sky now gray and cool, stood a cement placard engraved with the names of perished veterans from Podymakhino.

"You know what?" said Alexander, raising his bespectacled eyes from the names. "I often think how different our history would have been if we just hadn't let Stalin get away with 1937." It was the most infamous year of show trials, summary executions, and the banishment of millions of "enemies of the people" to labor camps across Siberia. Very few resisted; in fact, many Party members believed it was their duty to submit to their doom, for the good of the revolution. The year 1937 was a holocaust for the Russian people, and almost everyone lost relatives in it, but mentioning it stirs little emotion today. Alexander's suggestion was so obviously true that neither Svetlana nor Olga acknowledged it; if Russians hadn't submitted to their oppressors, history would be different and this village might be thriving. But they did submit. Then as now, Russians expected the worst from their rulers, and there was no point in getting upset.

They all walked me down to our boat, where Vadim was casting a fishing line without luck. From out of her dress pocket Svetlana pulled a snapshot showing their last graduating class and wrote on its back, "Remember us, your friends here in Podymakhino, on 24 June 2004!"

I shook Alexander's hand and smiled to Svetlana and Olga (men don't shake women's hands in Russia), thanking them all for their time and talk. I climbed aboard, and so did Vadim. They stood and watched as we pushed away from the bank, heading north for the channel.

Soon after departure, once we had passed out of sight of the village and found ourselves alone with the trees and the steepening *sopki*, we sailed under a troupe of clouds migrating south, trailing showers of cold pattering rain. A chill settled over the land, and we donned our rain gear. Vadim busied himself with his maps, saying nothing.

But the rain didn't last. At seven that evening, on a narrow bend in the river opposite a *sopka* with crooked beige veins of limestone running down its fir-forested slope, we landed on a stony clearing by a pine grove that climbed the mount behind us. We performed for the first time the tasks that would make up our daily routine: unloading the raft and pulling it half ashore; securing it to a tree stump with the bow rope; clearing a spot to make a fire; and setting up the tents (we each had our own). Tents had initially been a matter of controversy. Vadim saw no reason that the two of us shouldn't companionably share his two-man tent, as would any pair of Russian men thrown in together for a long journey. I, however, knew that I would want to be alone after sitting aboard the raft with him for ten hours a day, but to say so might cause offense, so I pleaded a writer's need for solitude. He argued but finally shrugged and accepted my caprice.

Vadim pointing at three sticks he had gathered.

"Recognize this?" he said, propping up a triangle of three five-foot-long pine switches, over the crux of which he had draped a yard of charred chain.

"How so?

"How so? It's from your Indians. It's like a teepee, but for cooking. We can build a fire underneath and hang our pots from the chains. I like this way of cooking better than our way, which is just to prop a stick up on a rock over the fire and hang the pot from it. Primitive, in my opinion. Your Indians were on to something. You should know that."

Vadim went on to narrate our evening's chores, delivering caveats that are familiar to every outdoorsman ("Sleeping bags must never get wet," "Building a fire is always the priority," and so on), and urging me to listen and learn. Then as later he would show a passion for every detail of expedition life. He was eager to discuss campsites, sleeping bag liners, the correct way to chop wood, how best to heat water. I nodded and now and then tried to ask detailed questions, more so that he would know I was listening than for any other reason, but to these I received curt, even rude, rejoinders: "Why don't you know that? Everyone does. You're just a writer living on paper."

I tried not to take offense. When he paused, I mentioned what I'd seen in Podymakhino and asked him what he thought of Alexander's ruminations about Stalin. He cut me off and continued bantering, almost to himself, about camping techniques. I dropped the subject, deciding that I should be glad of his enthusiasm. Like so many hobby masters — and remembering that in Moscow he drove a truck for a living (that, at the time, was how I saw him) — he wanted to show off what he knew. This could work to my advantage. I had always found it harder to get comprehensible answers from native experts (Bedouin or Congolese fishermen, for example) on getting by in their environments, because they grew up learning how to survive there and often took for granted too much of their knowledge to be able to explain it properly to an outsider.

An hour later, the camp was set up, the sun down behind the *sopki*.

"Okay, let's go get some firewood," Vadim said, grabbing the big ax and handing me the little one.

He didn't wait for me but stomped off behind some bushes and was gone. I walked down the bank a ways and entered the taiga — here a damp, dark pine grove carpeted with grass of an almost phosphorescent green. I stood for a moment in the half-light, wondering where I might find dry wood, but instants later mosquitoes assaulted fast and furious, ignoring my repellent, biting through my hair and jeans, clustering thick on my hands and face. I swatted and yanked at logs. All were damp, so I ran back out into the clearing. Realizing I had a lot of adjusting to do, I set out searching in drier places. Eventually I found a dry pine trunk and dragged it back to camp.

But Vadim was already there, and he had collected enough wood for two or three fires. He looked at my pine with contempt. "We don't need that sort of wood here. It burns black resiny smoke. Watch me and learn. Watch and learn."

He hung pots on his chains, one for tea, the other for our buckwheat and canned beef entrées, and placed cloves of garlic — we would chew garlic or onion every evening as a prophylactic against stomach problems — on a plastic table mat. An hour later, in a whining haze of mosquitoes, we were eating our dinner and sipping our tea. I stood in the smoke to avoid the insects, but they hardly bothered Vadim. After each bite of buckwheat or sip of tea he exclaimed lustily, *"O, krasota! O, dushevno!"* (Oh, beautiful! That really hits the spot!)

His pleasure equaled my bug-bitten misery; his love for canned food made me think of succulent mbuku fish, freshly caught, that I had tasted on the Congo. I scratched my bites, coughed in the smoke, and realized that, in fact, I would have to listen and learn.

3

MY TENT'S YELLOW WALLS blushed with the rosy light of dawn. I awoke cramped in my sleeping bag, perceiving the cranky approaching rumble of an outboard motor, followed by a boat's wake lapping against the shore. There was a pause, and then boots crunched gravel.

I sat up and peered through my gauze window. Surrounding Vadim's tent were three camouflage-clad young men brandishing AK-47s, their fingers on the triggers. Two were stout and blond; the third, thin and dark. It seemed they had not noticed my tent, which I had erected behind bushes some yards away.

"Come out of your tent!" the thin one shouted into Vadim's window.

Vadim unzipped his door and clambered out in long johns.

"Show us some ID."

They scrutinized his passport and handed it back to him. "Okay, all right . . . has anything disappeared from your camp?"

"No. Why?"

"A prisoner's escaped from Kirensk, downriver. He's armed. He's probably headed this way, and he may have his own boat. It's likely he'll steal to survive, and he may be violent. You're going to have to be careful."

"We're armed too," said Vadim.

"Well, we've warned you."

The men peered at the wooded hillside above our camp, still dark, said *"Ladno, udachi!"* (Okay, good luck!) and jumped aboard their skiff and took off, heading upriver, toward Ust'-Kut.

I climbed out.

"Ha!" said Vadim, in lieu of a greeting. "If *I* had escaped from prison out here, no one would *ever* find me. This criminal is probably stupid enough to stay along the river. Me, I'd head into the taiga. I wouldn't need anything at all from civilization. Okay, maybe I'd slip into a village now and then for matches and ammo, but that's about it." He grabbed his ax and the chopped-up wood he had gathered the night before and lit a fire. His voicing rising, he expounded on the certain urban obtuseness of the escapee, who would hew to the riverbank and get caught, and spoke matter-of-factly about his own taiga survival skills, which would allow him to evade capture.

The sky darkened with an approaching storm. We quickly breakfasted on bread and kasha, packed up, and shoved off.

As the wind rippled the water, the Lena, now as iron gray as the clouds above, uncoiled like a snake through the *sopki*, with sloping walls of gloomy taiga ever curving and straightening out ahead of us. Mist daubed shadowy dales and groves of rayless depth, creating a Brothers Grimm landscape of nightmares and lost childhood. Soon, on shoreside meadows, we saw the dying villages of which Alexander had spoken: Tayura, Novoselovo, Kazarki. Most of their izbas were abandoned, lost in high grass, their windows smashed, the children's swings in yards rusted, the surrounding fences hacked apart for firewood. Swallows had dug their nests in the clayey banks, and they sailed out to dip and dive around us, cheering us on with a chorus of incongruous chirps. Here and there, lone plumes of smoke trailed from steel stovepipes and waggled in the wind; some people, it appeared, couldn't bear to leave. Who could blame the holdouts, who had grown up knowing peace along this great river?

The wind blew down, cold and damp, from the north, and we pulled our jackets tight. At noon, the patrol speedboat bounced across the waters and overtook us. The soldiers pointed to a man sitting between them, handcuffed with head bowed — the escapee.

Vadim raised his head. "Ha! I *told* you he would be caught. I *told* you!"

That evening, on the grassy lee side of a deserted cabin at the taiga's edge, we camped on the bank opposite the village of Verkhnemarkovo. ("We can't stay on the village's shore, or drunks will bother us all night," said Vadim.) Svetlana in Podymakhino had suggested that I stop by the House of Culture here, for it was Friday evening and there was sure to be something on. Verkhnemarkovo, from the bank at least, resembled Podymakhino, with a long row of wooden houses running along a dirt road at river's edge.

Vadim drove me across the water and left me on the pebbly bank. I wasn't alone. In the ennobling light of an amber evening, ancient rusted skiffs and patched-up rowboats were departing a settlement a mile or so downriver and cutting across the still waters to converge on the bank where I had landed, carrying men with crewcuts wearing polyester jackets and clip-on ties, and short-haired women in chintz blouses and long skirts. Wondering what was going on, I climbed the path into the village, coming across clutches of garrulous teens in ballroom gowns and pressed suits hurrying down a dirt road toward a three-story brick building.

"Excuse me," I said to one of three well-dressed guys walking by me, a somber fellow with dark hair and drooping eyes, "is that building there the House of Culture?"

They all stopped. "Oh, no," he replied. "That's the school. Tonight's graduation night, so the House of Culture's closed." They glanced down at my muddied jeans and sandals. "May I ask where you're from?"

I told him. Showing no surprise, he shook my hand and invited me to the ceremony. His name was Luka, and, he said, he was going to live it up this evening, for in a couple of days he would leave for the mainland to study at a military academy. Once again, I thought, the feared "village barbarians" were turning out to be among the friendliest souls I had met in Russia.

We entered the school and found ourselves in the blue-walled and wooden-floored lobby, standing among a crowd of forty-two rambunctious teens and clutches of silent parents, some of whom had arrived with me by boat. In another country, the teens might have been selected for their comeliness, for their sleek builds and tanned skin, their jade and turquoise eyes; but here in Russia, they were typical. Only the homemade dresses worn by a few of the girls stood out as plain, as did some of the coiffures, which recalled 1950s hairdos in the United States. I sensed perfume and cologne, but mostly I smelled soap. Not one teen was overweight. As elsewhere in Russia, only the middle-aged were comfortably padded.

"Our Russian girls are beautiful, aren't they?" Luka asked. A bell rang. "Come on, the ceremony is about to start."

Inside the auditorium the evening sun washed through high, diaphanous pink curtains onto the entering crowd. At the door a matron handed students baldrics of red sateen announcing, in yellow letters, GRADUATE OF 2004. Girls with white and violet corsages, some holding bouquets of peonies, took seats in the front row of wooden chairs; the boys arrayed themselves behind them; and parents and grandparents, whose hands, I noticed, were callused and dirty-nailed, probably from working in garden plots, occupied the rear. As a backdrop to the stage, a white sheet painted with images of a couple performing a ballroom dance again reminded me of decades past in my own country. A red and gold banner hung above all, announcing GRADUATION EVE 2004. I thought about my own high school graduation ceremony, in 1979, and remembered painful metallic dental braces and rented pastel tuxedos, long sideburns, and female classmates (who usually ran about barefoot and in jeans) wearing dresses for the first time.

I told Luka that this ceremony reminded me of graduations belonging to the more decorous decades before my time.

"Really?" He chuckled demurely. "Well, our kids are serious now. But later, when we start drinking . . . let's just say we won't be very decorous, and we won't stop till dawn. We'll be greeting the sunrise, as is our tradition."

A boy with strawberry hair and a pointy chin came up and shook our hands. Adjusting his tie, he introduced himself to me as Sasha. "You're from the U.S.?"

"That's right."

"Well, we're against Bush and the war in Iraq. We think it'll be another Vietnam. We're surprised your country would get itself into the same mess as we did in Afghanistan. You Americans really —"

Luka motioned for him to stop. "Al Gore should really be your president. Everything would be different if he were."

"You're probably right," I said. "I'm against the war too. But President Putin and Bush are friends, at least as far as fighting terrorism goes. What do you think about that?"

"Oh, Putin doesn't have a choice," said Sasha. "He has to make do with whatever president you have."

"Russia has no friends," said Luka.

"Wait, what about Ukraine and Belarus?" asked Sasha.

"They're not real allies. Our only allies are countries we sell guns to."

"Well, Putin is a real good guy, a real *man*," said Sasha. "I can't even believe we ever had a president like Yeltsin. Putin's done a lot for us."

"Like what?"

He thought for a moment. "He's sober. Yeltsin was drunk."

"Fine, but what has he actually *done* for you?"

"Well, we no longer have to call Podymakhino for a militiaman. It used to take days to get a cop out here. Now we have our own militia station. Oh, look, the ceremony's starting."

Lights blinked on over the stage. The evening's MC was one of the vice principals, another matron with a clarion voice. She welcomed us and ordered the commencement of ceremonies.

A pair of female teachers recited in tandem a versified valedictory about there being no easy ways forward from now on, no second chances, and no orders to carry out, and those who thought otherwise were deceiving themselves. Eleventh-graders executed the arms-akimbo twirls and stomps of Russian folk dances; junior high school girls in bizarre *I Dream of Jeannie* outfits performed a Middle Eastern number. Then teachers, all women, I noted, with sensible hairdos and hearty voices, mounted the stage to award "surprise" prizes: the "UFO Award," for the graduating student least known to faculty members; the awards for all-around "Best Guy" and "Best Girl"; the "Most Studious" prize; the "Sunshine Medal" for the most cheerful. As teachers announced the winners, the students whispered excitedly, giggled, and looked back nervously on smiling parents.

A distinctly Russian skit followed. A teacher asks a police officer with a bandage on her head what happened.

"I was trying to guard the school!"

"From what?"

"From the students!"

A *biznesmen* in a shiny suit and dark glasses walked on stage, hawking bulletproof vests.

The parent chided him, "You never deliver the goods! You're a swindler, like the rest of the businessmen!" All the actors then turned to the audience and exclaimed, "Oh, the free market! Oh, reforms! Oh, democracy!"

Finally, after the vice principal reappeared to remind us all that there can be no one answer to Lenin's famous question "What is to be done?" a teenage boy emerged from the wings carrying a tiny first-grade girl in a white dress, a white bow in her blond hair, down the stairs and around the auditorium, jingling a bell, ringing out the *posledniy zvonok* (the last school bell of the year) to conclude the ceremony.

Out in the hall, after I had congratulated my hosts, Luka told me that this was the first time such skits were performed, such humorous awards presented.

"Why? What's different about this year?"

"Things have stabilized with Putin," he answered, "and finally we can relax a little."

The next dawn came on hot. A potent sun mounted the azure above Verkhnemarkovo, glazing the green river with glare, warming my tent and heating dragonfly pupae to hatch by our camp. Everywhere newborn insects, dun-colored and glistening with goo, were working free of their shells on twigs, unfolding their bent wet wings to dry, stretching their segmented legs. I took a bucket bath behind the cabin and then returned to my tent to order my jumbled effects, which included a bulky insulated suit, a knit cap, and heavy trousers against an Arctic cold I found impossible to imagine in this estival blaze. Vadim set about deflating the boat to repair a minor leak. Around noon Luka arrived on a sputtering old motorbike and invited us to lunch at his place. I accepted but Vadim declined; he would not leave our craft and gear unattended.

Just beyond the village proper, on a high grassy hillock overlooking the river's curve to the northeast, in the belfry-shaped shadow of a derelict church, stood the house where Luka lived, enclosed behind a larch fence. With its patched aluminum siding roof, weathered brown walls, and junk-cluttered yard, it had the gimcrack look of "home" so common in rural Russia — a place where Mom and Pop lived but from which the young generally flee as soon as they can. Before it spread a garden plot furrowed with rows of ripening tomatoes, potatoes, and cucumbers. In yard corners chickens pecked through odiferous piles of vegetable peelings, and from a shed somewhere in the back sounded the urgent oinks of pigs.

"We're here!" Luka shouted into the gate.

An old man and woman, both trim and tanned, with sparkling blue eyes and white wavy hair, came out to greet us. They had regal noses, high cheekbones, and arching brows — the lineaments of Polish nobility exiled along the river in the nineteenth century.

"I live with my grandparents," Luka whispered.

The elders walked across the yard and welcomed me. Dressed in a bright blue-white floral-print dress, Grandma had berry red lips and must have been a beauty in her youth; Grandpa wore a ratty T-shirt and moth-chewed flannel trousers, and when he spoke he shouted.

They gave me a tour of the house. Inside it had a close air, with its low concave ceilings and dark rooms cluttered with dusty bric-a-brac and antique furniture. In their cellar, jars of homemade jams and jellies and pickled cucumbers lined shelves along cold stone walls. Outside, opposite the house proper, stood a shed — the summer kitchen. The kitchen was as it might have been a hundred years ago, dominated by a wall-sized Russian stove, at the base of which snoozed a pair of Siberian huskies. A profusion of pipes ran along the ceiling. A window took up most of the southern side, letting in blue light and warmth and giving onto the taiga beyond a winding dirt road.

Grandma ushered me to a seat by the window table. Luka sat down and told me about life in Verkhnemarkovo. The lack of plumbing obliged villagers to draw water from the river and lug it up to their homes — a hardship. When the generator had fuel, they had electricity for six hours a day. It didn't have to be this way, he said: there is oil in the region, and the state had dug wells, but for unknown reasons it chose not to operate them.

"Some of the wells are in people's backyards," he said, "but the state gives them nothing for having drilled on their land. So people tap in to them on their own. They sell fuel made from a mix of crude oil and gasoline that works in the old Soviet cars people drive out here."

For the ever-dwindling numbers of young people in Verkhnemarkovo (those who can leave do, as Luka would in the morning), a "night out," he said, consists of gathering with friends in an abandoned cabin, firing up the stove, and smoking hemp or drinking spirits — often *pure* spirits. One acquaintance of his had died recently from alcohol poisoning. There's no work and nothing else to do.

Luka recounted all this with downcast eyes, yet he himself was fit and strong; his despondency seemed a matter of character more than circumstance.

Impatient with Luka's account of life, Grandpa cut him off and shouted to me, "Grandma's ten years older than I am! So you see, she's not my first wife. My first wife died." He glanced slyly at Luka and then at me. "Look, I'd like to treat you to *samogonka* [moonshine]. Can you handle Russian *samogonka*?"

Luka frowned and subtly shook his head at Grandpa, as if to say "No!" Grandma threw up her hands. "Oh, now it begins! Leave our guest alone, Grandpa!"

"Shut up, Grandma!" Grandpa leaned over to me, his eyes ablaze. "Well, what do you say? I make it with the finest yeast, potato shavings, and sugar around! It's as green as tequila, as smooth as ice!"

"Sure, why not."

Though I noted Luka's displeasure, it is impolite to refuse a drink in Russia from a host, especially an older one. Grandma set glasses in front of us. Grandpa scurried out of the room. He rattled around in the cellar and reappeared with a tall bottle of phosphorescent green fluid in one hand, a plate full of lard slices in the other. "Got to chase it with lard or else you'll get sick. Smoked it myself."

"Excellent."

He poured us fifty-gram shots.

At that moment Luka's friend Sasha walked in on wobbly feet, his eyes bloodshot, his hair mussed. Grandpa held up the bottle and shook it at him enticingly.

"Ooh, no!" Sasha groaned. "Please, put it away!"

He collapsed into a chair at the table. "Got any beer? I need to chase away this hangover!"

Grandpa turned around. "Grandma, pour this boy a beer!"

"Drunkards! All around me drunkards!" she said in a good-natured way that still rang true, for so often women here find themselves catering to alcoholic husbands, picking them up off the floor or street, guiding them home at night. Shaking her head, she pulled a tall plastic bottle of beer from beneath a table. She laid out *zakuski* (hors d'oeuvres): rolls of sausage, slices of cucumber, and the obligatory chunks of home-baked black bread. Luka was also nursing a hangover and so poured himself some beer.

Grandpa raised his *samogonka*.

"To our meeting!" he announced.

We drank to the dregs, as is customary, and munched on *zakuski*. (In Russia, freelance tippling is frowned upon: one drinks at the host's command.) The *samogonka* went down as smooth as ice, just as Grandpa said it would. He leaned over to me.

"So what did you think of the girls in the graduating class?"

"Beautiful, quite beautiful."

"We're proud of our Russian beauties here," said Luka.

"Beauties?" Grandpa shouted. "Skin and bones, all of them! Where are the meaty girls of my youth!"

I asked Grandpa what he had done for a living.

"You youngsters can thank me for the roads around here! I built them myself on a state bulldozer!"

"Grandpa, we have no roads," said Luka sadly.

"Don't listen to him!" Grandpa bellowed.

Grandma cut in. "Quiet down, you old drunk!"

A feeble female voice sounded outside, followed by the thump-and-drag of a cane on the porch. An ancient scarved woman appeared in the doorway, hunchbacked and shod in peasant felt boots. "I congratulate you young folks on your graduation!" She cleared her throat, and then recited lines from Stalin's national anthem: "*To our young all our roads are open! To our old, we give a respectful bow!*"

"Thank you, Maria Ivanovna!" Grandpa rejoined.

"She wasn't congratulating you, old drunk!" shouted Grandma.

Luka and Sasha stared at their beers. The old woman hobbled out, singing the anthem under her breath, to continue her rounds. Sasha and Luka smiled sadly at me, surely finding the lyrics preposterously inappropriate for the country in which they now lived. For the elders, the lyrics recalled a time of certainty and Soviet pride and mass killings, midnight arrests and state-sponsored famine — youth, in other words, a time to remember fondly.

"She's eighty-three years old!" said Grandpa. "Let's drink to her!"

We did. I looked around me. As the liquor warmed my throat, the wondrous taiga outside grew even more wondrous. The summery fields, the fat bees climbing lazily over flowers outside the window, the sleepy huskies at my feet, all seemed miracles I had never witnessed before. How I loved Russian villages! Homey and pleasant and as comfortable as an old slipper!

Grandpa poured us another round of *samogonka,* and the boys topped off their beers. We toasted to the future of the young men at the table. But then Grandpa turned somber. "Life here's gone downhill since the mishap in 'seventy-four."

"Shut up, Grandpa! You're drunk!"

"Mishap?" I asked.

"Oh, you know our country. Nuclear explosions. Eight of them in fact, and right under the earth here, in mineshafts. You see, they were doing seismographic research, looking for oil. They produced an earthquake that hit three on the Richter scale as far away as Irkutsk. This very house shook like mad. We've had many deaths here from cancer since then. Oil now contaminates our well water. It's probably radioactive as hell here, but no one'll tell us the truth."

"Shut up, Grandpa! You're drunk!"

"Oh, quiet down, old woman! Our guest should know the truth!"

In 1993 I had stopped in the Siberian town of Tomsk after a nuclear accident at a military installation nearby and had heard similar words from locals. Then, I was worried. What was the radiation level? Was I being irradiated? How long was it safe to stay? Now, after so many years in Russia, I received Grandpa's news with indifference. Perhaps age played a part in my apathy — at forty-three, I had lived half my life and felt blessed so often that I could hardly have wanted more. But certainly Russia had worn me down, confronting me with death, grief, and displeasure in so many varied, ingenious, and inevitable ways that fatalism was the only response. There really was only one thing to do.

"Let's drink to your health!" I suggested.

Za zdorov'ye!" he shouted. We upturned our glasses.

As the sun began casting oblique bronze rays through the big window, I remembered Vadim down at the shore. I had to get back. I stood up, rather unsteadily, and warmly thanked Grandpa (who gave me a jar of homemade blueberry jam as a going-away gift), Grandma, and Luka and Sasha for their hospitality. Luka walked me down to the bank, where Vadim was waiting for me in our raft, to see me off.

4

COAXED OUT OF SLEEP by the mosquito's whine, the horsefly's buzz, or the plaintive ha-*hoo!* ha-*hoo!* of a cuckoo perched somewhere in the taiga high above us, I now found awakening in my tent a languorous transition from dreamland into a pristine world without the carks, cares, or accoutrements that often intruded on my life back home. I had with me no alarm clock, no computer, no access to e-mail (or mail of any sort, of course), no telephone, no bills to pay, no deadlines to meet. Even the shortwave radio I carried proved less useful than expected, given that we were due north of China and heading for the Arctic; for the most part, the only news bulletins I could get were in Chinese. The civilized world lost its grip on me, and I lived according to the rhythms and exigencies of our voyage, immersing myself in the sounds and smells of the moment. So far, at least, far from vexing me with "wild villagers," the Lena was granting me a peace that I had rarely known.

Our fourth dawn found us camped on an incurved bank beneath a soaring forested slope. The scent of pine needles drifted down on the breeze and permeated my first moments of wakefulness. My eyes opened to focus on the silhouettes of more newly hatched dragonflies drying their wings on the walls of my tent. I unzipped the door and stepped barefoot onto rounded crunching pebbles to observe the river's crystalline currents flowing over a white stony bed. The sun had not yet surmounted the *sopki,* but it beamed its rays from beneath the horizon, tinting pink the puffy clouds set against a firmament of blue céleste.

Vadim had gone fishing, so I was alone on the bank. I turned to face the firs behind me: how silent they were, how deep the hollows beneath their majestic boughs! The noisy skylarks and magpies and crows of western Russia were nowhere to be seen. Several minutes passed before I detected audible signs of life: the faint dwindling screech of a hawk, the throaty grunt-caw of a raven. *Sleeping land,* I thought, *sleeping land.*

Fifty yards upriver a stream burbled down the *sopka* into the Lena, a cottony mist clinging to its surface like some sort of vaporous fur. At its mouth Vadim was rowing our boat among bobbing bottle floats, retrieving the fishing nets he had set the previous evening. Twenty minutes later he was standing at my side, dumping his catch, still twitching and gasping, onto the pebbles: okun' (perch), footlong and golden green; and krasnoperka, a larger, greener fish resembling a walleye.

He set about cleaning them, ripping out the gills, slicing open and gutting the bellies, hacking off the heads. "The krasnoperka, with its tiny scales, will be good for smoking," he said. "I'll salt the okun' and we can fry it for dinner."

"How are you going to smoke fish out here?"

He pointed with his chin at what looked like a charred metal shoebox with grass sticking out from beneath the lid. "In that. You'll see. You'll never have tasted better fish. It will be *much* better than that prefabricated *crap* Americans eat."

"Not all Americans eat TV dinners. I don't."

"America doesn't have its own cuisine. Your national dish is hamburgers. I just can't understand how you can stand it. And why do people rave about Italian or French food?" He grabbed a flapping okun' and severed its head. "Macaroni and snails!"

"Aren't you being a little close-minded? Don't you think you —"

"Westerners ought to look at how Russians eat and learn from us. What people has suffered the most in history? Russians! This means we've learned an awful lot, much more than peoples who live in luxury, like you all. So watch and learn."

Apart from excoriating city dwellers, Vadim had talked little since Ust'-Kut. But if the tone of his few words grated, he was here expressing stereotypical ideas about the West common enough in Russia. The morning was too beautiful for an argument. I dropped the subject and returned to my tent to pack.

· · ·

A day later we were sailing past rounded bluffs of tawny limestone, five hundred feet high and striated diagonally with reddened rivulets — what locals call *shchoki* (cheeks). In the West, where the peaks of the Rocky Mountains or the valleys of the Alps stand as examples of nature's artistic flair, the *shchoki* might not really impress, but they excited Vadim to cries of wonder; after all, mountains are rare across most of Russia, and *sopki* here generally repose under a dense layer of taiga. Throughout the trip he would display a zealous appreciation for natural beauty equaled only by his contempt for mankind.

The cheeks didn't last long, and eventually the taiga receded from the banks to leave clearings from which scattered trash and scrap metal announced the town of Kirensk, just around the bend at the confluence of the Lena and the Kirenga, a river emptying out of the wilderness to the south. Wrecked barges and ruined boats soon littered the shores, but between them stretched beaches teeming with bathers. Mothers frolicked in the shallows with their children; grandmothers in plastic bathing caps and one-piece swimsuits sunbathed standing, as Russians often do, posed like Hellenic statues with flabby midriffs and varicose veins; shirtless men with bronzed arms and sallow chests sat around campfires, roasting kebabs on skewers, now and then raising shot glasses for a toast and a gulp. Then a dirt road began paralleling the river, and along it putted 1930s-style motorcycles with sidecars, their leather-helmeted drivers bouncing up and down and swerving to avoid potholes. Finally, ahead, beneath more limestone bluffs, we spotted Kirensk, a colorful hodgepodge of slatted wooden houses interspersed with drooping poplars that formed a crown of foliage atop a hilly island in midriver. This was the old town; newer Soviet-era neighborhoods stood on the banks, marked with cranes and petrol barges.

Vadim grumbled.

"What's wrong?" I asked.

"I *hate* returning to civilization."

"Civilization? Kirensk is pretty remote."

"Well, there'll be drunks and thieves here. After all, it's a town. Where're we going to camp?"

A good question. We steered around Kirensk and made for a low island a half-mile downriver, and pulled up to the shelter of a willow grove at its head. Beneath the trees, tufts of chartreuse grass sprouted on soggy ground sloping up toward a meadow. Vadim steered us into an inlet that led right to the grove. Just above the mud, on dry ground, we put up camp.

"A lot of islands on the Lena disappear under the springtime floods, but not this one," he said. "I think it'll do for now."

Later I learned that this was Monastyrskiy Ostrov (Monastery Island) — home only to a shepherd, a cowherd, and a few bedraggled animals enjoying cloistral solitude beneath the limestone cheeks.

Greedy for *yasak,* in 1628 the Cossack Vasily Bugor quit Yeniseysk and headed east into the taiga, leading a division of ten men. Down the rapids of the Indirma River to the Kut they sailed and portaged, emerging — with much relief, to be sure — a year later onto the Lena's tranquil expanses. In 1630 they reached the Kirenga. Loaded down with furs collected on the way, Bugor returned to Yeniseysk, leaving four men on the midriver island to build a *zimov'ye* (an insulated, well-stocked shelter) in which to pass the winter. The next year the thirty-strong Cossack division of Petr Beketov arrived with orders to secure Muscovy's hold on the Lena by expanding the *zimov'ye* into a *pogost,* a noun that now means "churchyard" but that once probably meant "gathering place for a region obliged to pay tribute to the tsar." In Siberia, the Russian quest for wealth went hand in hand with the spread of Orthodox Christianity, as did the search for gold and proselytizing in the conquest of the New World taking place on the other side of the planet at the same time. Beketov christened the *pogost* in honor of Saint Nicholas, the patron saint of Russia and the protector of travelers, and charged his men with collecting *yasak* from the Evenks, animal herders roaming the surrounding taiga. (The *pogost* became Kirensk only in 1775.) On the whole, collection from the animist tribes went peaceably, and Cossacks married Evenk women, thereby acquiring knowledgeable guides who swore fealty to the tsar and helped in exploring Siberia.

Eventually Bugor returned to the Lena, but he and his men ended badly. Some years later, they sailed downriver to the *ostrog* of Yakutsk, fell out with its despotic Cossack administrator, and suffered imprisonment, but managed to escape. Once free, they turned renegade, plundering other Cossacks of *yasak,* boats, and provisions.

. . .

The next morning Vadim deposited me at Kirensk's antique green dock. Nothing had changed since my first visit in 2000. The aroma of sap perfumed the warm air. The sun transformed floating poplar puffs into snowflakes of gold that showered a dreamy languor over shack shops and izbas, mostly hundred-year-old candy green or bright blue hovels sinking crookedly into ashen earth. Other cabins had been painted in chocolate hues, with ornately carved white gutters and shutters, the nineteenth-century *rez'ba* (artistic woodcarving) of Siberian masters. Children's laughter rang out from behind larch fences; twosomes and threesomes of teens peddled past me on rusty old single-gear bikes, zinging their bells; young women, wan-eyed, fleshy and cream-complexioned, with thin wrists and ankles, heavy breasts, and pouting lips, strolled past arm in arm, the embodiment of fertility and domesticity. Many were métis, of Slavic and Asiatic blood. But Kirensk was not paradise: groggy alcoholics, their chests sunken in and blue-veined, their faces pink and swollen like overripe fruit, begged in shop doorways, asking for alms in coarse, hopeless voices.

Near the dock I took out my camera and snapped a picture of a *rez'ba*-covered house.

"*Muzhchina!* [Man!] Muzh*cheeena!*"

A woman called out to me from beneath the poplars.

I turned to face a diminutive red-haired woman in her thirties, with high Buryat cheeks and a button nose. Taking mincing steps, her arms chugging like the wheels of a toy choo-choo, she hurried over to me and grabbed my free hand, pushing her face to mine.

"Send that picture to President Putin! I want him to see how bad we live out here. Our town is a dump — just look at those drunks! We should be rich but our mayor is robbing us blind, stealing the money Putin sends to help us."

There has long been a tradition of *yurodivyye* in Russia, holy but mad souls protected by Providence whose insanity permits them to tell the truth with impunity. In a country with almost no public support system for the mentally ill, they subsist on charity alone. Judging by her manners and eyes, this woman was a *yurodivaya*. Holy or not, however, I tried to pull my hand free of her damp grip, but she tightened it and pressed her body to mine.

"I'm from Bodaibo. So I *know* what an honest administration is. Everybody all over the world knows about Bodaibo! You're of course from Moscow, right?"

"Not exactly."

She demanded to know my country, so I told her. She then licked her lips and wiggled her eyebrows, imitating Mae West — how could she have known that actress? — after a fashion that, I could only think, one needed more than a splash of verve and a dash of talent to pull off. And pull it off she did.

"Say, that bein' a pistolet in you pocket, or you be'in heppy to see me! Ah, me likin' you! You takin' me to America! Me sing-a-you song!"

In pidgin English that sounded straight from an equatorial port, she proceeded to render "Strangers in the Night," raising her arms and dancing with an invisible suitor; the effect was entertaining, and she had a gift of some indeterminable sort. The passing clutches of strolling women and cycling teens glanced at us and smiled; in such a small town, they must have known her. She took my hand again. *"You a wondiful distoorbin' kinda guy! Me likin' you muchy, takin' me to America!"*

"I think my wife might object." I felt bad that I could think of no more artful response to her lines.

She reverted to Russian. "Just my luck. An American makes love to me on a sunny morning in June, and he's married! Come back to Kirensk when you're divorced!"

She let my hand go and walked back to the poplars, where she sat down and put her head between her hands, a grievous frown contorting her features. She looked up at me, though, her eyes red and despairing.

Vadim had given me a list of perishables to buy — bread, fruit, vegetables, and so on. But one glance at the stores' names told me shopping wouldn't be easy here: DOM BYTA (House of Appliances), PROM- TOVARY (Manufactured Goods), PRODUKTY (groceries) — names portending unreconstructedly Soviet-style establishments scantily stocked with stale goods, run by sullen clerks, clicking with ancient abacuses and smelling of bad plumbing. But I had no choice, so I dropped into the first one. It lacked most of what I needed, but I bought a loaf of black bread, and also a Mars bar, which I ate while the pretty but glum attendant knocked her abacus beads about in an angry Morse code of clicks, as though she was being forced to compute the cost of half the store's items. (There was in fact a cash register, but a pale thin fellow with dark hair stood over its disassembled parts, conducting repairs.) Peeved, she closed her eyes and blurted out the amount I owed: a whole dollar's worth of rubles.

I paid. But I didn't really want to leave just yet: as grumpy as she was, I wanted to talk to her. Days of travel with taciturn Vadim had left me yearning to hear a human's voice. So, I unpeeled my Mars bar and ate it, and asked where I might find the other foodstuffs on my list. "Don't know," she snapped.

At that I saw there was no point, and I started walking out.

"Hey, *muzhchina!* Clean up after yourself!" she barked in a sharp voice. "I've got enough to do without sweeping up your garbage!"

"I'm sorry," I said, picking up the wrapper I had left on the counter.

She shook her head at my unforgivable negligence. "*Sorry!* Everyone is *always* sorry. Put your trash in the trash bin over there where it belongs!"

I did so, thinking, *Civilization! Vadim was right!* The thin man finished with the register and told the clerk he'd be back soon with the spare part. He walked out with me.

"Quite a militant salesgirl, isn't she?" he said with a smile.

"Yes. She doesn't exactly charm her customers, does she."

We started talking. He introduced himself as Ivan, manager of a cash register repair firm; he was making the rounds of his clients' shops. Waiting for him down the block was his technician, Pavel, a blond fellow with a stevedore's build. Both were in their twenties. Ivan invited me back to their office nearby, a two-room affair on the second floor of a lopsided larch tenement, the first floor of which served as the DA's headquarters. There, in a musty room bathed in sunlight and strewn with metallic shells and keys and the assorted plastic widgets of defunct registers, they attended to the complaints of a sweating, Sumo-shouldered Buryat woman whose toes crisscrossed crookedly in cheap sandals and whose beet-red helmet of hair showed an inch of black root.

Done with her, they asked if I'd like to see the town. I said yes.

We chatted as we walked Kirensk's dusty streets, with the river glinting from behind the poplars at many a turn, with *sopki* rising to the north. I told them I found the town charming.

"Oh, it's not really paradise out here," said Ivan. "Everything is falling apart. Moscow is trying to sell off our river fleet, which is all we have; this town lives off transporting oil to Yakutsk. Our sailors aren't paid for months on end" — their salaries ranged from $160 to $300 a month — "and sometimes go on strikes, taking their boats out and blocking the channel. And in 2002 a huge flood hit us in the spring. Moscow offered us a thousand rubles [about thirty dollars] a person to cover losses. Think of it! You lose your house and get a thousand rubles! Nothing's improving."

"Nothing? In fact, I see a lot of women with young children here. That's got to be a sign of hope."

"Okay, some things have improved, you know. At least we're capable of manufacturing some things now, when we couldn't under Yeltsin. For instance, we haven't bought foreign cash registers since the [economic] crisis of 'ninety-eight. Our Russian companies have gotten their act together, with foreign stuff being so costly. Prices have stabilized and some are having kids now. There's not much else to do out here."

"Has Putin restrained the *mafiya?*"

He looked around. "Well, they don't really bother those not involved in" — he cleared his throat — "in dark dealings."

"They don't bother you?"

"No, no," he said quickly, inhaling and looking around, as if searching for a new topic of conversation.

Our first stop was a ruined two-story brick building standing alone above a plot of wild, tangled grass, near the bank of the Kirenga. Its roof had collapsed, and sunlight streamed through its empty window apertures. Vandals had long ago stripped away the doors and stolen anything else of value. We entered and picked our way down a derelict staircase, emerging in a stinking basement strewn with spent beer and vodka bottles, shards of glasses, and old clothes befouled in a way that hinted at binges, violence, and death. This foul place, my guides told me, was the old NKVD office (the predecessor of the KGB), and it had made Kirensk infamous in the last days of Soviet rule.

I asked why. Pavel casually recounted what he had seen here in May of 1991. "I watched them bring the corpses out of the basement. It was interesting, you know. They had been buried in 1938" — during Stalin's Great Terror — "but since they were mummified, preserved, that is, you could tell who was who. People found they could still recognize their relatives, even after fifty years."

We were standing in dungeons. In 1991, tipped off by the deathbed confession of a former NKVD officer, citizens of Kirensk rushed here and uncovered eighty-four corpses — people executed by a blow to the head with a blunt object. The NKVD had arrested them in 1938, and later that year informed their relatives that their loved ones had — all of them, on a single day — succumbed to "cardiac insufficiency." But a document found in the pocket of one of the victims stated the charge: "Active participation and activity in a counterrevolutionary . . . organization" — a common, but preponderantly false, accusation in Stalin's time. The sentence was death.

I asked my hosts what they thought of the unjust killings. They shrugged. Not quite so impassive later on was Olga Kuleshova, the director of the Kirensk Regional Museum. Olga herself was descended from tsarist-era exiles, and she told me that one of her uncles had been found among the exhumed. Though he was the chairman of a local collective farm (and so, presumably, was a loyal Communist) he had been denounced in an anonymous letter to the NKVD as a "wrecker" and an "exploiter of farm laborers" — more lethal charges common in Stalin's day.

"Siberia is the prison of nations," she said, sighing. Her voice shifted from calm to despairing, and her gaze deepened. "The executed were our best minds, the light of our nation, the cultured people among us. There were rumors that others, who were never found, were put on barges and drowned in Pyanyi Byk" — a narrow winding stretch of the Lena downstream.

Why had no one demanded vengeance when the implausible death notices arrived? I asked.

"In those days people who complained shared the fate of the murdered. Children denounced their parents. Everyone feared for their lives. Remember, Siberia is the prison of nations. What could you expect from inmates?"

Only the macabre element — that the faces of the executed could be recognized a half-century later — stood out as unique in this story; I had heard many like it during my years in Russia. But with President Putin assuming powers that many fear may eventually recall those of Stalin, I was becoming increasingly alarmed by the indifference Russians displayed toward both atrocities in the Generalissimo's day and the renewed potential for repression now. The NKVD headquarters could have been preserved as a monument to repression, but the befouled execution site in the basement showed what little importance people attached to the murder of innocents. Every time I confronted such sights, I tried to suppress my inclination to follow the lead of my Russian hosts and shrug and accept them, but for now I kept silent.

I invited Ivan and Pavel to lunch in Kirensk's one functioning café-restaurant, the Luch. Though built of cheap-looking panels of white steel, the place was clean and bright, and its Buryat waitress served us tasty chicken and fries.

Their nonchalance about the killings and Putin's growing power wouldn't let me rest.

"Could the Terror repeat itself?" I asked them as we ate.

"Oh, all that could never happen again," said Ivan. "We have our freedoms now. Everything's permitted."

"What do you think, Pavel?"

He raised his eyebrows and took a bite of chicken.

Everything is *not* permitted in Russia now, of course, as Putin's curtailing of liberties has shown, though if you're twenty-seven the murders in the basement must seem part of a distant past. In fact, they stalk the present. The fears and executions of the Stalin years further entrenched an already potent fatalism and generated a comforting misconception that prevails still: as long as things don't get *that* bad, as bad as they were during the Terror, say, they're not really bad at all. This fatuity, by inducing complacence, could enable the rise of a new tyrant, and is especially inexcusable in Kirensk, where three NKVD prisons had functioned and corpses with recognizable faces had been unearthed, and where, moreover, plaques on houses announced that so many Decembrist revolutionaries had passed sentences of exile. Here the past coexists with the present in a way that no sentient being could ignore.

Reformist-minded revolt in fact began with the Decembrists, though not in Kirensk. Named after the month in 1825 during which their rebellion broke out in Saint Petersburg (then capital of Russia), the Decembrists, Russian army officers enamored of Enlightenment ideals, launched their country's first revolutionary movement. They hoped to bring down autocracy, establish a republic, and abolish serfdom; in short, they wanted to Westernize Russia. In reprisal, Tsar Nicholas I hanged five of them and banished hundreds of others to Siberia. But, fearing the spread of the Western contagion, he then went further and "reformed" Russia in a way of which Stalin would have approved. Since the dissident officers had been "infected" with liberal ideas while in Europe during the war of 1812, Nicholas I forbid Russians from traveling abroad. He expanded the powers of the secret police, issuing them a mandate to "report about all occurrences without exception"; he instituted Russia's first state ideology, "Orthodoxy, Autocracy, and Patriotism." He strengthened censorship, even creating censors to censor the censors. He expanded Russia's already gargantuan bureaucracy, the incompetence of which (then as now) was only superseded by its venality. In sum, Nicholas I instilled throughout Russia "the quiet of a graveyard, rotting and stinking, both physically and morally," as one disillusioned reactionary of the time put it. The graveyard today looks less lugubrious, but Russians' overwhelming submission to the Kremlin's growing powers shows that they may be standing on their own tombs nonetheless.

After saying goodbye to Ivan and Pavel, I returned to the river to await Vadim. I alternately seethed with frustration and despaired, thinking of how Russians even after centuries of despotism would not likely resist reimposition of something similar, even now, when the country is more open to the West than ever. I remembered a passage from Alexander Solzhenitsyn's *Gulag Archipelago* about how millions of Russians passively suffered arrest, imprisonment, exile, and execution during the Stalin decades:

> How later, in the prison camps, it burned to think that if only every officer, on his way to make an arrest, had doubted whether he would return alive, and found he had to say goodbye to his family? If during the times of mass arrests, for example, in Leningrad, when a quarter of the city was being imprisoned, people had not huddled in their lairs, overcome with horror at every slamming of their apartment building's entrance door and at every footstep on the stairs, but had understood that they had nothing left to lose, and had lain in ambush, in groups of threes and fours, armed with axes, hammers, pokers, with whatever they had? Because you knew anyway that these [officers of the night] were not coming with good intentions you would not have done wrong in breaking the murderer's skull . . . then the [secret police] would quickly have begun losing staff, despite Stalin's thirst for blood, and the whole damned machine would have ground to a halt!
>
> If only . . . if only. We simply deserved everything that happened afterwards.

5

BENEVOLENT SUN AND INVIGORATING BREEZE! Before my expedition down the Lena, I had never taken such visceral pleasure in light, which, at our high latitude, slanted through the atmosphere as though cast from the divine torch of a solicitous deity aiming to warm but not burn. Neither had I relished each breath the way I did here on the Lena, where every inhalation (at least near the taiga, when the breeze was right) refreshed with its bouquet of pine scents and spruce aromas.

The river wound northeast in lazy loops, widening and narrowing and widening again. Islands that had been submerged in the spring spate now, during the summertime ebb, stood lush with alders, silver-leafed and shaggy, and began dividing the channel into watery lanes. I reclined on my bench and turned south to gaze at the alabaster crescent of the matinal moon above the taiga staggered on the *sopki*'s rising shelves. The sky beyond was a feast for the impressionist's soul, displaying manifold soft hues. Now, at noon, it was robin's-egg blue; at dawn and dusk, salmon pink. And during the four-hour (and shrinking) night, the passage of which I hardly noticed at times, it spread from horizon to horizon a glowing canopy of lavender.

Before we set out from Ust'-Kut, I had steeled myself for hardship. It hadn't occurred to me that this expedition could actually be *enjoyable*. Was traveling the Lena so for Cossack explorers? The written records (mostly official correspondence with the tsars) suggest it was not. To begin with, however courageous and free-spirited the Cossacks were, they served a despot. Cossack commanders thus had to address their sovereign in servile locutions, referring to themselves as *kholopy tvoi* (your humble servants, or slaves) and reporting back to them by means of *chelobitnyye* — petitions, but literally, "a banging of one's forehead" (against the ground), as in a bow of submission, a custom Russians had adopted during days of subservience to the Tatar-Mongolians. In such *chelobitnyye* Semyon Dezhnyov, for example, dwelled on the miseries and perils he suffered on the Lena for his master in the Kremlin, citing suspiciously numerous and near-fatal wounds sustained during battles with benighted indigenes unwilling to offer up *yasak* peaceably. For their many troubles (and, of course, their loyalty), the tsars paid him and his comrades salaries known as *zhalovaniya* — a mix of bread, salt, lead, and rubles.

We had it better, of course, though not everything was sweet. In places the Lena now stretched a mile or even two miles across, yet the distances didn't daunt horseflies — green-eyed beasts almost an inch long, with wasplike carapaces striped black and yellow. One or two always managed to stay with us, circling, landing, and circling again, until they caught us unawares and drove their proboscises, a quarter-inch long and curved like scythes, through our clothes and into our skin, provoking us to murder them with angry swats. Small consolation it was that they were too heavy and slow to escape.

All morning we coursed through islands, beneath ridges covered with a stately mélange of cedars and pines, until we caught sight of the tiny hamlet of Petropavlovskoye, on the north side of an elevated bend. There, we stopped so I could look up Leonid (a friend of Ivan's), a collector of artifacts and an amateur historian. Locals directed me to his house, an izba with blue and white *rez'ba* window frames and a gabled roof of aluminum siding. A picket fence enclosed both his house and that of a departed neighbor, plus a shed stacked with firewood and a garden plot of tomatoes, onions, and cucumbers.

I rapped on the door. An old woman called out in a feeble voice. But the door swung open forcefully, with a loud creak.

"*Zdorovo!*" a husky man's voice called out from the dark.

"*Zdorovo!* Leonid?"

"*Da.*"

I introduced myself. Leonid stepped out into the light, his thick, dark-rimmed glasses glinting. He shook my hand with a shockingly powerful grip, and nodded as I described my expedition, looking down and saying "*khorosho, khorosho*" (fine, fine). His shoulders sloped vertiginously, but his forearms rippled with muscle and vein — he later told me that he had been a weightlifter in his youth and had even traveled to Moscow to compete in national competitions. Now in his late fifties, he had the look of a brainy proletarian. On his breath I detected a sweet-sour smell of vodka.

I finished explaining myself. He continued nodding. "Ah-ha. Hmm. Say, you play the accordion?" he asked. Alcohol or no, his speech was precise.

"Ah, no."

"Come!"

He grabbed my hand and pulled me across the yard, along a plank walkway (useful during muddy spring and autumn months) to a room in the back of his cabin — his retreat, apparently. He opened the door. Through filthy glass windows yellow light poured over stacks of old photos and dozens of accordions, ancient and dusty, plus bayany and tal'yanki, the wind instruments of Russian folk music. He seized an accordion, huffed away the dust, and squeezed out a tune, breaking into song. I sensed he wasn't so much drunk on vodka as he was excited to have someone new to perform for.

A groan sounded from the front of the cabin.

"I'm coming, Mom! Come with me!" He pulled me back outside and launched into a history of the village. "You know Zakharka?"

"Who?"

"The Cossack Zakharka Ignat'yev founded us in 1646. Our original name was Zakharovo. The village grew and grew until it became the capital of a *volost'* " — an administrative division in tsarist days. "Then of course they built the Church of the Two Apostles" — Peter and Paul, as *Petropavlovskoye* translates — "and it was the tallest church on the Lena, with two belfries thirty meters high. You know about it?"

"No. I didn't see a church from the river."

"It stood right there, right where the public library is now, across the road. Well, Soviet law protected it as a landmark, but during the Stalin years our leaders encouraged people to destroy it as part of the struggle against religion. Brick by brick they took it apart, for building materials. I'll show you something."

He walked me down the block and over to the museum room in the school. There, coins and old flags and documents lay in scratched glass cases. On the wall were black-and-white photos showing the gradual reduction of the magnificent church to rubble.

Without warning he sang, in a dreamy baritone, a verse from Pushkin. "'*Ya Vas lyubil! Lyubov' yeshcho, byt' mozhet.*' [I used to love you! Love may come again.] You a musician?"

"No."

"I need to sing sometimes or I'd lose my mind." His voice cracked on the last word, and he paused. "There's too much grief in our history out here. Anyway, as I watched fellow villagers take apart the church I became obsessed with saving our heritage. Look here." He pulled a paperback-size icon off the wall. It showed the apostles Peter and Paul, dressed in robes now the color of dried blood, their faces obscured by grime but with their eyes clearly scratched out. It must have been painted a century ago. "I rescued it from the church's entrance. Villagers used to burn precious icons like this for *fuel* in the winter! Imagine! Icons hundreds of years old, and *zap!* into the fire, for five minutes' heat!"

I studied the scratched-out eyes and thought of the church's history in Russia. There was a connection. In the year 988 Prince Vladimir of Kievan Rus' accepted Christianity from the Byzantine Greeks and began converting his pagan subjects to it. If he chose Christianity because it was the faith of the advanced, wealthy empire to the south, benefits beyond better trade relations soon followed. A pair of (Bulgarian) monks developed an alphabet for the Russians based on Greek letters; and Byzantine social customs, law, and literature spread throughout Rus', enhancing their Russian counterparts. But Vladimir's choice of Eastern Orthodoxy over Roman Catholicism, natural given Kiev's proximity to the Greeks, bore heavy consequences. After 1054, the year of the Great Schism (the rift between the churches of Rome and Byzantium), Russia found itself estranged from Europe and, eventually, isolated from the Renaissance, the Reformation, and other developments that would lead the West out of the Middle Ages and foster the Enlightenment and the rise of democracy. Ivan the Terrible and later tsars increasingly subjugated the church and turned it into the ideological arm of despotism. The clergy thus made easy targets for Soviet propagandists aiming to rile impoverished peasants; in fact, the KGB infiltrated the Church, and many priests served as agents. The Church is still basically an adjunct of the state and as such enjoys privileges, including the right, granted by presidential decree in the mid-1990s, to import cigarettes, alcohol, and luxury cars tax-free.

Leonid continued. "I went house to house, collecting what I could

—coins, tsarist rubles, even this bloodletting device" — he pointed to a rusty pair of pincers that, he said, could be used to bleed a patient and reduce hypertension. "See, our life here has always been tough, and we've had to improvise. We suffer from vitamin deficiencies and sixty-below frosts. We've never had doctors out here. Anyway, everyone was happy to get rid of their 'old junk.' Incredible!" He paused and inhaled, and hummed briefly. *"Ya Vas lyubil!"*

I walked around, examining the artifacts. I found a photo of Leonid in his twenties, proudly standing on Red Square with his burly arms crossed. Next to him hung Stalin's portrait.

Leonid walked over. "We can't get rid of history, so I've hung Stalin here. Some say he was a tyrant, others, a good ruler. Whatever he was, we won the Great Patriotic War going into battle shouting, 'For the Motherland! For Stalin!'"

"You sound proud."

"Look, like everyone else, I cried in 'fifty-three when he died. Those who remember Stalin remember the order, the discipline! We hoped Putin might establish the same. But *no.* As things stand, we have *no* government in Russia, *no* real courts, *nothing.* You've got to remember how tough life is out here for us. We *need* help from the state, just to survive. But we have only six hours of electricity a day. Bears kill people: my own brother-in-law was eaten by a bear. Another man I knew was scalped by a bear. We're all hunters here, as a result. But now when we go after the bears we have trouble: our dogs have been so interbred that they fear them." He paused. "We call our government for help and get no answer. We're entering the twenty-first century losing our phones and electricity and still fighting bears!"

"But what about all the blood Stalin shed, the injustices? How could you possibly want another dictatorship?"

"It's better to serve in a battalion with discipline, right? Look, we're half Asiatic, half European. We need to maintain our traditions, and for that we need a *strong leader.* We need *discipline.*"

"You don't think Putin fits the bill?"

"He's changing things — for the worse. Definitely for the worse. We don't expect much from him. He is, after all, Yeltsin's heir."

We walked back outside. The sun showered soft golden light over the river; a breeze rustled the birches and fluffed up the lank grass; his mother's cry echoed from down the lane. Leonid favored a dictatorship, but a dictatorship had encouraged the destruction of the patrimony he made it his mission to salvage and caused the "grief" he decried, the grief that made him sing and possibly drink. Had any other people on earth done so much to destroy itself? Tens of millions of Russians were complicit, either actively or unwittingly, in their country's ruin, and yet to this day were unrepentant, even defiantly yearning for more of the brutality that ruined them.

Leonid continued. "All we've had since the end of the Soviet Union has been a criminal revolution," he said. "In a hundred years there won't even *be* a Kirensk or a Petropavlovskoye left. We were three thousand people here in the village and surrounding land. Now we're down to seven fifty. Our people have lost their faith. Before, we lived to help others, we had a sense of duty. Now, money has become our god. Our parents' generation knew *golod i kholod* [famine and cold] and had to fight to survive. Now they've set up these unemployment offices in the cities, so who wants to work? We've degenerated, and we've raised our young to be dependent. Theft is our biggest problem out here. The young steal for booze money. They're drinking themselves to death. For all this I blame state policy."

At the path leading down to the river I thanked Leonid for his time, and we said goodbye. I hurried to the raft. Vadim was starting up the engine.

Out on the water the wind picked up, and we lurched through low waves, dowsed in glittering spray. A few hours later, in a clearing amid firs on a mountainside, Vadim and I spotted a manned guard tower with a Soviet flag flying above it at full mast — a startling sight, since the Russian Tricolor had replaced the red banner thirteen years ago. Nearby, from what looked like two-story cement barracks, glowered down a thirty-foot-high portrait of Lenin, painted in red and white, in the stark style of socialist realism. From beneath Lenin's chin, a shaved-skulled youth in what resembled a blue prison uniform launched into a run down the bank toward us, waving. An officer in khaki then emerged from a cabin high above, peered at us through binoculars, and motioned that we approach.

"This looks like a labor camp," said Vadim. "Don't tell me you want to stop here."

I wondered whether it would be wise to stop and decided that we should, since we had all our permits and fleeing would only arouse suspicion.

The shaved-skulled fellow reached us first, panting. He was smiling. He shook our hands and welcomed us to "Zolotoy Correctional Labor Settlement."

"You're an inmate?" I asked.

"Sure am."

"You seem awfully cheerful about it."

"He gets to live in the taiga," said Vadim defiantly. "So he's happy."

Out from the barracks marched a line of ten inmates, tanned and healthy-looking; one whistled to our accoster.

"Oh, sorry, roll call!" he exclaimed, and trotted off to join them.

The officer, a lieutenant colonel, judging by his epaulets, finally walked up and asked me warily to explain our presence. I did. He listened and nodded, interested but, to my surprise, not alarmed.

Vadim needed to fix something in our motor, so the officer and I stepped away from the boat to let him work. We began chatting. He was a dark-haired and brooding type, in his midforties. It turned out he was the commander of this camp, where inmates served their sentences logging in the taiga.

"They don't look very dangerous," I said on hearing the news. "Are they petty criminals?"

"Oh, they all robbed someone or beat up people," he said. "They're here for a good reason."

He found nothing wrong in our visiting and offered to walk me up to the camp store, where I could buy bread. I accepted. Zolotoy, he said, had once been a logging settlement, but its timber plant had died with perestroika, and the remaining villagers, now mostly pensioners, lived in the derelict huts up on the bank. As part of their duties, the inmates helped them with their chores. All this would have seemed thoroughly pleasant except for the vicious, chained-up attack dogs that lunged barking at us from every yard.

But what about the Soviet flag? I asked.

"Excuse me, what's wrong with the Soviet flag? It's *always* pleasant to see it. It reminds of how things were before all that crap with perestroika began and killed this village."

As we walked back to the raft, he talked about his disillusionment with reforms, about the one year he had left before retirement, and about the beauty of being posted out in these wilds. Yet he grew curt once we reached the shore; he clearly didn't want us to hang around. With no ceremony, he shook our hands and saw us off.

The officer's frank air and the casual atmosphere of his camp surprised me; he hadn't even glanced at my passport. The free rein the prisoners enjoyed and the alacrity with which the inmate had approached us gave me to think that, with the death of Soviet ideology and the collapse of the police state, perhaps prisoners might be treated with the relative lenience they knew during the tsarist centuries. The air of secrecy, even paranoia, that would have surrounded this camp fifty or even twenty years ago had vanished. No matter what the officer said, something had definitely changed for the better since perestroika.

From Zolotoy the Lena narrowed and curved north. As the day aged, clouds and mist drifted in, lacing the dark green *sopki* with white, softening the crisp, sunny landscape into a shadowy, oneiric domain. We chugged ahead, and I slipped in and out of sleep, finding my dreams vivid, all voices and visions from my past. Oddly enough, Rabelais came to mind, along with his lines, from somewhere in *Gargantua and Pantagruel,* about mysterious voices assailing travelers in the far north — snippets of speech frozen by frosts and thawing out in spring.

But a battering of waves jarred me awake. The river was now dividing again into channels running between wooded islands; the *sopki* were rising, with rocky patches scarring their faces. The wind had shifted and drove down from the north, hurrying toward us a front of dark clouds and chill air.

Vadim unfolded his poncho and slipped into it. "We'd better quit early this evening and look for shelter. A storm's about to hit."

The waves and gusts affirmed his prediction, as did the thrashing pines on the bank. A cabin came into view on a finger of land jutting into the river beneath a *sopka.*

"Let's see if we can stay over at that cabin, and meet its owner," I said, expecting Vadim to protest. But he didn't.

"Good idea. I'd like to meet someone who could teach me about hunting in these parts."

We veered off and pulled up to the bank. I wondered how much of a shock our sudden arrival would inflict on the hermit who no doubt lived here. Feeling it would be safer to announce my presence, I shouted hello. I jumped out and thrashed through waist-high grass, examining the cabin's windows, which were dark.

I called out again. No answer. I cautiously walked around back and discovered that the windows there had been smashed; inside I saw chairs, tables, clothes on a peg. I turned around to shout again but spotted a tombstone beneath two birches. The cabin's owner had died years ago. Someone had buried him but not touched his effects.

I hurried back to the boat.

"You're out of luck," I said to Vadim. "Your hunter is dead."

We headed downriver a few miles. We set up camp on an elevated isle of sand and pines, facing *sopki* to the southwest, just as the rains hit. The cumulus bearing them, purple-gray, rolled out of the east and over our heads, drifting away to melt above the sunset.

During the night the weather cleared. Circled by chipper swallows, we traveled all morning, stopping for a lunch of tea, bread, and sausage beneath the sheer limestone cliffs to which the birds had affixed their nests, hand-size pouches of mud from which peeked cheeping black mandibles. After our meal, we moved on. Soon we rounded a bend and saw a majestic larch edifice standing alone on a promontory.

"Look, a bell tower!" Vadim shouted.

Our first church on the river.

Vadim grabbed his map. "This is the village of Mutina. It's not marked as abandoned. There should be people here."

"I thought all the churches had been destroyed. We've come three hundred miles and not seen one."

"Oh, who cares. We were pagans anyway. The tsars forced Christianity on us. Most Russians didn't know what Christianity was until Ivan the Terrible. Which was probably good. Nothing's brought the world more pain and suffering than religion."

We pulled up to the bank and got out. Mutina was tiny. In the brilliant sunlight stood a half-dozen izbas and shacks amid tangles of uncut grass. We poked around, and I looked into the church, the bell tower of which rose from a gable-roofed nave. The interior had been gutted, probably by looters. I guessed its age to be around a hundred years.

There were no people about, however.

"What could have happened to the villagers?" asked Vadim. He stared across the fields through his binoculars. "Look! Graves!"

We loped down into a valley, plodded across a stream, and hiked a hundred yards up the other side. Behind bent steel fences almost lost to high grass we found tombstones, emblazoned with black-and-white portraits of the deceased, as was the Soviet custom. The first was "Svetlana Karmadonova 1956–1988." She had been a beauty: the picture showed long dark hair curving around an oval face and a svelte neck, delicate earrings, a floral-print dress. What could have taken her life at such a young age? Next to her were tombstones without pictures but with inscriptions: "Luker'ya Svetlolobova 1896–1969. Sleep, Dear Mother!" and "Raisa Ramazuyeva 1928–1969. Sleep, Dear Sister, Mother, and Wife!" Just behind them lay "Andrei Sveltolobov 1964–1990."

"What could have killed the young ones?" Vadim asked. "People should have been healthy here."

A gust of wind chilled us. Historians and writers have long occupied themselves with Moscow and Saint Petersburg, written about the Volga and the steppes, and described the parts of Siberia along the railway. Even Kolyma, a gulag zone farther to the east, had found its littérateurs among the intelligentsia exiled there. But the Lena? Its shores have known no chronicler, its villages no hallower in verse, its deeds and deaths no novelist. Lives had begun and ended here — no more.

We headed back down to the boat.

Like flamboyant schooners of eiderdown, elaborately tufted but flat-bottomed cumuli, harbingers of hot weather, were moving across the sky when we pulled in at Korshunovo, a village of some two hundred souls just south of the border between the Irkutsk oblast and the Republic of Sakha. As usual, Vadim steered us to a spot on the stony bank opposite.

After we set up our tents, he ran me over to the village and left me. I climbed up the path to the clearing, some twenty feet above the river. Houses bore fresh coats of paint, and their windows glinted spotless in the sun. Siberian huskies dozed on cut grass by picket fences. Echoing through the fresh air came the banging of hammers and the *put-put* of tractors, the staccato buzz of a power saw. Farther in, men and women tilled crops in plots spreading in checkered formation across the clearing to the taiga's edge. In contrast to so many places we had seen so far, Korshunovo was alive and vibrant.

By chance I had debarked in front of the modern, almost Scandinavian-looking wooden house of the mayor, Vladimir Ryutin, whom Leonid had recommended I meet, so I knocked on his door. Within an hour I was sitting in his rustic but well-appointed kitchen, sipping tea and gazing onto the river below. Vladimir was in his late forties, hale and muscular, with glossy white hair and a dark mustache and brows. His wife, an attractive, tanned blonde in a white scarf, served me scrambled eggs and sausage.

Still spooked by our stop in Mutina, I asked Vladimir what had killed off the village.

"Ah, Mutina! I tried to get the church there disassembled and moved here. But the priests told me it was built on holy ground, and it would be a sin or bad luck to touch it. Now, I was a Communist, of course, but I also believe in God. So I respected their wishes and left it alone."

"What happened to the people?"

"You saw the tombstones? It was a tragedy, a real tragedy. Young Andrei died of meningitis. Svetlana was a beauty, but, well, she took to the bottle. She was married. She used to invite her vodka friends over to the house, and her husband didn't like it. So he forbid her to drink. But one evening he came home and found them all drinking and laughing. He went in his room, got his shotgun and loaded it, and came back out. He fired a blast right through her heart. She never knew what hit her."

"What happened to him?"

"He did time in jail. But then he was released on good behavior and joined the army. He was killed in an accident somewhere on duty. That ended the history of Mutina."

For the rest of that afternoon and most of the following day, while we sat in his home, visited his office, and toured the garden plots, I put questions to Vladimir about life in Korshunovo, and he responded avidly. Founded by the Cossack Stepan Korshunov some three hundred years ago, Korshunovo was more than a remote Siberian village. The empress Catherine the Great (who ruled from 1762 to 1796) ordered the laying of the Prilensky Trakt (a postal carriage road along the Lena, now defunct) to Yakutsk, and Korshunovo was designated a way station where officials checked travel permits and issued carriages with fresh horses. During Soviet times, Korshunovo, with nine hundred heads of cattle, produced meat and milk for LenZoloto, the state gold-mining enterprise to the south in Bodaibo, until it closed down in 1993. After that, it lost a third of its inhabitants. Twelve-seater planes on their way to Lensk downriver used to land on the tiny runway nearby, but in 2002 the local air company went bankrupt and flights stopped, isolating Korshunovo for months on end during the mucky spring and fall *bezdorozh'ye* (roadlessness). As in Cossack times, hunting for sable, especially the valuable black barguzin, provides able sportsmen and trappers with relatively substantial income, sixty-five dollars a skin (a season's take might be from twenty to a hundred skins) — still of course far less than the $175 to $1,000 the furs bring on the international markets. Bears here as elsewhere pose an increasing danger.

"The problem is," Vladimir explained, "no one patrols the river anymore. Drowned people wash up and the bears get them. Once they've eaten human flesh, they become man-eaters. You're going to have to be careful out there. Say, how have people been treating you? How are they living upriver?"

I told Vladimir about my talk with Leonid and his pro-Stalinist comments. He dismissed them.

"Oh, our people are used to complaining," he said. "The past is always better. It's the same with my residents. This village is on federal handouts, so it makes sense that the government doesn't do much for us, and everyone here complains. We don't give the federal government meat, vegetables, gold, or anything. Our people don't understand that you don't get something for nothing."

"But it seems prosperous enough."

"Yes, it is. I work hard to keep good relations with the oblast authorities, and that helps. But as for Putin, I don't think he's doing much of anything, good or bad. He's just a pawn. The real actors are offstage, shadowy figures, and we don't even know who they are. They run the country for themselves, for their own aggrandizement. And anyway, as always in Russia, by the time Kremlin orders make it out here, they're out of date and no one enforces them. What does worry me, though, is that our media are glorifying Putin, just as they glorified Stalin and Lenin. That's dangerous. We just need our courts to function as courts, our police to be police. That would make us a normal country. The solution is pretty simple. But we're nowhere near it.

"As for our people, it's easier for them to complain than do any actual work; they could get a three-year interest-free loan to start a farm, but no one does. That would take work, and who wants to work?"

His words sounded true. And Korshunovo's order and relative prosperity showed that he was a rarity in the former Soviet Union: a local leader who cared about his people, knew his job, and performed it well.

"Look," he said, "Gorbachev should have instilled discipline before breaking down the socialist system. Then he could have introduced privatization in a humane way. The new generation is growing up in anarchy. They don't need to work to survive; life for them is about getting drunk and sponging off parents. My generation grew up on patriotism and the work ethic. Once my generation is gone, the young here won't be able to survive.

"You know," he said, "I think the cold war had some advantages. And not just because that without it the world would have sunk into some sort of feudal system. The cold war gave each side a reason to strive and build and improve. We Russians *needed* that competition to force us ahead."

While I sat in Vladimir's kitchen drinking tea, a chatty and affable redhead with Rubenesque curves stopped by to let him know that she was holding a *diskoteka* in the village club: it was Friday. Her name was Irina. She ran the event and invited me to it — with a caveat. "Old people like us" — she was twenty-two — "don't usually come to the *diskoteka*. We're all married and have children. But the kids will be excited to meet you."

I accepted her invitation. So later, under a honey-colored evening sky, I made my way from the riverbank up the footpath, treading between columns of swarming midges, and wobbled down bouncy planks tossed over puddles to a green shack marked with a crooked sign reading KLUB. Behind it was a larch pigpen raucous and shaking with oinks and grunts and bangs — the club abutted a farm.

Irina met me at the door. The club was paneled with dark wood, buzzing with mosquitoes, and most of the windows in its dance hall had been shuttered to keep out the white nights. The partyers soon began arriving, toting plastic cups and jumbo-size bottles of potent Tolstyak (Fat Man) beer. The eight or nine teenage girls (the youngest, thirteen, the oldest, eighteen), many still plump with baby fat rippling over the waistbands of their below-the-navel jeans, outnumbered a grim threesome of shaved-skulled boys in leather jackets. Most village youths, it turned out, preferred a straightforward, manly regimen of vodka and salted fish to a frivolous evening of girls, dancing, and beer.

One of the girls brought a boom box and set it down in the corner. After much fussing, they managed to connect it to a pair of old speakers, and threw the switch. Saucy Russian pop blared forth, and a funky red bulb sparked to life, casting a seedy infernal glow through the dark room. Several girls jumped up and danced in a circle, their lipstick and blond-streaked hair, their feline poise and bared midriffs and sinuous gyrations, confounding notions of age.

Irina poured thirteen-year-old Galina a cup of beer. Galina took a gulp and sat down, smiling at me and cocking her head, as if not truly sure of what she was seeing.

"Thirteen-year-olds drink in Korshunovo?" I asked.

"What thirteen-year-old in Russia nowadays *doesn't?*" said Irina, stating a fact, not criticizing. "Look at these kids. They're the accelerated generation, I like to say. Everything's permitted. It's not like in *our* days."

She was right. Soviet generations grew up reading *Crime and Punishment* and *War and Peace,* exhorted to moral fortitude, enjoined to sacrifice for the Motherland and the bright Communist future. Nowadays Russian youth come of age to B-grade movies from Hollywood, to sex-and-gore television series, to a lionized *mafiya* and the wildly popular pop group Tatu — two Russian teenage girls who profess to be lesbians in love and who kiss and fondle each other in music videos so steamy that there had been talk of banning them from the airwaves.

Irina told me that in Siberian villages girls often bear children at fourteen, so getting drunk scandalized no one. Given the lack of alternative recreation, such debauchery was comprehensible.

"All our social life consists of here is walking up and down the two roads," she said, "swatting mosquitoes and drinking beer and smoking here, smoking there, until it rains or we get tired and go to bed. Unless of course it's *diskoteka* night."

All the partyers, including, eventually, even the grim guys, took great pleasure in being together, passing around the Fat Man (the group drank one big bottle at a time) and trying out moves on the dance floor. In short order eyes went glassy, and chairs and a bench were pulled up to Irina and me. My foreign presence — the first for most, if not all — generated intense curiosity. Soon I became the cynosure of many pairs of glazed and friendly eyes, and I was assailed with questions. Did I like Tatu? Had I tried *samogonka?* Did villages in America have electricity and running water? Did Americans live in log cabins? Were there clubs like this in the United States? Was life in general better or worse in America? That I live in Moscow and am married to a Russian — I showed pictures of my wife — won me bear hugs and praise. Maybe it was the Fat Man, but all at once I felt that I *belonged.* Once again, the Lena was offering me human contact and warmth that I rarely found among strangers in Moscow.

Hours later, just after midnight, the village generator cut off and the power went dead, killing the music and the light. One of the guys offered to drive me down to the river on his motorbike. After saying goodbye and thanking everyone for showing me such a good time, I stepped out into the white night, startling a couple necking on the back porch. They straightened up, but I urged them to continue and walked on, almost tripping over a pair of girls taking a companionable pee by the pigpen, from which oinks and grunts still sounded. The girls giggled, pulled up their pants, and ran inside, waving goodbye to me. I felt content that by just showing up I could please so many people.

6

A DAY OUT OF KORSHUNOVO, we found ourselves floating beneath the *Lenskiye Shchoki* (Lena's Cheeks), thousand-foot-high escarpments of moss-mottled limestone and bronze-tinted dolomite intercut here and there with ravines that brought the taiga, here aspens and pines, down to the riverbank. Often from these ravines flowed brooks frigid and pure, and we made a point of filling our thermoses there. And, finally, on the northern faces of distant *sopki,* trees were thinning and shrinking, and patches of leaden rock were appearing — grim harbingers of the sixtieth parallel, the bourn of Vadim's True North toward which we were inexorably drawing near.

In a sun-washed stone hollow beneath the Cheeks we halted for lunch. As we did every day around noon, we pulled our boat partly ashore and spread foam mats on the bank. Vadim made tea, emptying a thermos of brook water into our cups and tossing in Lipton tea bags. Most of our staples came from store shelves: sausage, tins of condensed milk and steamed meat, Finnish bitter crackers that would have gone down well with beer, and various brands of oats. This was bland fare, as far as I was concerned, but the Cossacks would have felt differently. They frequently fell ill and died from scurvy, and sometimes starved, finding rivers in places devoid of fish, the taiga empty of game. But today, instead of preparing our usual snack of sausage and bread, we opened the charred metal box filled with smoked pike, remnants of Vadim's catch from the day before.

"Like a true poacher," he said, "I set my nets where no one can find them, near underwater holes, where the predators are."

I had shuddered as I watched him bludgeon, behead, and gut the squirming fish, which, once cleaned, he tossed into a plastic sack and dowsed in salt. But the procedure drove home an oft-forgotten truth: we kill to live. In any case, as I ate, my objections dissipated. The pike, raised in waters clear enough to see the pebbly bottom twenty feet down, was succulent, white-fleshed, with a deliciously charred layer of scaleless skin.

That afternoon we left the cool Irkutsk oblast and descended into the Republic of Sakha, onto the muggy Central Yakutian Plateau, a wilderness of barren *sopki,* frost-stunted taiga, and impassable bog some 350 feet lower than Ust'-Kut and a full 5,000 feet beneath the Lena's source west of Lake Baikal. Though inhabited by only 970,000 people, Sakha covers two million square miles — roughly equivalent to the size of Western Europe — and accounts for a fifth of Russia's landmass. Harsh land it is — 40 percent of Sakha lies above the Arctic Circle, and permafrost runs nearly five thousand feet deep in places — far from moderating ocean winds and currents. The greatest known temperature variations on Earth occur in Sakha, in Verkhoyansk near the Lena, where Soviet meteorologists have recorded both −90 and 105 degrees. Though dotted with 700,000 lakes and veined with another 700,000 rivers and streams (all flowing into the Arctic Ocean), the combined length of which exceeds half a million miles, Sakha's climate is relatively dry, especially in winter, influenced by persistent high-pressure fronts that limit snow- and rainfall. The almost ubiquitous permafrost compensates, retaining moisture from precipitation.

As my thermometer's mercury edged into the eighties, the river widened into glassy sheets of glare. Fish grew more plentiful, often splashing on otherwise still water, but so did horseflies, which here resembled wasps and were augmented by other varieties bearing olive and brown stripes and bulbous orange or green eyes. Now, from our departure around ten in the morning till we pitched camp at eight in the evening, ten or fifteen bloodsuckers would circle us relentlessly, awaiting a chance to land and strike; every time I dozed off I suffered a painful puncture, or two or three. As the day aged, we swatted and swatted, finding that it took a powerful strike even to stun, let alone kill, these monsters, and tossed corpse after corpse overboard.

"Watch this," said Vadim.

He held out his arm and waited. A horsefly dutifully alighted, and just as it reared up and prepared to jab its quarter-inch beak into his skin, he cupped it in his hand, and thrust it a foot underwater. Then he opened his fist. Within a few seconds, the fly swam to the surface, shook its wings, and buzzed airward, droplets from its carapace splashing into the river, and resumed its circle-us-and-dive quest for lunch.

And then there were the midges — clouds of bloodthirsty gnats that feared no swats but alighted, began gnawing into our skin, and perished en masse as we struck at them, leaving our arms and faces streaked with a paste of guts and blood. Plain old mosquitoes, as common as they were, now of three species (all swift and giant) seemed like the least of the insectoid evils.

In Sakha, we found that our choice of campsite would bear directly on the number of bloodsuckers we had to endure. The rare spot of grassy shore meant mosquitoes, which arose in clouds as we approached, often flying up our noses or into our mouths, causing us to gag; the commoner pebbly banks, midges. Larch and birch forests sheltered an abundance of man-eaters, whereas pine groves, scented with sap, proved anathema to all manner of insects. In any case, biting bugs have played their role in Siberia's history, deterring or even killing escapees from the gulags; swarms can suck up to three ounces of blood a day from their victims, and their venom causes swelling and even asphyxiation.

"In Old Russia," Vadim said, "people were put to death by being tied to a tree, naked. The bugs would suck all the blood out of them." Sakha's thousands of rivers, streams, and lakes assured no scarcity of breeding grounds for executioners.

I found that the only sure way to escape bites was to stand in the acrid plume of campfire smoke; Vadim, to avoid them, chose not to shave or wash. ("The Yakuts of the taiga don't wash," he said. "Traditional peoples know that clogged pores don't attract bugs.") But he seemed impervious to the bug-imposed discomfort. Often, as I stood coughing and red-eyed in the smoke, shaking my legs to scare mosquitoes from my ankles, my arms swollen with red welts, Vadim would strip naked and, followed by swarms of bugs, stroll down to the water and jump in.

"I ask you," he would demand, without irony, "what sort of idiot would prefer a week in Paris to a month in this taiga! Oh, *krasota!*"

· · ·

A day after entering Sakha, on a torrid morning of incandescent glare, we set up camp on a midge-infested isle opposite Vitim, a logging settlement strung out atop the Lena's steep and clay-faced northern bank. A sawmill gulag once operated here. In tsarist days, known popularly as *razboy-selo* (robbers' village) for the bandits who preyed on passing gold prospectors, Vitim owes its existence to the vengefulness, farsightedness, and mercy of Russia's greatest statesman — a figure who, like Ivan the Terrible, devoted as much energy to the grandeur and expansion of Russia as to the ruin of his enemies.

In the late seventeenth century, as often happened in Russian history, a tsar's weakness fostered machinations among rivals for power. Within a fortnight of his crowning in 1682, when he was only nine years old, the inquisitive yet green Tsar Peter witnessed a savage revolt by the *strel'tsy,* the permanent musketeer units formed by Ivan the Terrible to destroy the khanate of Kazan. The *strel'tsy* slaughtered Peter's relations and forced him to delegate the greater part of his authority to their protégé and favorite, his brother Ivan. His mother, and later his elder half-sister, Sophia, sympathized with the mutineers and acted as regents.

The revolt scarred the young tsar's psyche. But soon the *strel'tsy* met their match. Peter grew into a seven-foot giant with a violent temper. When he angered, a tic contorted his face, lending him the terrifying air of a madman; he became a debaucher, an aficionado of torture, and, to the shock of Muscovites, an admirer of all things Western. He was also a tireless autodidact; in fact, he was tireless in every respect. Between drunken orgies, Peter the Giant devoted his considerable energy to mastering the arts of war, shipbuilding, and a dozen other trades from those who knew them best — the Westerners in his capital's "German" Quarter. From the infidel (i.e., non–Russian Orthodox) German Westerners Peter also learned of his country's backwardness vis-à-vis Europe, and he came to nurture a hatred of Old Muscovy. Soon, for the Russian elite, the heretical Westernizing tsar incarnated the Antichrist, and the *strel'tsy,* Muscovy's defenders, began plotting with the regent Sophia to overthrow him.

In 1697 Peter embarked on an eighteen-month-long journey around Western Europe, during which he endeavored to learn all he could about how the West was run and why it prospered. During his time abroad, he hired hundreds of Dutchmen, Germans, and others to come to Russia and modernize it. But the *strel'tsy* seized on his absence and staged another uprising, with Sophia's support. Peter rushed back to Moscow and exacted vengeance, strappadoing, burning, hanging, and whipping to death more than twelve hundred *strel'tsy*, and had their mutilated bodies strung up around Moscow, where they hung for months, rotting proof of the tsar's newly preeminent political power. Sophia he banished to a convent.

After this massacre, nothing could stop Tsar Peter in his obsession to do away with Old Russia and build a country outwardly resembling those of Europe, but with himself as uncontested autocrat; his version of Westernization aimed to strengthen the state, not liberalize it, all the while creating the appearance of modernity. His reforms affected every facet of Russian life. He personally cut the beards of his nobles; instituted a Western dress code for state officials; adopted the Julian calendar (Russia had till then dated years from Genesis); modernized the Russian alphabet; founded Russia's first secular university; and sent Russians to Europe to study shipbuilding and navigation. His reform of the Orthodox Church spawned the reactionary "Old Believers" movement. He instituted a table of ranks and enacted administrative and military reforms. He raised taxes and further entrenched serfdom, economically necessary concomitants to the almost continual wars of expansion in which he engaged Russia. He launched the Great Northern War against the Swedes and seized the Baltic coast, where he dragooned hundreds of thousands of serfs (tens of thousands died) to drain the swamps and build Saint Petersburg, to which he moved the capital in 1712. He suppressed the rebellious Cossacks of the south, killing thousands. The result: in 1721 Russia officially became the Russian Empire, a redoubtable European and Asian power; and Tsar Peter, "Peter the Great," "Father of the Fatherland." President Putin keeps his portrait on the wall of his Kremlin office.

The thousands of *strel'tsy* whom Peter the Great spared he exiled to Siberia. Most landed in Vitim, where they founded a community that won regional renown for its discipline and industriousness. Following them to Vitim came their wives and children, runaway serfs and fugitive Cossacks, fortune-seekers of all kinds, banished Decembrist officers and convicted revolutionaries (mainly Poles, of whom Siberia would count nineteen thousand by the mid-1900s out of an exile population that had reached half a million) from Russia's European possessions, and ex-cons and other riffraff bent on striking it rich prospecting for gold. Vitim evolved into a town of exiled nobility, wealthy merchants, and pleasure dens like no other in the Lena's southern reaches, with a "Wild East" atmosphere that won it the nickname Razboy-Selo.

Early the morning after our arrival Vadim dropped me off at Vitim's dock. The sun was already punishing, burning at eye level through a cloudless sky. For the first time since Ust'-Kut, I was exhausted. Dawn had come almost as soon as I had fallen asleep; my tent had heated up; and an assault of mosquitoes and midges had turned my morning bucket bath into a tortured session of scrubbing off dirt and swatting, leaving my towel streaked with blood and crushed bugs.

From the dock a rickety staircase wound up the clay bank over a gully to a boxy green building I took for a barn. I ascended the steps with trepidation, noticing that every third or fourth plank was missing or broken. Up at the barn two men, one in a pale green doctor's surgical outfit, the other, who looked Chinese, in a white smock, stepped out into the sun and let the door slam behind them. The surgeon lit a cigarette and coughed hard, his lungs wheezing and squeaking like a demented accordion.

Back in Korshunovo, Vladimir had suggested I look up a friend of his in Vitim who might like to show me around. So, after saying hello, I asked the doctors if they knew how I might find Vladimir Mikhailovich, dock superintendent.

"You'll have to head out to the technical zone to find him," said the Asiatic one in thickly accented Russian. "You can take the bus from in front of the hospital to get there. It's the last stop. Here, let me show you the way. By the way, my name is Toktor."

Toktor and I set off for the station. He turned out to be a dentist practicing in the barn, which was of course Vitim's hospital. Black-haired and of wheaten complexion, Toktor had a benevolent, gold-toothed smile and looked fortyish. Always grinning as he talked, he enunciated his words with the open vowels and rough consonants of Central Asia's Turkic languages. I wanted to ask him his provenance, but in Russia such inquiries now sound racist, so I refrained. He didn't question me about where I was from or how I had arrived in Vitim in the absence of the ferry from Ust'-Kut, so I told him what I was doing on the Lena. He nodded at the news and offered no comment.

As soon as we reached the road, a bus rocked down the battered tarmac — a boxy twenty-five-seater spewing fumes and listing to the left, coated in a quarter-inch yellow-brown dust. Its filthy windows, I noticed, were streaked with clear rivulets left by trickling rain. Rain! How wondrous was the thought in this dry heat!

The bus stopped and its doors clanked open. Toktor leaned inside. "Dear passengers! Please let this man know when he gets to the technical zone. He's looking for Vladimir Mikhailovich!"

Smiling, he held the door for me and I climbed in, thanking him and saying goodbye. I felt embarrassed by his kind gesture, but the passengers nodded greetings to me and returned to their conversations. From the lively chatting going on, it seemed they all knew one another.

I took a backward-facing seat up front. With a roar and the toot of a sick horn, we pulled out down the lane. Houses, all low and of unpainted larch, a crude gulag gray-brown, stood desolate in the glare against a ragged taiga backdrop. Fences of vertical boards, also of larch, leaned hither and yon, as if disturbed by an earthquake long ago. Partly submerged tires separated the road from plank sidewalks, and all kinds of junk and refuse cluttered clearings. Larch and pines grew at random, often casting zigzagging shade on the dusty earth. Farther on, derelict small boats appeared, tossed up here pell-mell, I later found out, by a recent flood. Giant hawks circled and swooped against the brilliant turquoise sky, their eyes angling toward the litter, searching for mice. One bird alighted on the fence and set it wobbling; it was as big as a toddler.

Perspiring in the ninety-plus heat, a teenage redhead in socks and sandals sloughed over to me, collected the fare, and sloughed back to her seat in the rear. Bouncing around with us was a crowd that looked as rugged as the village. Men had haggard faces riddled with wrinkles and spider veins, matted hair, and scarred hands missing digits. (From logging accidents, I supposed.) In the front rows, middle-aged women sat and chatted, their synthetic gray or pink dresses dark in fleshy hollows with sweat, their makeup coagulated, their hair frizzed out.

My gaze came to rest on a young tough sitting opposite me. He wore a soiled sailor's blue and white striped shirt. His head was shaved, and his cranium a mass of lumps; his eyes glazed, piss yellow; his hands gnarled and grimy; his biceps sunburned at the halfway mark. He was probably twenty or twenty-three, but Siberia's climate, and probably booze and cigarettes, had aged him doubly. How many youths across Russia resembled him! Yet standing next to him, her left had gripping the vertical bar over her head, was a woman his age with alabaster skin, clear and dry and somehow fresh. Her hair hung in black curls around sad hazel eyes. She wore black pants and a white T-shirt with no brassiere; her nipples dimpled pink the fabric. She was, I thought, as luscious as he was foul. But both shared a despondency, a resigned weariness in the eyes.

No one was looking at my goddess — Russia is a land of gorgeous women, and female beauty comes cheap. But she put me in mind of the gold prospectors who coined the saying *"Peleduy mimo duy, a v Vitim poletim!"* ("Let's blow past Peleduy" — the next settlement downriver — "and hurry to Vitim!"). The women of Vitim, many of aristocratic blood, have historically been considered some of the Lena's most attractive.

A huge beetle sailed through an open window and struck the young woman on the cheek. She shrieked and stumbled back onto the young tough, recoiling at the writhing, golf-ball-size bug at her feet. He leaned forward and picked it up, noted its two-inch-long antennae, and tossed it back out.

As Toktor instructed me, I alighted at the technical zone, but learned from the dispatchers' office that Vladimir Mikhailovich was out for the day, sailing one of the Lena's tugboats. So I walked back to the bus stop.

Half an hour later another bus arrived. As I got ready to board, I met Toktor, who was stepping out.

"Oh!" he said. "You didn't find Vladimir?"

"No. He's out on the river."

"Ah-ha. Well, I have to go to my other office. Would you like to see it?"

I said yes, but inwardly I shuddered at what sort of horrors a dentist's office here might offer.

It was only a short ride north to the suburb of Geografy (Geographers). The authorities had done well by these specialists: nothing was collapsing here, and the taiga came up to the houses, cool and fragrant.

Toktor's office consisted of two clean, airy rooms in a spiffy larch house. It was nicely furnished and inspired notions of dentists' offices in the West: its walls were painted an antiseptic green-blue, its floor tiled in warped but intact linoleum, and a new microwave oven pinged as it sterilized instruments.

The first patient of the afternoon was waiting in the anteroom: a young Russian woman in a Chinese-made décolleté dress of purple and white patterned chintz that reached her bug-chewed calves; her sandals exposed cracked heels and abraded toes with flecks of purple polish on the nails. As with the tough on the bus, the extreme climate or an early indulgence in cigarettes and alcohol had aged her prematurely.

I sat down on a bench in the hall. She settled tremulously and squeaking into Toktor's plastic-wrapped chair and opened her mouth, her lower jaw quivering, her eyes looking up.

Toktor smiled, his gilt rictus flashing reflections of sunbeams from the window. He brandished his tiny pick and leaned toward her. She pulled back, her skin squeaking more on the plastic.

"What are you going to do to me?"

"Afraid, eh? Keep your chin up," he said. He flicked a fluorescent light on her face. Its bulb emitted a whine like that of a jumbo-size taiga mosquito, the very soundtrack of anxiety (and of my growing queasiness). "Ah-ha. Hmm. Well, the number six has rotted away."

"The what? Please don't dig around in my tooth. Just fix it."

"The number six. Hmm. And the next one's rotted too. I'll put a filling in the first one for now. Just got to clean out that hole a bit. But first let me give you a quick shot of painkiller."

She gripped the sides of the chair, her toes curling in her sandals. All notions of Western dental offices vanished when he switched on his drill, which sounded like a hand-size model of a taiga chainsaw. I slipped back into the waiting room, and when she began squealing and squeaking and whimpering, and he grunting, I suffered an urge to cover my ears and run.

When finally he released her, she had calmed down, perhaps thanks to the painkiller. She squeaked her way out of the chair, thanked him, and walked out, trailing a faint odor of sweat.

Toktor tossed his instruments into the microwave and set it pinging.

"Most people out here can't afford to eat enough fruit or vegetables, so they suffer vitamin deficiencies that rot away their teeth. Either that, or periodontal disease gets them. Anyway, no more patients today. I've got to go to the store for some bread, and I'd like a beer. Want to come with me?"

It was already well after noon. We left his cool and shady office and walked out into the burning sun, toward a scattering of shops. Toktor finally told me that he was from Kyrgyzstan, working in Vitim to earn two hundred dollars a month (a decent salary in the outback) instead of the twenty dollars he'd make back in Bishkek, his hometown. In larger villages up and down the river, I would see that educated people from the poorer regions of the former Soviet Union were moving into places Russians were happy to leave. Though there were a few notorious ethnic conflicts in the defunct empire, for the most part its diverse peoples got along, sharing the Russian language and Soviet-Russian education and culture, plus several centuries of history.

Toktor told me about his life. "In Vitim I earn enough to put my daughter through law school back home. Tuition is five hundred dollars a year. But soon I'll have to pay for my son's schooling too. The clinic has given me a great apartment here, and since it's on the second floor it doesn't flood when the water rises. But whatever improvements Moscow says are happening in Russia, they don't make it out here. My salary still comes three months late."

"You don't complain?"

"We're a patient people."

Bureaucrats, he said, were obstructing his request for Russian citizenship. Maybe they were obstructing the bakers' work too. In the nullifying heat, shielding our eyes from the sun, we visited various larch-shack shops, each with its white lace curtain hanging in the doorway to keep out bugs, but we found no bread. Market culture with its deceits had yet to make inroads here. The large and grumpy saleswomen, their peroxided hair stringy in the heat, groused at customers but offered surprisingly frank advice: "I sure wouldn't buy our cooking oil. It has a funny smell. . . . Those rolls of ours are no good. They're all crumbly. . . . Don't buy my peanuts; they must have lain around here a year. . . . You really want this mustard? It's cheaper in Olga's shack down the street."

They did have beer, however, so we bought a couple of cans and walked back outside so I could catch the bus back to the dock. As we ambled along the dusty streets, Toktor remarked on the beauty of the women trudging past, the handles of bulging plastic sacks cutting red into their white hands, their eyes exuding a tragic charm. Many greeted him by name: Toktor had won the respect of his adopted hometown's citizens. For Toktor, Vitim was not hell or purgatory but a promised land.

By the bus stop I made my departure, leaving him grinning and proud of having shown me around his corner of the country he wished to make his homeland.

7

AT NOON WE CROSSED the sixtieth parallel — the latitude of south-ernmost Greenland, and the boundary of the True North, according to Vadim. Soon afterward, as if to imbue an otherwise arbitrary geo-graphical designation with menace, storm clouds began massing in the northeast, where we were headed. Cool winds advanced over the wa-ters, first rippling dark their bright azure surface and then lightening it into waves with foamy crests that caught and refracted the sun, still shining in the southwest, into a churning spray of diamonds.

Vadim swerved us port and starboard to take close looks at one or another bald *sopka* or protuberant boulder. He commented on their rich, tawny shades; marveled volubly at the palate of reds and grays and browns presented by now frequent taluses; mused aloud about the origin of the myriad brooks tumbling down from ever steeper banks; and pointed out that stalwart larches here finally outnumbered less hardy birches and pines — a sure sign we were approaching the Arctic. So much did the north delight him that he couldn't sit still in his seat or stop talking about it.

"I need to have another person along with me that I can express my love of the taiga to," he said. "I can't bear it alone. The north! Tell me, how could anyone want to live anywhere else?"

"It is beautiful, you're right."

"I'm asking you a question: tell me, why would *anyone* want to live anywhere else? I detest all those idiots who spend their salary on beach vacations so they can bronze their asses on the Mediterranean."

"Well, I wouldn't call them idiots. Different people —"

"They *are* idiots; they're just cattle in a herd. Don't you appreciate what I'm showing you here? Where else can you find this beauty?"

"You have a point. But not everyone who —"

"People who don't appreciate this beauty are narrow-minded and limited and I don't have any use for them."

The farther north we got, the more Vadim inveighed against the multitudes back on the *materik* and declaimed his love for Siberia and all he associated with it. Every time he jumped into the Lena to rinse off the day's sweat, he shouted, *"Krasota!"* (Beauty!) At each initial sip of tea — commonplace tea-bag tea sweetened with cube sugar — he closed his eyes and murmured, *"Dushevno!"* (Oh, that hits the spot!) I marveled at his enthusiasm; it was an unalloyed sentiment. He seemed to expect similar elation from me, but I was inclined to admire silently, take notes, and shoot pictures.

He interpreted my reticence as indifference.

"I have to tell you, Jeff, that I'm luckier than you are."

"Oh?"

"I have a passion, the north, and I'm free to enjoy it."

"I'm glad you are. But you haven't even asked me if I have a passion."

"Oh, come on. You're not going to tell me that the Congo or the Sahara can hold a candle to the north? That your Bedouins or Africans can cook a meal as tasty as what we're eating out here?"

"I wasn't comparing the Lena with those places. I see no reason that one can't find beauty in all these things, even in Paris or Rome. Why —"

"Ridiculous. It's an insult to compare any city with the wilds. It's just absurd. Cities are the same all over the world. People are the same *everywhere.* Wherever they are, they create hell for themselves. Only nature differs, only nature is pure."

"Vadim, that's just not true. Anyway, you're going on experience in Russia alone."

"Ha!" he shouted, his voice sharpening. "There's the herd that does what everyone does, and then there are those who can enjoy this beauty. Look, I'm luckier than you. I have a passion in my life. I make friends only with people who share that passion, whom I can tell about it. You don't have that."

"How would you know?" I answered, growing angry in spite of myself. I understood his words to be professions of almost religious conviction, and therefore impossible to argue with, but still I responded.

"You're not trying to understand me, and anyway, rejecting people just because they don't share your passion isn't right."

"I'm only guiding you because I wanted to learn about the Lena. I never take a job, even in the north, unless I can learn from it."

We — pointlessly — continued trading sharp remarks until I managed to silence him by stating the obvious: that I *was* pursuing my passion out here on the river; that as a writer I worked for myself, answered to no boss, and thus met his criteria for nonherd status. But his temper was quick, his scorn deep. What had caused it?

In his categorical assertions about the masses I discerned the same contempt for the hoi polloi voiced, if privately, by Russian dissidents advocating democratic ideals. Liberal parties ceaselessly lament the restrictions on freedom of speech Putin has reimposed, but when have they ever hit the road to agitate among the masses they hope to uplift, to deliver stump speeches to the "commoner" in whose name they say they are acting, to create bonds with Russians living outside the capital? Very rarely. Possibly they know they would face a hostile reception from the likes of Leonid and others. Or possibly they remember how, in the 1870s, some two and a half thousand followers of revolutionary *narodnichestvo* (populism) decamped to the countryside to "awaken" the peasants slumbering in adulation of the tsar? Many activists found themselves collared by those same peasants and turned in to the authorities as subversives. Mass trials put an end to their well-meaning crusade, Russia's first and last experiment of the sort.

But Vadim's scorn reminded me of my Cossack friends, who, at times, call other Russians "serfs," and adduce "free man" as the original meaning of the putatively Turkic word *Kazak,* which is their people's name in Russian. If this assertion has never been proven, the Cossacks' devotion to liberty has certainly won them fame throughout Russian history. After the revolution of 1917, Cossacks refused to submit to the quasi slavery the Bolsheviks were establishing — with the collaboration of millions of commoners, the "herd." They also served as the elite guards of the tsars. For these reasons Lenin destroyed and dispossessed millions of them.

Still, maybe Vadim was right in his own way. In a country where murderous despots are regarded as national saviors, the honest fools, the rich thieves, and the poor losers, why should he not disdain his fellows?

. . .

At a bend in the river, Lensk announced itself boldly, its nine-story apartment buildings towering white into the azure. But as we approached we saw that beneath them swaths of the city lay in ruins: during one night in May of 2001, the Lena rose fifty-five feet, its currents swelling with the spring flood and powering house-size ice blocks that bulldozed away entire shore-side neighborhoods, leaving a thousand people homeless.

Yet for decades Lensk was a byword for promise in Soviet history. Geologists discovered diamonds in the region in the 1950s, an event that in a few years converted the lantern-lit village of Mukhtuya, a lonely stopover on the Road of Shackles to Yakutsk, into the frontier town of Lensk, the "Gateway to the Land of Diamonds." Diamonds unearthed to the north of Lensk and elsewhere in Sakha comprise some of the bulkiest ever discovered, including the 127-karat "Yakutsk-350," the 137-karat "Sixty Years Since the Foundation of the Yakut Soviet Socialist Republic," and the 235-karat whopper, the "Yakutian Star" — stones so valuable they constitute a national treasure guarded behind the Kremlin walls. Diamonds finance 60 to 70 percent of Sakha's budget, and Russia now provides a fifth of the world's supply. Only De Beers sells more diamonds than Alrosa, the Russian company authorized as the monopolist in the country's gem trade.

To reach the diamond deposits, Soviet laborers, during the winter of 1956–57, laid the *Doroga Muzhestva* (Road of Courage) from Mukhtuya 145 miles north through icebound taiga to what would become the settlement of Mirny. There was no hyperbole in calling the road by such a name: Soviet laborers hacked down forest and shoveled ballast during polar nights with –70-degree frosts, with tents as their only shelter. Neither would it be an exaggeration to call the truck drivers plying the route heroes, the swashbucklers of the taiga, for piloting giant primitive Soviet lorries required muscle, mechanical skills, and sheer guts. The Soviet authorities once glorified these workers for obvious political reasons; nonetheless, across the north their many similar achievements were spectacular, and veterans of such labor deserved respect. In New Russia, they did not get it. It hardly surprised me that for years Vadim had driven a truck in western Siberia, in the oil-soaked taiga around Tyumensk. There, as here, one needed to be a knowledgeable zealot to survive and get the job done. Yet in Moscow's cash-flooded glitz, who would care? No wonder he was bitter.

· · ·

It was another searing Sakha afternoon. Once we pitched camp, Vadim ran me over to the beach beneath the apartment towers and handed me a grocery list. With the low but fierce sun prickly hot on the back of my neck, I climbed the cement stairs up the bank to get my first look at the town's center: a mess of low wooden houses, concrete tenements with collapsing balconies and crisscrossing laundry lines, and lopsided Ladas rattling along through a miasma of dust and exhaust fumes. Searching for a store, I came across a sign on the post office door warning that pensions would be paid late once again. Yet next to the whitewashed modern building housing the all-important municipal administration stood an array of SUVs, jacked up and gleaming, with tinted windows — property, to be sure, of bureaucrats grown rich on the diamond business. The juxtaposition of wealthy state officials and impoverished townsmen was nothing new in Russia, but its flagrant nature here inspired me to investigate. I decided I would like to meet someone in the municipality and discuss it.

I soon found the bread and onions I needed, but through the Lensk museum's director, a heavyset blonde in her forties with furrowed brows, I learned that I could not arrange a meeting with the mayor or anyone else in the city administration during my stay.

"It's useless trying to meet government people here today or tomorrow," she said. "Tomorrow is the mayor's birthday, so everybody's getting ready for his party, which will begin around noon. They'll all be looking for a present to give him, and thinking of a toast to say in his honor. In fact, I've got to go out and get him a present myself, so, if you don't mind . . ."

Lugging my sack of bread and onions, I walked back out into the heat to find a café. I wanted time away from Vadim, so I decided I would sit and have a meal by myself and watch people go by.

I ended up at an outdoor café across from the State Park of Culture and Rest. Grand pines provided shade for yellow plastic tents and white plastic chairs, a bar slapped together out of aluminum siding. A blacktop dance floor ringed with flattened beer cans, old bottles, and other trash took the sun and held the heat. It was already six, but here, where the sun set close to midnight, no evening cool was yet descending; in fact, it was 92 degrees, according to my pocket thermometer.

Behind the bar a girl in her midteens leaned on her elbows, smiling beatifically, her chin on her palms. Raven bangs curled over an alabaster forehead and topaz eyes, longer locks fell astride dimpled cheeks;

her cutoff T-shirt exposed a taut belly. She looked as innocent as she was delectable.

"*Zdrasst'ye!*" I said.

"*Zdrasst'ye!* What'll you be having?"

"A can of Zolotaya Bochka and —"

The checkered curtain leading to the kitchen flew open. Out stepped a barebacked brute with a laborer's tan, his muscles oily in the heat, his skull a prickly pear of three days' stubble. He grabbed the girl around the waist and shoved his tongue through her lips, waggled it around, and slapped her hard on the rear. "Get him his beer!" he grunted, shoving her toward the fridge. He then turned to me.

"Some meat with your beer? We got kebabs."

"Yes, in fact, I was just about to order."

He slapped her rear again and stepped back behind the curtain, yanking it shut. There followed a racket of cleaver hacks and a spate of sizzling. The bartender, still smiling, handed me my beer and asked me to take a seat; she would have my order brought out to me.

I picked a tent and sat down. A tiny black mutt came up and begged, but I had nothing to offer him but beer, so he turned away and trotted off.

Music came on. "She goes to the disco to forget her problems!" blared the song, in Russian, from monster speakers at the dance floor's edge. A teenage girl stepped out from an adjacent tent, a tattoo on her pimpled left arm, wearing black knee-length tights and a soiled white T-shirt two sizes too small, her feet in black socks and rubber sandals padding the concrete, her torso turning in lazy tact with the tune. In midfloor she halted and raised a cigarette to magenta-painted lips for a languid drag, her eyes half closing as she sucked; she waved away mosquitoes, pushed back her bobbed black hair, and shimmied some more. She was probably no more than seventeen or eighteen but she exuded the slutty assuredness of a hooker, which maybe she was. She went on shimmying and smoking, her sandals squeaking on the tarmac, her hips gyrating. A Yakut girl with a geisha face joined her, in pink hot pants and a black halter-top, her legs spotted red with mosquito bites. A table away, in the shade, three Russian girls in their midteens chatted and passed around a Tolstyak beer and smokes, coughing, their breasts shoved up high in their low-cut blouses by turbo bras, their slacks clinging to long slender legs, their makeup caked and glistening in the heat. From another table out lurched a Yakut youth, sweating and drunk, his T-shirt tied around his waist. The dog returned to pester the dancers, jumping around in their midst, hoping for a handout. He got nothing.

I remembered Irina's description of Korshunovo's young people — "The accelerated generation! Everything is permitted!" — and sipped my beer. My own sheltered childhood hadn't equipped me with the street smarts these kids had. Watching them, I felt, oddly, younger than they, more naïve, through I was almost thirty years their senior.

A waitress, dressed in a blue smock and pink tights, blue socks under white sandals, brought me my kebab. Her jaws chewing something indistinct, she waited by me as I bit into it. It was as tough as rubber.

"I'm sorry," I said, almost choking, "but do you have anything else?"

"The chicken kebabs are just as tasty," she said.

I looked up at her. She was a teen, yet her lineaments were matronly in a sensuous sort of way; she looked far wiser than her years. She spat out a sunflower seed and smiled.

"*Ty Superdevka!*" ("You're a Supergirl!") was the next song, and it was followed by a Tatu tune, "*Nas Ne Dogonyat!*" ("They're Not Gonna Get Us!") During my first trip across Siberia, in 1993, Western songs provided the soundtrack to which everyone bopped. But faces even then showed something of a cynicism, or wisdom, that my sheltered Western upbringing had not given me. How many foreigners arrived in Russia in the early nineties, determined to teach them something yet leaving themselves instructed!

I had lived in Russia ever since. My life was passing in the shadow of cities built by heroes but now populated by angry pensioners waiting for the grave, by sex-obsessed youngsters bent on getting buzzed or high — on living a Western-style life, in other words. Tatu ruled.

8

DURING THE BRIEF NIGHT, the heat broke and rain poured down, pummeling our tents. We awoke to drizzle and a 60-degree cool, to a dour lowering nimbus and dank air swarming with giant, gangly-legged mosquitoes. Stepping out of my tent, I took a breath and inhaled several of them straight into my trachea; the gags that followed did nothing to dislodge the beasts. I quickly put on my hat with the netting, which offered some protection against new attackers, but I spent the next hours irked by a clot of bugs just south of my larynx.

For the first time Vadim and I dressed in our rain gear — he in a camouflage poncho, I in a blue Gore-Tex suit. Saying little, slogging about in the grasping mud, we broke camp, loaded the boat, and set out, with Lensk now mostly obscured by drifting banks of fog.

"The weather's rotten today," I said as we made for midriver, wanting to make conversation though still smarting from our previous day's exchange.

"Oh, this is *nothing*. It'll get worse, *much* worse. You'll see." His tone shrilled and he raised his eyebrows. "This is the north. Here nature decides whether we move or stay put! I don't think you could have seen anything like it in the Congo or the Sahara."

"Well —"

"Look, what would you do if I walked off into the taiga and never returned? You couldn't survive out here without me. Surviving out here's an art."

"I know. That's why I hired you to guide me."

"So, tell me, what would you do if I disappeared?"

"Vadim, I think I could manage. There are risks in everything."

I understood him to be both asserting his taiga-trained superiority over me (unnecessary, for why else would I have hired him?) and affirming his own identity as master of uniquely inhospitable terrain. But it was early in the morning, I had slept poorly, and I found his insistent banter grating. I wished he would shut up.

He checked his map and thrust it back under his poncho. Our bow cut through the fog, the dark green expanses of water surrounding us dappled by raindrops, unruffled by breezes. After a while, he adjusted his poncho, pulling the hood over his brow. "If ever I needed to, I could drop everything and move out here and *never* go back to civilization."

"So why don't you?"

"I'm married, and like all women my wife loves civilization. But I hate it. I detest city life."

"You've said that many times. Look, why rant on to me about it? Why not do something about it?"

"I *have* found a way. I drive my truck for one month, then spend the next month in the north. I'm never idle. But *everyone* in Moscow tells me I live wrong. Everyone, all the time. But not *one* of them could survive out here."

Now I understood — or thought I did — what was bothering him. With the fall of the Soviet Union, the he-man proletarian culture the Communists promoted was rejected as phony; manual laborers, once paid better than doctors or lawyers, dropped to the bottom of the wage scale; and hard work itself became the object of ridicule, the lot of losers. The point in the New Russia is to get rich quick, no matter what, no matter how. Clever swindlers are glorified, the *mafiya* exalted, conspicuous consumption idealized. After seven decades of deprivation and enforced socialist ideology that vilified individualism, a swing toward the once-forbidden made sense, but this left honest toilers like Vadim foundering and angry.

That evening, some seven hundred miles and almost three weeks out of Ust'-Kut, under a sky stirring with thunderclouds, we pulled up to the sandy beach beneath the village of Nyuya. Floods and ice floes had devastated Nyuya's lower reaches, leaving only the foundations of cabins, the odd fence stake or two, and driftwood.

In Nyuya I hoped to meet Volga Germans. During World War II Stalin deported en masse forty-four Soviet ethnic minorities to Siberia and Central Asia. The Germans were among the first to go; others were exiled later, on suspicion of treason or collaboration with the Nazis during the occupation. Yet Germans had a long history in Russia. In the late-eighteenth century, Catherine the Great, herself of German origin, invited her former countrymen to settle lands recently conquered from the Turks along the lower Volga. Thousands heeded her call, and they established communities along the river, maintaining their language and culture. In recognition of this, in 1924 Lenin established the German Autonomous Republic (one of the many sham entities the Bolsheviks created to convince minorities that they had been "liberated" from imperial Russian rule), and it lasted until Stalin's deportation. Thanks to the Soviet campaign to collectivize agriculture — that is, to dispossess millions of peasants, including Volga Germans, of their lands and reenslave them on state farms (sovkhozes) and collective farms (kolkhozes) — Stalin probably had good reason to fear how Soviet Germans would receive invading Nazis. Yet despite two world wars, Germans today still enjoy respect among Russians for their tidiness, punctuality, and sobriety — stereotypical generalizations, perhaps, but ones that neither people fears advancing.

Nyuya's mayor, I assumed, could introduce me to Germans, so I decided to drop in on him at his house, which first I would have to find. The afternoon of our arrival, I hiked up the trail from the river, heading for rows of cabins on higher ground, but the farther I got, the more disappointed I became: little about Nyuya suggested that it differed from other villages we had seen. In fact, it looked entirely desolate. There were no people about, only cows grazing over decaying shards of fences, feeding on grass sprouting among half-collapsed houses. I listened for voices but heard only moos, the wind, muffled peals of distant thunder, and the caws of ravens.

I reached the corner of an izba on a badly rutted lane — the main street, judging by the number of old houses and long-closed shops along it — just as it began to drizzle. Who owned the cows? Where had the people gone? Perplexed, I started down the road.

A powerful, sandpapery hand gripped my forearm and yanked. Startled, I recoiled and broke free to find myself facing a man sitting on a bench in front of the izba. His face was streaked with grime, his muscular hands cracked, the crevices in his nails black. He wore an engineer's cap and stained overalls.

"*Zdrastvuy!*" he shouted hoarsely, his lungs wheezing. He grabbed my arm again and pulled me with such strength that I fell down onto the bench beside him. His eyes were wide-pupiled pools of mucus, his lower lip loose like a chimpanzee's. "Who you looking for here?" he said, exhaling a reek of vodka and rotting gums.

"The mayor."

"What you want him for?"

"Could you tell me where he lives?" I asked, freeing myself and standing up.

He grabbed my hand and pulled me back onto the bench. "Sit *down!*" He turned to the open gate next to him and croaked, "Vera! Vera!" Silence. "Vera, get your ass out here!"

"I'm not dressed," a girl's voice answered. "And it's about to rain!"

"Little bitch, get your whore's ass out here *now!*"

"Oh, *daddy!*"

A dishwater blonde some fifteen years old emerged from one of the shacks, pulling a T-shirt over her shapely but sallow torso. She wore tattered gray running pants and ripped rubber sandals. Following her was a pudgy Yakut girl of the same age, dressed in a dirty white blouse and shorts. Mosquito bites covered her calves.

"Take this guy up to Marikov's!" her father ordered.

Saying nothing, they set out sloughing down the road, their shoes splattering mud. I nodded thanks to the drunk and fell in behind them.

We walked up a succession of mucky rising roads rutted from tractor wheels. Finally the daughter spoke.

"How'd you get here? The ferry isn't due for a week."

"I have my own boat."

They both stopped and stared at me.

"You from . . .?"

"I'm an American."

"American!" said the Yakut. "What on earth brought you to our *glush'*!"

"I'm traveling down the Lena. I'm actually here in Nyuya looking for German exiles. Survivors of Stalin's deportations."

They began giggling. "But an American? How is it possible? Why would you ever leave your country?"

I told them I had married a Russian and moved to Moscow. This seemed an easy way to answer their question.

"Well, okay. Hmm. Germans," said the daughter. "The ones sent here in 'forty-one. You landed in the sovkhoz part of Nyuya. To meet the Germans, you should have landed across the way, over there, where they live."

"Sovkhoz" said it all: the most miserable places in Russia were state farms; they were little better than agricultural gulags.

We found mayor Marikov at work in his yard, and the girls introduced me to him. Solicitous and pleased to have me as a guest in his village, he told me most of the Germans had emigrated to Germany after 1991, but he asked that I return in the morning to meet two who stayed. They could tell me about the deportation.

The German side of Nyuya looked nothing like the sovkhoz quarter; in fact, it seemed to belong to a different village entirely. Its houses, though built in squat Siberian style of unpainted larch, sported windows of polished glass hung with bright yellow and green curtains. No trash littered plank walkways or dirt lanes. No drunks were about, and cows grazed only in their pens. German exiles had clearly put much effort into building their own prison village.

At noon the next day, I found myself sitting in the low-ceilinged kitchen of two of the mayor's friends, Sophia and Jacob Deisling. Both were in their midseventies. Their faces were wizened. His eyes were teary and fixed, yet hard. Her gaze was heavy and disconcerting, and conveyed something akin to suspicion at my interest in their past. As we sipped tea, their cheerful middle-aged daughter, Anna, round-cheeked, with wiry blond hair, served me sliced-up tomatoes and cucumbers grown in the garden.

Sophia told me how they ended up in Nyuya, three thousand miles from their native village on the Volga. "We were living near Saratov, near the kolkhoz Krasny Partizan [Red Partisan]. We heard about the order for deportation signed [on August 28, 1941] by Foreign Minister Molotov, but we wondered if it could be true: after all, how could anyone deport an entire people? And what had we done? But then on September seventh, the troops came, and told us to pack lightly, we were going on a trip. They loaded us and everyone else aboard cattle trains with only narrow, high barred windows, and we had to sleep on shelves. For a month we traveled cooped up like that, eating only gruel and drinking only tea."

Thus began a yearlong odyssey of hunger and filth, disease and abomination, that took Sophia and her family through various labor camps, to Ust'-Kut, and eventually aboard a barge up the Lena. During the course of these sojourns and transfers, the authorities impressed her father and all the other young and middle-aged German men into the TrudArmiya (Labor Army). Her mother fell ill, and several of her brothers and sisters sickened and died from malnutrition.

On September 19, 1942, the guards ejected the survivors from the barge, axes in hand, at the Yakut huts and yurts of Nyuya, and told them to start hewing down the forest — or else.

"We were little girls and children and old people. How could we cut down trees! But they told us to meet the timber quota or they'd take away our rations — just four hundred grams of bread a day!"

Exiled Finns and Lithuanians soon joined them. In a measured tone, Sophia told me that they would all have perished from starvation and overwork if a new director, a man named Kul, had not been assigned to oversee their labor. When I asked if she was angry about the deportation, she answered with praise for Kul and the government of Sakha, which, in accordance with legislation passed in the Soviet Union's last year, grants survivors of Stalin's atrocities material compensation for their travails — free electricity, firewood, and a hefty pension. "May God grant peace to those who called us fascists!" were the harshest words she had for her tormentors. Did she or others consider resisting? No. "Such was the time then. What could we do? How could we run away out here, in the taiga?" The deportation hit them like an earthquake or a tsunami. "How could anyone have fought back?" she asked. "What was the use of blaming anyone?"

They fed me sausage and eggs, all delicious and homemade, and we sipped tea. Jacob spoke more vehemently about Stalin's decision to exile them. "Our republic was the breadbasket of Russia. We could have fed Russia and America too if Stalin had let us!" To my shock and surprise, he said he had actually *volunteered* for the hated TrudArmiya but was rejected: "They told me, 'We don't hire fascists here, we kill them at the front!'"

An old clock ticked on the wall, and clouds were descending from the north, grazing the summits of the *sopki* visible through the window. I waited in vain for one of my hosts to criticize Stalin, to express grief or even a remembrance of grief.

"Do you harbor no grudges at all?" I finally asked. "After all, the Soviets destroyed your lives."

Jacob did harbor a grudge. After the war, the German Autonomous

Republic was never restored (unlike minority republics of other deported peoples), and the authorities had outfitted them so poorly for subarctic exile that they had to fill the bottom of their boots with heated sand or lose their feet to frostbite.

But that wasn't what I meant. How, I asked, could he find himself banished to Siberia to spend his youth at hard labor, and yet complain only about the demise of a sham republic and his footwear? What about anger? Rage? *Resistance?*

"Stalin was unjust, of course," he replied calmly. "But who could we attack? The bosses here were just following orders. We all worked together to fulfill the plan!" He paused, and then his voice trembled. "I've preserved my Catholic faith. I pray that God will forgive Lenin and Stalin. I know this: I can't enter heaven with enmity in my heart. We must forgive those who harm us. We must."

Sophia cut in. "Who should we be angry at? We never supported Hitler, and we hardly knew what Germany was in those days. We can talk about this forever, but why? Why complain? I can't say anything bad about my fate."

The Russian national anthem — which is now, thanks to Putin, the Soviet anthem with a few verses altered — came on the radio. Jacob's eyes welled with tears. The very faith the Soviets had tried to extirpate had induced in him a docility that had him praying for his tormentors' souls. I sat back, frustrated, beyond pity.

Anna stood up. "Well, can I show you around the village?"

"Of course."

"We'll take my car," she said. "You can come to work with me."

I thanked her parents for their time and help and wished them Godspeed. Jacob massaged his face and said he would pray for our safe arrival in Tiksi; Sophia regarded me with hard eyes, as if still wondering what could have merited my attention in Nyuya.

I felt bad about leaving Jacob so distressed, but Anna pulled me along outside. "Don't worry about them. You can't change what they went through."

"If I were in their shoes, I would want revenge. No one's been put on trial for these deportations, and a former KGB agent is president now. It's infuriatingly unjust."

She shrugged. She opened the door to her car, an old red Niva jeep in good repair.

Soon we were bouncing around Nyuya, and she was cheerily pointing out its sights. "There were barracks there, and there. I grew up in those barracks, down that way. Of course the houses you see now are pretty new. And over there you see the clubhouse where they used to unload prisoners from the barges." Lenin's portrait still hung glowering and fierce over its door.

We veered past some pines. She pointed to a waist-high rock in a clearing amid them. "That's our Stone of Grief — our memorial to the exiled. But no one really pays much attention to it."

"You seem pretty happy here," I said finally.

"I am. I grew up here. I have a good job. We have to work to make our lives better, don't we? We can't just sit around fretting over the past."

We jolted down a road between cabins destroyed by floods. A gentle rain started falling.

"Across the way," she said, "where you first landed, we have our *sovkhozniki*. Of course, the sovkhoz itself broke up a decade ago, and people were given a couple of acres of land per family."

"They looked miserable."

"Of course. No one's adjusted. It was too late for them. But in fact, since there's no work in Nyuya" — the sawmill that once employed three or four hundred people went bankrupt in the 1990s — "farming is the only thing for a man to do. It doesn't provide enough of a living to lead a decent life, though. So the future for young people is in leaving for the *materik*."

Anna was the director of SEL'PO, the cooperative that keeps Nyuya supplied with consumer goods shipped from Ust'-Kut. SEL'PO's office, a respectable cabin with many rooms and a freshly painted interior, stood on the village's outer tier, by the taiga. There Anna issued directives to the two accountants, women her age laboring over books. She then drove me down to a store she also ran — one of the many sheds with shelves I had seen, but clean and orderly and joined to a larger building of some sort. There she stormed in, demanded to know where a certain Lena was, and fumed on hearing that she was still at lunch.

"Come this way," she ordered, still in her directorial mode. We passed through another door into what looked like a restaurant. Two women in white smocks and white chef hats stood over trays of tea cups, filled and steaming. Behind them were plates of dark bread slices and pots simmering on stoves.

"This is a cafeteria for our schoolchildren," she said. "They're arriving now."

Forty kids aged five to twelve charged noisily through the doors. On Anna's command they fell silent, stood still, and then took their seats, careful not to screech the chairs on the floor. The women in chef hats served them tea and bread. What struck me about the scene was the Germanic obedience to authority; Russian children would have been more rambunctious.

After lunch we heard thunder. Worried about the weather, I asked if we could cut our tour short. She agreed and drove me down to the river. There I signaled to Vadim, on the other bank, to come get me.

Anna was a talented administrator, cheerful and optimistic. "You seem so energetic and efficient," I said.

"Oh, I've always been active. I was a pioneer and a member of the Komsomol [the Communist Youth League]. So I'm used to responsibility."

"I'm surprised you've stayed on in Nyuya."

"In fact, my husband and I want to move to Novosibirsk. And only because everything's so expensive here; everything has to be brought by barge from so far away. Our pensions will only be a hundred dollars a month. Too little for out here, but enough, just barely, to get by on in Novosibirsk."

"What do you think will happen to Nyuya?"

"It's sad, but I wonder if it will be here in a hundred years. The pressures to leave are intense, and so are the isolation and the inflation and the unemployment and all that." No regret sounded in her voice. She was just telling me how it was.

Vadim pulled up and I jumped aboard. Anna watched us pull out, waved goodbye, and got back in her Niva. Maybe she would be happy anywhere she could use her administrative skills and indulge her penchant for keeping others in line. She had succeeded under the Soviets, and she was succeeding now.

The next morning, as we pulled away from the shore in a cloud of biting horseflies and mosquitoes undeterred by rain or cool, I reflected on what I had heard in Nyuya. To part with all notions of freedom, hope, control over one's life — this was nullifying. To desire no revenge, to seek no justice, to wish forgiveness for one's tormentors, struck me as symptoms of emotional and moral defeatism, of a broken soul. I could explain them only by remembering that in Russia, after Ivan the Terrible, terrorist governments repeatedly attacked their citizens, atomized society to impede any potentially threatening unity, and did all they could to foster a culture of resignation and sacrifice, a worldview in which mere survival counts as success. Homo Sovieticus has survived the demise of the Soviet Union, and with Putin in power, this bodes ill, as much for Russia as for the world.

I felt I needed to share my incredulity with Vadim. As the weather cleared and we chugged ahead, I told him the Germans voiced no anger, were not radicalized by their sufferings, and had not pursued their tormentors.

He answered with venom. "As I've been telling you, Russians are a herd that can only be ruled by force. You know, Stalin got it right for the most part, though I won't justify all the murdering he did. Our people are too undisciplined to achieve anything without a ruler whipping them ahead."

"You couldn't lead the life you have now if you were born in Stalin's day."

"Maybe. But all I want from my government is that it leave me alone. In Stalin's day the only hope I'd have had would be to escape into the taiga. Anyway, I'm more worried about how we're killing off our wildlife than about how people suffer from their own mistakes. As long as the government doesn't bother me, I really don't care what happens to people."

If men as strong as Vadim felt no interest in helping their fellows, where could the weak turn for help?

An anvil-shaped cloud formed to the south, behind us. But it would not stay there for long. We were veering southeast, negotiating the river's last curve before the great northward bend. The air trembled, lighting ripped from *sopka* to *sopka,* and we sped into water peach-colored and glassy, toward blue skies, and then away from them, back into the storm. A few minutes later the sky blackened. Rain fell, first plopping heavy singular drops into the water and eventually hiding the river behind us in wavering curtains of silvery white. A brown hawk flew out of the forest toward us, its claws holding a chipmunk still twitching. Killing to live was as natural as it was cruel, but killing for other reasons? Fear, coercion, violence, cynicism, and grief defined life in most of Russia; when they were absent, the memory of suffering, if not in one's lifetime then in one's parents' or grandparents' day, obtruded and hemmed in ambition, made one cling to one's family — the sole sanctum — and fear one's neighbor.

The wind roared through the forest, picking up the scent of pines and granting us respite from the flies.

The storm died by evening, leaving the air cool and fresh, and we camped a few miles east of the village of Macha, on a beach of round white stones, beneath a grove of pines high atop a cliff. There, not a single mosquito or midge bothered us. We could find only pine for our fire, which thus churned out billowing smoke oily black with resin. A huge orange midsummer's sun burned over the river and distant ridges, setting the waters aflame, but the scent of pines and cool gave the place an autumnal ambiance and enhanced the flavor of the lenok and okun' Vadim had fried.

After we finished eating, Vadim reached into the big blue food sack. He pulled out a bottle of clear liquid.

"Vodka?"

"Close," he said. "Pure spirits. Well, should we have a drop?" He decanted some into another bottle and added river water. Then he dolloped in sugar and honey, shook it, and let it settle.

"This looks about right," he finally said.

He poured an inch into my steel tea cup. For himself he used a discarded film canister, saying, "Just big enough for a shot."

As was customary, I waited for him to sit down and raise his canister.

"Za zdorov'ye!" he said. To our health. We downed the drinks. But I choked: it was powerful stuff.

He poured me more. "You toast now!"

"Well, may the second half of our trip be as successful as the first."

"No, no. You can't say that. It's bad luck to wish well for the future. So let's just drink to you becoming enamored of the north. There's no more beautiful place in the world."

We drank.

As the spirits did their work, Vadim's hard eyes softened, and he smiled. "So, what news are you hearing over your radio?"

"Paul Klebnikov" — the American editor of the Russian edition of *Forbes* magazine — "was just murdered in Moscow. *Svoboda Slova*" — the last Russian television program on which political opinions could be freely expressed — "was just canceled. And in Chechnya —"

He smirked. "Enough!" He shook his head. "You know, I live an entirely separate life out here in the wilds, as soon as I go home to Moscow, as soon as I see the windows of my apartment from the courtyard, I know that nothing has changed in the world. You see, with people, people in the cities, nothing *ever* changes. There is *never* any good news."

I didn't argue. We looked out over the Lena, now rippling molten orange with the beams of the late-night sun.

9

AROUND MIDNIGHT THE SUN slipped behind the pine-serrated ridges. The orange sky shaded into lavender, glowed phosphorescent green for two or three hours, and then, finally, lightened into the rose of dawn. All these gradations of color washed over the land as if beamed down through a kaleidoscope with a softening filter, loosing the spirits of the taiga's unseen prowlers. At times we heard the echoing roar of a brown bear (one night a hungry male tore open an anthill fifteen feet from our tents and gobbled up its inhabitants); the thudding steps of a moose on mossy rocks; the lorn lingering howl of a lone wolf. Was it any wonder that shamanism originated here, among Yakuts and Evenks dwelling alone, scattered throughout the wilds, for months on end, with their reindeer? In the fine, tremulous light, trees and stones, rivers and brooks, all acquired spirits, all breathed with a hidden life force.

Though he did not aspire to create, Vadim possessed an artist's eye and sensitivity. Now frequently turning churlish when I asked him practical questions about the expedition, and mostly silent at other times, he livened up recounting, whenever the desire visited him, past forays into the Russian north — hiking odysseys through the frozen waterfalls of Taimyr, catamaran runs across the iceberg-riddled White Sea, ski outings in Kamchatka. He loved reading about the north too, even when he was there. On our expedition he had brought along the memoirs of a Soviet geologist named Fedoseyev, who had surveyed parts of eastern Siberia after the Second World War. He pulled this tome, gold-embossed and grass green, from his pack as he climbed into his tent at day's end; he emerged clutching it in the morning; he consulted it at lunch. This was the habit of a romantic and reminded me of my own need to keep close at hand Kazantzakis's *Zorba the Greek*, a maroon, cloth-bound edition of which, stamped with the authenticating seal and signature of the author's wife, I had chanced upon and bought in Corinth on my first trip abroad, in 1982. Convinced that liberating truths resided in foreign lands and determined to follow them, I had left the United States of my own volition, but I found the transition overseas agonizing nonetheless and often felt I had no life anywhere. *Zorba* became my bible. I read and reread it dozens of times, memorizing entire passages, finding solace and guidance in the mix of Greek carpe diem and Buddhist philosophy espoused by the novel's two protagonists. For a decade I traveled with this book, and it still stands, much abraded, on my top shelf in Moscow.

Here on the Lena, however, I had no energy at the end of the day for reading. The white nights tired as much as they inspired, and I slipped into a sort of delirium whenever I lay down, safe from mosquitoes, beneath the light-infused walls of my tent. Almost as soon as I shut my eyes, I found myself dreaming, slipping back into my past, laughing with my cousins by their oak-shaded swimming pool on Long Island, visiting with my grandfather in his musty, book-lined study in Maryland, stumbling alone at midnight up the stony trail to the Acrokorinthos, *Zorba* in my pack, wondering how I was to live true among rocks and brambles and distressed that so few Greeks I met cared for my fictional hero or the life-affirming philosophy he spouted. Out on the river during the day, I set my eyes on the taiga and watched for animals, but, wearied by the lack of sleep, I succumbed at times to the spell of the dark vales and hanging mists and dozed off. I often came close to falling overboard.

But whenever I started awake, I always confronted Vadim's stolid stare, his blue eyes unblinking in the breeze, fixed on the river ahead.

The next day broke cold and overcast, but blue infinity shined through chasms in the clouds. We were soon on the move, gliding over turquoise waters silvered with eddies near the shore. I huddled in my sweater against the breeze. Drowsy as I was, I perceived the subarctic wasting of the world around us — trees shrank, birds grew few, lichen began proliferating over grass. I felt pangs of primal alarm. With our progress north, the landscape hinted more and more at death and dying, at loss mounting upon loss.

"This is empty land, isn't it?" I said. "Not a bird, not a squirrel."

"No, this forest is filled with life," responded Vadim, his voice pierced with pique. "*Why* would the animals come out to the river, where hunters could get them? This is *rich* land. Just because *you* can't see it doesn't mean it isn't."

There were no hunters about, but I nodded and said, "You're probably right."

"Of course I am."

He scowled at the ever-choppier waters ahead. The cold was souring our moods; and it was affecting the few living things astir. Flies with exquisite camouflage patterns on their wings flew out from the shores to land on my navy blue Windbreaker, the dark color of which held the sun's fugitive warmth. They didn't try to bite me, and they looked so vulnerable that I let them stay. For the first time I felt compassion for insects.

The cold didn't last. On a subsequent morning of sun and hot wind, the river divided into channels and islands where sand dunes five or six feet high rippled above swaying reeds, fulvous Saharan humps and oasis greenery beneath a steely sky.

"This looks like the desert!" I said, astonished.

"No," replied Vadim. "It's a sign that we're approaching the Arctic. The trees shrink, the river gets clearer, and the soil turns sandy." He raised his binoculars to his eyes. "Oh, I see steel roofs! There's Olekminsk!"

Olekminsk! Though I had no recollection of dunes, I remembered the last evening of my ferry trip to Yakutsk, in June of 2000. The white nights and copious doses of vodka had intoxicated a majority the people aboard, including, most distressingly, the captain. I was sober, however, and, leaning on the deck railing, I watched the bare clay banks redden and draw higher and higher. Around me the passageways teemed with flirting teenagers and bumptious soldiers. Two privates seized a third by the legs, upended him, and dangled him overboard — the terrified fellow, himself drunk, screamed and thrashed against the hull upside down, his eyes bugged out. His tormentors relented. They dragged him back up and tossed him on the deck. He scrambled to his feet, banged into the wall, and stumbled away.

Word got out that I was from the States, and I soon found myself in conversation with Sveta and Anya, Yakut teenagers who had never met an American before. After apologizing for their rough Russian, they said they wanted me to drink with them. Anya pressed a tumbler of vodka on me: "You must drink vodka like we do in our village!"

Then Almira came up. She was a Tatar, in her early twenties, with broad freckled cheeks and limpid blue eyes. She pulled me away. "You're really a writer from the States? Listen, I manage the best break dance troupe in all of Olekminsk! Please, write a story about my break dancers! Take them to America!"

I would have liked to hear more about these dancers, but just then, a drunken brawny teen in camouflage grabbed me in a bear hug. His head was shaved and dented, his knuckles were scarred, and his breath reeked.

"My name is Sergei. You know what? I'm going into the army now," he declared. "The army . . . to Chechnya!"

He cursed and swayed, hanging on to me. Mention of Chechnya sobered everyone up. When he released his grip, Almira and I talked, and though I couldn't promise her I'd take her troupe to the States, I'd certainly look her up if ever I returned to Olekminsk.

Now I would have my chance.

Though it reposes on nine feet of permafrost, Olekminsk enjoys regional renown as the capital of an oblast blessed with a (Siberialy speaking) moderate climate: average January temperatures range between −35 to −40 degrees but in the summer rise to a positively infernal (again, by Siberian standards) 65 to 67 degrees. The Cossacks of Peter Beketov founded the settlement in 1635 as a stockaded town opposite the mouth of the river Olekma, and it would supply other Cossack divisions pressing northeast. It hosted leftist revolutionary exiles in the tsarist era, but it has never been heavily populated, possibly because many of its first residents belonged to an exiled religious sect called the Skoptsy who demonstrated their love for the Lord by castrating themselves. They did manage to raise bumper crops of wheat and potatoes, and ever since, and for whatever it's worth, the Olekminsk oblast has been known as the "breadbasket of Sakha." Bogs and soggy forest isolate the town and delayed the arrival of Soviet power until 1922 — five years after the Bolsheviks took over in western Russia. Olekminsk was a bleak place before the revolution — a mere 126 wooden cabins, 26 yurts, and 2 churches, according to a tsarist-era encyclopedia. It is a bleak place now, and scarcely much larger, as I discovered while walking into town from the riverbank.

In a broiling wash of sunlight, beneath nonsensically hortatory red and white banners (EXPAND AND GROW STRONG, OLEKMINSK ON THE LENA!) sagging over crooked, cement-slab lanes, dust floated, catching the glare and sticking in the throat. Ancient izbas lurked behind plots of drooping reeds and overgrown bushes, crisscrossed by yard-wide planks serving as sidewalks or leading from back doors to outhouses. Heat-struck cows mooed at crossroads. The usual shaved-skulled toughs stomped down the sidewalk planks toward me, spitting sunflower seeds; Yakut women trudged by lugging plastic bags of produce, their eyes wearied, their teeth capped in gold, their black hair dyed blond except for an inch of root. Sweat stains spread under the armpits of both sexes. Snippets of conversation from passersby assailed my ears and befitted this steaming dirty hell: *"Oy blyad', prostyla!"* (Oh, fuck! I've caught cold!) *"Yob tvoyu mat', ne poydu ya!"* (Fuck your mother, there's no way I'm going!) *"Pizdets, blyad'! Vooshche!"* (Fuckin' incredible! C'n hardly believe it!) Russian has always abounded in expletives, but the Siberian gulag did much to spread their usage by introducing prisoners, from fallen gentry to unlucky laborers, to the speech habits of the stevedore.

I wanted to locate Almira and her dancers, so straightaway I made for the state House of Culture on the main square; if her group was as big as she said it was, it would be registered within the House's dingy cement walls. In the lobby I asked a cleaning lady about the group. She pointed with her broom to a side room, and I knocked and walked in.

Inside, behind a steel desk, sat a wiry youth in his late teens. His hair was cropped, but his demeanor was frank and affable. "Ah, Almira left earlier this year," he said. "Moved to Kazan. I've taken her place now managing the dancers." He pulled out a chair. "Have a seat!"

Misha, as he was called, spoke expletive-free, educated Russian; he hoped to go to law school soon. He fiddled with a computer mouse and, on the screen in front of him, stanzas of verse popped up and faded away. We chatted. Almira and her brother had started the break dance group five years ago, modeling their moves on those of Western rappers they saw on television. Soon Flygirls and B-boys (he used the English terms) were all over Olekminsk, rapping and dancing.

"For us," he said, "hip-hop means freedom, and it's somewhat anarchistic. We're an underground movement, really. In our songs we talk about what matters to *us;* the government never asks us what we need or want or think. They only try to crush our freedom so they can keep their SUVs. If we perform in public, we have to show our lyrics in advance so they can censor them. We want to tell the truth, they want to coat everything in sugar."

"What, exactly?"

"Look at this dump we live in. It's not a city but a village! Cows graze at our bus stops. Not one traffic light. No indoor plumbing anywhere. Imagine using an outhouse when it's forty degrees below! All our youth can do here is hang out and drink. That is, the kids of *average* folk. Government workers here officially earn tiny salaries, but we see what they do. They send their kids to study abroad! They build cottages for themselves! You can't do anything here without their permission: everything here is done *po blatu* [through personal connections]. Without *blat,* everything's closed to us. You can't have a life or be anything here without *blat.*"

"Well, at least you have a computer and an office provided by the city."

"Fat use we get out of it. Our Internet is so slow, the chat room is closed by the time your e-mails get through."

"Yet the city gave you this office. How many break-dance troupes have an office anywhere?"

"Oh, this is really the House of Culture's press office; they just let us use it sometimes. As for the dance troupe, the city authorities tried to get us to campaign for local elections. I came up with a song for them and sang it for them at rehearsal. They called it 'depressing' and canceled it."

"What was it?"

He printed out the text and showed it to me.

> A gang of fuckers is running our city . . .
> Bastards destroyed our country
> Jerk-off politicians are to blame for it all
> Leftists, rightists, communists and democrats!
>
> This terrifying machine is devouring us all
> Hello, capitalism, able men are now in power!
> . . .
> Our cannibalistic government is hot on our heels!

"You sung this to the people you hoped would give you money?"

"Yes."

"Well, I can see how it might ruffle some feathers. So they canceled your engagement?"

"Yes. I got really angry and stormed out."

"At least you stood on principle."

"Yes, but, well, okay, I did write another song. In the end, they gave us five hundred rubles [about fifteen dollars] for our performance, while the folk dancers got twice that. We needed the money, so we had to sing something."

"Those are pretty revolutionary lyrics to write and then sell out."

"Sell out? Look, we think of other things too, not just our songs. Hip-hop and dancing would be *good* for our students' lives. It would take them off the streets, away from gangs and drugs and booze. We're trying to save our youth from crime. That's why we want the city administration to give us space in a government building, and some funds. Anyway, our dances are the most entertaining thing in this dump. You've got to understand. Hopelessness turns our kids into savages, and our country is hopeless. We can't change anything here. We're not really anarchist, come to think of it. Anarchists want utopia. We just want to have good elected officials who do their jobs. We want respect from our government."

"So what do you think of Putin?"

"He's the first president to give us hope. At least our salaries out here're paid, and we're starting a mortgage program. But we're against the Khodorkovsky trial [in which the multimillionaire head of the Yukos oil company was sentenced to nine years of prison, ostensibly for fraud but really for opposing the Kremlin]. Why should he be jailed just because he's rich? He's better and cleverer than some bribe-taking bureaucrat, that's for sure."

"Do rappers belong to any political party here? Do you have any definite political ideas?"

"Yes, oh yes." He raised his chin, as if ready to make a defiant announcement. "We'd like to abolish left- and right-leaning parties and have one unified party."

"One party?! That's what you had in Soviet days!"

"One party would let all people work together — all the smart and educated people, that is — to solve our problems. Our goal should be simple: to better our lives."

"And for that you need a strong leader, like Putin?"

"For that you need an intelligent *people*. See, since 1991 the government here has robbed the people and destroyed the country. But back in Soviet times, well, *everyone* was happy and the stores were *full*."

"How would you know? You're only eighteen. You were born when the Soviet Union was already coming apart."

"This much I do know: we lived *well* in Soviet days and we were *happy*. My parents tell me all about it. Okay, we had no freedom of speech, and that was a minus. But to live so happily again we need to get rid of all our prejudices. These days, an honest man is left with empty hands."

"And you think Putin is going to help?"

"Moscow doesn't care about what goes on out here. Olekminsk produces nothing, you see, so they don't care about us. That's why I hope to go to law school in Novosibirsk."

I asked him to show me the town — a tour from an angry insider like him would prove edifying. We set out into the decimating afternoon sun. But quickly he grew nervous and began glancing about, as if suspecting that we were being followed. I tried to get him to talk, but he turned taciturn. And no, I could not meet the other dancers because, he said, many were away from town, this being summer. Finally he "remembered" that he had to meet someone somewhere, shook my hand, and was off.

I wandered back to the riverbank through the hovels, down the cement-slab streets, passing a limping dog, a bloated dead rat, a twitching, half-paralyzed girl sitting in the sun-bleached dust, staring at her pretzel legs. My talk with Misha had depressed me. How much Russia had regressed — had it ever progressed? — since Putin arrived in the Kremlin. During my early years, older people pined after the Soviet days and the young were optimistic about the free, Western-style future they were sure awaited them. Now the most vocal youths spout angry nonsense yet search not to form true "underground" movements (as the Communists had done) but to find a way to the dole. The gist was simple: the Soviet state had left its subjects as impotent as the Skoptsy.

I sat down on a stone by the water, eager to get back on the river. Horseflies whirled around me and mosquitoes droned. Feeling queasy from the heat, I put on my sunglasses and waited for Vadim.

· · ·

An hour later, Vadim and I were motoring down the Lena. Giant strat-
ified cumuli mated and parted in the vaulting sky. The heat was dizzying, and I checked my thermometer: 114 degrees in the sun, 90 degrees
in the shade. There was a rumbling, and soon, across the taiga, over the
sopki, bolts of lightning ripped free of the clouds, flashing and stab-
bing. I put on my waterproof kit as rain spattered down, scintillating
with sunbeams shooting through lacunae in the clouds, and the river,
surmounted by a rainbow, ceaselessly, dreamily unwound its coils,
leading us north.

10

THE LENA SPREAD into a lazy waterway two to three miles wide, flowing like liquid mother-of-pearl under cloudy skies, its course directed northeast by the steepening, granite-faced *sopki* of the southwestern bank, its currents nourished by countless brooks and tributaries burbling out of the misty bogs of Sakha's northern plain. The aqueous lairs of reclusive sturgeon, kharius, and man-size taimen trout, these streams bore indigenous names — Basytakh, Markha, Tuolba — the non-Russian phonemes of which bespoke prehistoric forest dark and deep, Evenk archers in bearskin boots and reindeer robes, chanting shamans beating drums and coiffed in moose antlers. Here, Russia seemed far away, modern, European. Here was Sakha, a separate land, a primal world apart, where people were few and legends many. Storms brewed above the plain, and the Lena, stirred by erratic breezes, glittered with flashes of lightning.

Serpentining away into an infinity of swamp, the tributaries held our gaze as we passed them, and they especially enchanted Vadim. "You or I could pick one of these streams, sail up it, build a cabin, and live off the land," he said in a dreamy voice. "We would be lost to the world. No cares what anyone does out here. It's now abandoned land; no one counts anyone or anything out here."

With each new mile covered in Sakha our sense of solitude deepened. Ever since tsarist times, when Cossacks scoured this wilderness for furs and the natives from whom they could requisition *yasak,* the Yakuts have hidden their settlements away from the shore, behind the cover of trees or cliffs. Now, often only a pair of tiny piebald Yakutian horses, stomping the grass with their stout hooves, their wispy black manes teased by the breeze, signaled that we were not alone on the planet. For all its notorious ecological disasters, Russia leads the world in acreage of land unsullied by man's presence — which has vexed imperially minded rulers of Moscow and Saint Petersburg ever since the Cossacks began annexing Siberia. Always the country has lacked enough people to exploit its resources, or at least enough people willing to work for the pittance the state could pay them; hence the network of slave-labor camps Stalin built to mine, log, and drill for all Siberia had. The problem is worsening. According to present demographic indicators, Russia will lose a third of its population by the middle of the century.

That evening thunderclouds threatened us, rolling off the bogs like churning boulders of iron. We drew close to shore. The taiga loomed haunting and silent above, occasionally breaking to reveal crags where ravens perched, their plumage puffed up against the cool. Finally, opposite a high curving wall of *sopki*, pine-covered in the lower and middle reaches, but stone bare toward the summits, appeared the dark izbas and broken fences of Uritskoye, a village of a few hundred people. Uritskoye was founded during the reign of Catherine the Great as a way station called Chekurskaya along the postal route to Yakutsk. The Soviets renamed it in honor of Moisey Solomonovich Uritsky, "one of the most humane people of our time, a fearless warrior and a person who never compromised," said a contemporary, adding that he was "possessed of the gentlest soul and most impeccable purity." The contemporary was Gregory Zinoviev, the longtime Bolshevik whom Stalin had executed in 1936 on trumped-up charges at the beginning of the Great Terror.

The head of the secret police in Saint Petersburg following the revolution of 1917, Uritsky had spent three years in exile here sometime just after the turn of the century. Relatively little has been written about this monocled former student of the Talmud. We know that he was born in 1873 near Kiev to a family of merchants. The delicately featured youth joined the revolutionary movement in his teens; graduated from law school (as did Lenin); spent years in exile in Denmark and Germany, working as the private secretary of the first Russian Marxist, Georgy Plekhanov; made common cause with Trotsky; and helped plan and execute the Red Terror (the murderous response to the "White Terror," as the Bolsheviks called a wave of assassinations launched against them by their opponents) in the Saint Petersburg region. His murder, possibly an act of vengeance carried out by a friend of one of his victims, or a contract hit ordered by his eulogizer Zinoviev for reasons still obscure, accelerated the massacre of untold thousands of "enemies of the people." In any case, Uritsky typified the educated, middle-class, progressive Russians turned Bolshevik revolutionaries who used violence to force the masses toward a "bright future" and who ultimately perished in bloodbaths of their own making.

With the weather worsening, and anyway needing bread, we decided to stop in Uristkoye. As we approached the village, an easterly wind rocked us and roiled the waters, but soon, some fifty yards from shore, we began hissing aground and off again, bouncing through a mosaic of shoals rendered invisible by the waves. Rowboats anchored here indicated that this was as close as we would get. Vadim halted to let me off. I set out wading through knee-high shallows, my eyes on the houses and cabins silhouetted on the raised bank ahead, against the blackening sky.

Descending the bank was a young woman, Rubenesque and ruddy-cheeked, with a shock of wavy blond hair flowing over a loose black dress, pulling along two blond little boys. She had a towel thrown over her shoulder; she must have been on her way to bathe in the river. She was singing, her spirits not dampened by the gathering gloom.

I reached the sandbar leading to the bank.

"*Zdorovo!*" I shouted to her. "Is there bread in your village?"

She paused, some twenty yards away. "*Zdrasst'ye!* I think so, but you'd better hurry before the store closes."

As I sloshed toward her through ankle-deep water, she cried out directions over the wind. "Turn right at Pavel's workshop, go past Granny's goat pen, ignore Uncle Vanya's invitation to drink vodka —he should wait at least another couple of hours before hitting the bottle! — and cut right by the principal's house," and so on. I watched her graceful gesticulations and enjoyed her mellifluous lilting Russian, caring not a whit that I could never follow her words to the bakery or anywhere else. She said that she didn't want me to get lost, though of course in such a tiny village, she added, getting lost was difficult, and I would find the store anyway. I nodded in agreement, noting that her back was strong, her eyes emerald orbs, her cheeks flushed; the boys at her side were green-eyed cherubs. Perhaps none of them had ever breathed city air, ever eaten food laced with preservatives, ever spent a night in the cramped concrete tenements their urban compatriots knew so well.

Heavy drops of rain started plopping onto the river around me, so I thanked her warmly and climbed up the bank. She returned to her song, and it faded on the wind.

From the cabins and fenced-off yards scattered pell-mell over lumpy grass knolls resounded children's laughter, disembodied on the wind. Rain came lashing down, and I hurried around a corner, nearly stumbling over a pair of twelve-year-old girls, both with the straight black hair, high cheekbones, and milky skin that meant a mix of Yakut and Russian blood. They at first froze and stared at me and then set off running, disappearing through a gate and slamming it.

As I walked by, the gate creaked open a crack. A single brown eye fixed on me.

"*Zdrasst'ye!*" I said. "Please tell me where your store is!"

Giggles. The gate slammed again, but then it opened and a petite hand pointed the way.

A handwritten sign flapped in the wind, announcing the cabin behind it as the village store. Inside I found two middle-aged women in green smocks. On seeing me, they stopped chatting and straightened up.

"I'm sorry, but we're all sold out of bread," said the younger one, in a tone of genuine remorse. "We . . ." She paused and looked me over, noticing my waist-high boots, mosquito-netted hat, and foreign-made Windbreaker. "Excuse me, but where are you from?"

I told her. She turned to her assistant. "Olya, give him your loaf. They need it out on the river."

"Of course! Of course!" Taking mincing steps, Olya hurried to the back room and rattled around, emerging with a fine dark loaf.

Her colleague questioned me, alarmed. "Are you really from America? Do you think it's safe to travel alone on the river like that? What about the bears? The bandits? How are you handling the storms?"

I was beginning to disbelieve all this talk of peril. But rather than risk jinxing myself by saying so, I told her that so far — so far — things were going well.

"Well, you're lucky. Anyway," she said, "you must have come to see the Uritsky House Museum. It burned down, but the school principal set up a little museum in our school. You should go find her."

An hour later, I was standing with Elza Odintsova, the principal, in the shrine she had set up to Uritsky in her school, a solid, single-story shack like many others in the village. Her pageboy cut and frank eyes gave her the stern demeanor Russian women often develop in middle age. Broad cheeks hinted at Tatar blood, but then, as the folk saying goes, *kakoy russkiy ne tatarin?* (What Russian isn't a Tatar?) Many Russians, including Lenin and Yeltsin, carry facial features inherited from Asian invaders who arrived seven centuries ago.

Elza flicked a switch near the door, and a diesel generator chugged to life somewhere outside. The lights came on. Old black-and-white photos showed scenes from Uritsky's days in Ukraine and Saint Petersburg. Elza explained how she had contacted his relatives to find out who was whom in each picture and pressed them to tell her all they could about the man.

While banished here, she went on to say, Uritsky organized a strike of local coachmen — his most memorable achievement, given that Chekurskaya once played a vital role on the postal route. It seemed he fell in love with another political exile in the nearby village of Naktuysk. One day, he "went for a swim," leaving his clothes on the bank, and never returned. To local officials it appeared that he had drowned, when in fact he escaped downriver, aided by his lover. He later showed up in Saint Petersburg and continued his revolutionary work. Tsarist authorities dealt leniently with political opponents such as Uritsky (and Lenin, and Stalin, and so many others) who managed repeated flights from exile. The Soviets, of course, learned their lessons from the tsar's tolerance.

Uritsky may have lucked out in missing the culmination of the revolution two decades later. Many of his relatives perished in the Great Terror. Doubtless Stalin would have gotten around to him too; the dictator put to death most of the Old Bolsheviks who had accompanied him to power, as well those who actually opposed him, including "Trotskyites," Mensheviks, and other "devationists." The last thing Stalin needed was committed ideologues (of whom Uritsky was one), preferring instead slavish younger men and women who owed their positions and status in Soviet society to him alone.

Not wanting to give offense, I pointed out to Elza that she had built a shrine to a murderer.

"Well, this is our *history*," she answered. "We can't erase it and we shouldn't try to."

"Doesn't it strike you as troubling, though, that this history is so filled with blood?"

"Look, we all had to be Octobrists, Pioneers, and members of the Komsomol and Party to get ahead in life. My generation didn't know about Stalin's purges, you know. We were taught for so long that we lived better than anyone else on earth. Then in one sweep, with the end of the Soviet Union, this was all erased. What should we do then about our past, once we learn the truth? I'm trying to preserve it here. We must not forget. Ever."

Much of what she said was untrue, if oft repeated. For seven decades after 1917, Russia's history amounted to a national obituary, an unparalleled chronicle of bloodshed, theft, and misery — an "abyss of evil," as Nabokov put it. The revolution, Red Terror, civil war, collectivization of agriculture, man-made famine, and Great Terror killed people in almost every extended family. Claims of ignorance of these atrocities have never convinced me. Although the press wasn't free, Russians did know that Grandpa was taken away in the middle of the night; that Mom was arrested and never released; that Brother starved to death because the state requisitioned his wheat crop; that the family once had a decent-size farm and lived well but now barely survived in the kolkhoz; and that clothes, food, and almost everything else had been better *do revolyutsii* (before the revolution). And contrary to what Elza said, no one "had" to be a Communist to get ahead, though it did make things easier. The Communists' most enduring legacy has been a society in which almost all citizens, in one way or another, if only by their silence, were complicit in the murder and dispossession of their fellows. In the early 1990s one could state this truth and it would not have shocked, but the ensuing years of "reformist" mayhem, mass impoverishment, and endless war in Chechnya have left most people searching for scapegoats, eager to forget.

I was sure she knew all this, but I chose not to press the issue; she was my host. "How do young people here react to your museum?" I asked.

"They don't care at all about politics. Why should they, when our history has all been proved a lie? Since the Soviet Union collapsed we've had no political orientation at all." She started walking out. "Come, let me show you something."

In the adjacent classroom she had hung a painted banner above a blackboard showing two girls, one Yakut and one Russian, sitting in a grassy field, gazing enraptured into each other's eyes. Above them were the words I CREATE MYSELF. I STUDY AND GROW IN ORDER TO AMAZE THE WORLD WITH MY ABILITIES.

"This is what matters to me that our young learn. I'm not sure where I found these words, but I put them up on the wall. The president of Sakha visited us in 1993, and he chose them as the slogan for our Year of Education. They seem to fit our times, no? We can no longer believe in anything but our own abilities."

As we were walking out, a frayed old magazine in a dusty glass case caught my eye. It was a 1979 issue of *Frei Welt* — a now defunct Communist monthly of the German Democratic Republic. Its lead story was an article entitled "Two Thousand Kilometers Down the Lena" (from Ust'-Kut to Yakutsk). Photos in primitive pastels with painted-on flesh tones showed smiling peasants and villagers tending campfires on the river, strolling along the banks, laboring with pride in their land's historic mission to build socialism, and otherwise enjoying a material and spiritual prosperity about which the West could only have dreamed. The pictures were staged; the *Welt* beyond the iron curtain was anything but *frei;* but looking at them, I could imagine that it felt better to believe the lie.

11

FINALLY THE LENA VEERED due north and we embarked on the last hundred miles to Yakutsk, the capital of Sakha, just beyond our journey's halfway point. The sky, a canopy of rain cloud and mist, pressed earthward; a malevolent electricity charged the sticky noontime air. Our bad moods told us that the barometric pressure was dropping. Gripping the steering shaft with his left hand, Vadim turned around on his perch astern and, with his right, raised his binoculars to scrutinize the southern horizon.

"Oh-ho! *Now* we're in for it! *Now* we've had it! *Here* we go! That's it, we're *really* done for!"

These words he had uttered at the genesis of each new storm that morning. Born of summer heat in regions to the south, showers were fomenting above the horizon at our backs and rolling toward us across the bogs and *sopki,* dowsing us in pellets of warm rain, flickering lightning into larches shaken by unstable breezes. Thunder rumbled in, long and low, sundering the silence, echoing off cliffs now rising higher and higher on the eastern bank. The weather excited Vadim to repeat boilerplate admonitions concerning the perils of wet sleeping bags, the priority of building a fire for tea and warmth, the need to keep well rested or risk falling ill, and so on. Each peal of thunder or bolt of lightning heralded doom and affirmed what he had been telling me since Ust'-Kut: the dangers of the Russian north would overwhelm and destroy all but the most skilled and determined survivalists.

The rain, steady but not heavy, soon soaked us through our "waterproof" kit, the seams of which, it turned out, could not be waterproofed. As we chugged ahead, I huddled on my bench, rocking back and forth and stretching my legs to ward off stiffness.

Vadim relished the storm.

"Whoa! There goes a bolt of lightning! Feel these waves! There may be times ahead when Mother Nature pins us to the bank. Here, Nature decides and man submits."

"I'm sure you're right."

In fact, I was enjoying the storms, which soothed the land, sending raindrops pattering through the larches to the forest floor, here a mat of moss and ferns, and providing a soundtrack for the quiet taiga. I had begun to find the silence oppressive.

"I *am* right. You don't know what the north is." He put down his binoculars. "I don't think there's anything in the Congo or the Sahara that I couldn't handle. Right?"

"Right," I answered.

"After all, I'd learn all I could about what I'd need to do to survive there, and I could handle it."

"I'm sure you could. It's hard to make comparisons, though. The Congo is tough even on Africans. Diseases and malnutrition and crocodiles make traveling there completely different from here, to say nothing of civil war and bandits. And in the Sahara, well, Bedouin spend their whole lives learning the trails through the desert. There, surviving is more a matter of lifestyle and experience than skills."

"Oh, you're not saying I couldn't handle the same thing as those ignorant Arabs who showed you the way, are you?"

"They weren't ignorant."

"Well, I wouldn't want to see the desert with a bunch of Arabs. I'd rather learn all I could and go it alone. I fought in the *Afganka*" — the Soviet war in Afghanistan — "and got enough of Eastern 'culture' there to last me a lifetime."

He smirked. Political correctness is not in vogue in Russia, and insults about the "East" are common. Tsarist- and Soviet-era colonization of Central Asia and the Caucasus have bequeathed to Russians both a disdainful familiarity with Islam and firsthand experience with jihad and religious animosity extending back centuries.

But the *Afganka* . . . I didn't know he was a veteran.

As evening came on, the storms died away and the clouds dispersed, and the low beaming sun bathed the land and river in soft golden orange light. The buff-colored cliffs on the southern bank stood rutted with stony protrusions and widening chasms — the precursors of the

Lenskiye Stolby, or Lena Pillars, famed as the haunts of shamans and Sakha's mythological heroes.

Just south of Sinsk, we pulled up to a rocky beach at the cliffs' base, facing the sun. We would reach the Pillars in the morning, but their precursors excited Vadim.

"These rocks are incredible," he said. "Only here can you find such formations. They're astonishing, don't you think? They're more beautiful than anything we've seen so far, wouldn't you agree? They're works of art only nature could have made, right?"

"They are beautiful."

As we set up camp, he repeated his plaudits for the artwork wrought by eroding wind and water, always asking me if I agreed. I said yes, yes, yes, though eventually his words came in such redundant waves that they failed to register. My mind wandered, my responses dwindled into affirmative grunts.

He kindled the fire and grew cross. "I don't understand why you're not getting excited about these rocks. I can hardly tell you how much I love seeing them. You can only see these rocks here, in the north, on the Lena, and you don't care."

I looked up from the tent poles I was assembling. "I *do* appreciate them. But I don't really need to express my feelings aloud. Besides, you're doing so well on your own, what could I add?"

"You don't really care about the beauty of these pillars or of this river," he replied. "You always want to stop in villages and meet *people* — the one thing I do *not* want to do out here. The landscape is more than enough."

"Well, there's a story to tell about this river — the story of how Siberia made your country a superpower, how its resources here keep Russia important to the world, how so many people died in the slave labor camps to extract them."

He tossed his stick into the fire and his voice turned shrill. "I don't give a *damn* about all that, or about anything to do with what *people* have done out here. Only a foreigner could be so interested in Russia. My country is a disaster. It's not *worth* such interest. But these pillars! Well, they're another matter! They're worth an entire book!"

"So write it, then!"

The fire was roaring now. He had already expounded on his contempt for foreigners — people incapable of fixing a flat tire, finicky spoiled rich folk who ate TV dinners and hormone-fattened beef and could never survive in the taiga. He was content with these stereotypes, and he now began arguing their validity anew, citing examples. He wouldn't quiet down.

"I accepted this job to guide you so I could learn all about the Lena. You as a person can't teach me anything. For me, being a member of the stronger sex is all about knowing how to survive in the taiga, about defending one's life against nature and enemies. Being a man is about *survival,* survival in the Cossacks' style. They were a *courageous* people. Just look at how people are degenerating nowadays. Most people now are *nothing* compared to them. Most of the guys my age just boast about how they get drunk and screw women and sun their asses on the beach. They're not *men.* And yet how many of them tell me I'm living the wrong way." His face reddened, and his hard eyes bored into mine. "Do I really give a damn about what car this or that guy drives, what girls he's screwed? In our country, a businessman can only brag about how much he steals. I just won't accept any of that. I refuse to live my life *po-blatu.* Why the hell —"

I had had enough, and I threw down my tent poles. "Look, you're ranting on, making wild generalizations and asking all these rhetorical questions. I'm sick of it. You talk and never listen. Why do you care so much about what all these other people do? And you lump me in a category you have in your head: weak Westerners. Maybe, by the way, you're right: Westerners might not be the greatest survivors now, but they don't have to be. They've built states governed by the rule of law. That's an accomplishment. What would be the point of civilization if, in the end, all we did was value people who knew how to survive in the taiga, like in prehistoric times? There's more to life. Your vision is very limited. By the way, frontier spirit was not unknown in the States. The Cossacks and American settlers had a lot in common."

He lowered his head. "That was a long time ago," he said, the shrillness leaving his voice. "But, well . . ."

"And the Bedouin and Africans you so disparage: they're survivors in the wilds. You should respect them for that."

"Oh, I *do* value aborigines," he said pensively. "If a nuclear bomb went off, we'd perish but they'd survive, because they don't need anything from our world." His voice hardened. "But *you* value history and the deeds of men. I tell you this: governments don't give a damn about their citizens' lives. You have only one life, and they waste it! I *know* this. My government sent me to the *Afganka*."

His shoulders slumped. The *Afganka!* It should have been obvious to me. I couldn't figure out why, exactly, but I now perceived that he had been saying something quite reasonable all along that I had missed, that his belligerence had concealed.

"What happened to you in the *Afganka?*"

He lowered his head. "It was back in 'eighty-six," he said. "I was driving the lead vehicle in a convoy of fuel trucks in the mountains. We were coming out of a tunnel, above a ravine. From out of nowhere the *dushmany* [Mujahideen] attacked, and hit my truck with a grenade. It caught fire. I jumped out — there was shooting all around from up in the cliffs, but I managed to turn the wheel to the side and steer the truck over the cliff. I had to do this: being the first in the convoy, my truck would have exploded and trapped all the others, and the *dushmany* would have picked us off one by one — that was their tactic. When the truck hit the bottom of the ravine it exploded, and the shock wave threw me forty feet against a rock wall. I hit my head and got burned all over. I don't know how I survived. They told me I could have died right there, but somehow, I didn't."

I sat down next to him. "They must have given you a medal for that. You saved a lot of people."

"Oh, yes, they did, a huge medal. When a government has nothing else to give you, it gives you medals." He smirked. "Our lives mean *nothing* to the government, absolutely *nothing*. Well, since then, only one thing has helped me: nature. Nature, it's never false, it never betrays you. People betray you, your government betrays you. Eighty percent of our people live like animals, and our leaders take advantage of that." He looked at the fire. "I know this: human relationships are insincere — except in war. In war, first you have to stay alive, and second you have to cover your comrade's back. You can't find such *man-to-man* relations anywhere — except in war. It's a paradox, I admit. But the best relationships I've had came from the war."

"I've never been in the army or fought in a war."

"Be grateful for that. They aren't experiences any human being should have."

Vadim silently prepared dinner. The sun sunk, the sky flushed with lavender, and tiny birds flitted about the cliffs above us, cheeping.

We sipped tea, consumed a meal of lenok, and ate, for dessert, bread smeared with the blueberry jam Luka's grandfather had given me in Verkhnemarkovo. For the first time I felt I was beginning to understand Vadim, his hard edges, his truculence. He was five years younger than I, but a decade older in spirit. His own government had forced him through a crucible of fire and lead that had damaged him. I had come of draft age after Vietnam was over and the conscript army was no more. I could not have been dragooned to fight and risk death in a pointless war, as he had been (or as young Americans are being now, in Iraq). The *Afganka* had made him; it had forged his strengths and molded his prejudices, burdened him with a past of pain and bitterness the likes of which I could never know. To escape he turned to the taiga. I would have too.

His contempt for "city folk" (to whose ranks he assigned me) may have exceeded reasonable bounds, but I could see that, for him, it made sense. After all, he had grown up in Moscow and associated urban life with the lies, absurdities, and perversions of Soviet reality, with the predations of the state, and with the rancor and cynicism pervading the old system almost as thoroughly as the new. Just as the Cossacks did, he fled for the wilds.

Yet he himself was not wild. He spoke without using *mat* — obscenities that in Russian sound harder on the ear than four-letter words do in English. He was belligerent but never actually threatening; he understood limits. He seemed to me, like so many strong Russians I knew, a tragic figure.

He finished his tea and raised his eyes to the cliffs. "I'm going to be doing a lot of mountain climbing. A lot of climbers die in the mountains, you know. I'm sure for me it will all end up there, amid the peaks. Mountain climbers rarely die in their beds." He smiled and looked into his tea cup, smiled again, and looked back up at the cliffs.

The next morning we set out early, hindered by northerly gusts and by waves foaming white on waters dark with the stormy sky. We passed Sinsk and drew within sight of the Pillars — a limestone canyon of soaring colonnades, lumpy totem poles, massive donjons and windowless belfries, formations in buff-hued rock dating back to the Cambrian period (some 500 million years ago), the stony embodiment of this land's ancient spirit, the product of hundreds of millions of years of erosion, of −60-degree frosts and 90-degree heat. At their base, low groves of mountain ash and Siberian pines, here and there splashed with the white blossoms of cherry trees, alternated with yellow-green carpets of moss speckled with a confetti of Mongolian dandelions and roses, red whortleberries and the thin green stamens of wild onions.

Awed by the canyons and disquieted by the inscrutable grins on totemic columns staring down at us, we halted for lunch. Somewhere around here, caves in the cliffs held prehistoric wall paintings, proof that humans had dwelled under the Pillars thousands of years before the Yakuts arrived in the tenth or eleventh century. That the Yakuts had taken these geological formations as the enchanted land of myth seemed fitting. Once, eons ago, legend has it, the Pillars were castles of gold, the demesnes of a vicious flying dragon. The dragon terrorized the Yakuts and extracted tribute. Hearing of a Yakutian beauty named Kere Kyys, the dragon demanded they hand her over. They did. But the chaste Yakutian maiden happened to be born to a great shaman and engaged to a fearsome hunter named Khorsun Uol, and had no intention of remaining the beast's concubine. She tricked him into revealing the locus of his magic powers: his tail. During the fateful duel between Uol and the dragon, Kere shouted this vital piece of intelligence, and — *whop!* — Uol lopped off the tail. All at once, the castles of gold metamorphosed into the Lena Pillars, Uol turned to stone, and a tree sprouted where the shaman stood, on which Yakuts to this day hang shreds of cloth for good luck.

More than anything we had seen so far, the Pillars excited Vadim and set him talking. I felt protective of him, and glad of his joy, which was as true as the beauty of the Pillars themselves.

12

NORTH OF THE PILLARS, the earth flattened out, the taiga dwindled and browned, the sky, its azure deepening as the sun's diurnal arc sunk, rose, and broadened. The Lena now stretched five or six miles across and abounded in low reedy isles with shoals proliferating in their wakes. On these we often ran aground, and had to jump into the river and drag our craft back to the channel; with the strong currents and steep, almost invisible drop-offs, we floundered and flooded our hip boots more than once. Ashore there were changes too. The soothing *ha-hoo!* of the cuckoo all but vanished, as did the few hawks and swallows that had been keeping us company since the sixtieth parallel. Now our only regular companions were the solitary seagull or croaking raven, the cheeping manic sandpiper. Even in the latitudes around Ust'-Kut animal populations are scant — for every 6,200 square miles, there are, for example, on average only fifty squirrels and ten sables — but here the wilderness was even emptier. As we approached the Arctic the world grew grander to the eye, but also more desolate.

Yet Vadim and I welcomed the changes. If night disappeared — at two in the morning it was as light as an overcast winter's noon — the sun no longer burned. The Lena now sparkled and flowed cooler than ever; and though the mosquitoes were fat and rapacious, frequent cold snaps kept them out of action for hours at a stretch. This all presaged our arrival in Yakutsk, where we would restock our provisions, refuel, and steel ourselves for the second half of the journey ahead, north into the Arctic, where I knew things would be different. But floating through this boreal paradise, I could not imagine what awaited us beyond Sakha's capital.

Late the next afternoon, we found an idyll in which to camp, a white sandy beach under pines giving off a tangy scent that kept the bugs away. We chatted freely now, our talk about the *Afganka* having (I thought) lessened the tension between us. With our tents pitched, Vadim set about making a fire for dinner, hanging his kettle over the flames on his teepee-shaped triangle of sticks. He reached into his bag and pulled out clusters of pink berries called bagul'nik and dropped them into the tea. "We need the vitamin C in bagul'nik as a prophylactic against colds," he said. "Do you like bagul'nik?"

"I've never tried it."

"What, you don't eat bagul'nik in the States?"

"I don't think so. Herbal medicine is less common there, since people tend to go to doctors and pharmacies."

My ignorance of his berries struck him as an affront, as a denial of their curative properties — how could I *not* know about bagul'nik and sing its praises? The long-standing Russian cult of herbal medicine has its roots in prehistory and flourished especially during the Soviet era, when almost anything manufactured, including medicines, was in short supply. It persists today owing to a lack of qualified doctors and the high price of drugs.

The irritating shrillness returned to his voice. "How can you *not* value the medicine in these berries, the vitamin C in them?" he demanded. "You should know that Russian and Chinese herbal traditions go back more than a thousand years, and should be valued. America is only two hundred years old. You're young and should learn from our traditions."

"Well," I said, dearly tired of being lectured to but, to keep the peace, trying not to show it, "now I'll know. Thanks for telling me."

He shook his head. He turned to his tea and kindled the fire. Soon he was chuckling at his mispredictions about the weather, pointing out a hole in a boot he had told me was indestructible — words I accepted as subtle apologies for his outburst. His combative zeal vanished.

I was glad of this, for I was in no mood to argue. The sun slanting above the ragged taiga opposite cast an autumnal glow over our campsite, infusing the tableau before us with the sepia tint of an old photograph. I sat down on the sand and closed my eyes. The light, the piny smell, the fine-grained sand between my fingers, brought to mind the eastern seaboard, where my family owned a house on the beach when

I was little. Back then, in the 1960s, the names of the towns on the way from Washington, D.C. (where I grew up), to Ocean City, in Maryland, stood for strange, fascinating places where there was so much to discover, if only we would not speed through. Annapolis, Easton, Salisbury . . . in these towns were dime stores where old men with southern drawls sold baseball cards different from the ones I could find in D.C.; there were Howard Johnsons staffed by friendly ladies with billowing hairdos I never saw at home; there were gas stations where crewcut teenage attendants looked nothing like the long-haired guys from our neighborhood. We never took the turns signposted for Rehobeth Beach or Dover, so those towns seemed to repose in mystery at the very end of the known world, and to my mind, then, were more fantastic than subarctic Sakha seemed to me here. Their inhabitants, if only I could have met them, would have looked more foreign to me as a child than the Russian *Afganka* vet cooking my dinner did to me now.

A rainbow impressed hazy bands of red, blue, and yellow on the turquoise firmament to the east, near where a sole storm cloud lingered, dropping a load of dark rain onto the bogs. I gazed into the waters now shimmering with the prism's colors. By now the elders in the dime stores had certainly died; the waitresses had reached old age; the teens were in their middle years, probably with short hair, paunches, and grown-up children. The Lena back then lay deep in the territory of a hostile and threatening superpower and was closed to Westerners, but now here I was, sailing it unhindered, and I felt myself insufficiently moved.

Vadim sipped his tea. "Oh, *dushevno!*" he said. "The bagul'nik makes it *so* sweet! Come and have some tea!"

He must have tasted the berries hundreds of times before, yet he savored them still. He had not lost his sense of wonder, and there was a gift to me in this. I sat down next to him and poured myself some tea.

A cormorant called out from somewhere afar over the waters. By the time we finished dinner, the rainbow had dissolved and the sky was a big top of baby blue velvet inlaid with a red diamond sun.

"That boat is Russia, all right!" said Vadim the next afternoon, pointing to the rusted hull of a ferry beached on a marshy shore, the port bow of which was painted with chipped white letters ROSSIYA (Russia). "Look at it. Burnt out, wrecked in a swamp, and looted! Why bother to cart it away when it so accurately depicts the state of our nation?"

We were twenty-five days out of Ust'-Kut. Just beyond the wreck we spotted dock cranes, nine-story apartment blocks, and messy suburbs of izbas sinking into permafrost — Yakutsk, some 250 miles south of the Arctic Circle, and home to 200,000 people. The Yakuts, driven northward by aggressive Mongol tribes, migrated to Sakha from Central Asia in the eleventh and twelfth centuries. They have never been many, and still number only 370,000 out of the Republic's 970,000 inhabitants, the majority of whom are either Slavs or members of other indigenous peoples. Yakutsk, however, is largely a Russian creation and was founded as an *ostrog* in 1632 by thirty Cossacks under Peter Beketov's command. Within a year, two hundred merchants and state functionaries had joined them, ready to make a new life among the bogs and taiga. It wouldn't be easy, of course. Flooding prompted them to move the fortress twice from points just upriver before settling on the current location. From the 1700s on, Yakutsk has served as the administrative and commercial hub of northeastern Siberia, from here to the Bering Strait.

Which is not to say that it has ever been more than a remote and dismal outpost of adventurers, lost men, exiles, and taiga-weary natives. Famous in Russian as the *"tyur'ma bez zamkov i reshotok"* (prison without locks and bars), Yakutsk, according to the 1904 Brokgauz-Yefron Encyclopedia, "resembles more a well-off settlement than a city. There is not one beautiful building or paved street, neither are there street lamps; on some streets planks have been laid instead of sidewalks, and even these suffer frequent gaps. Mud is deep everywhere, and no one thinks to drain the streets of water."

If Yakutsk developed since then, I now found that little had changed since I last saw the city in 2000, apart from the pastel façades of newly renovated buildings in the center. Though I eventually managed, this time I had trouble at first getting hotel rooms for us. Sympathetic but unyielding receptionists told me that local authorities had ordered them to keep open all rooms for potential participants in the Children of Asia sport festival that was to be held later in the week. No one offered them any compensation, but proprietors obeyed, fearing the possible consequences of insubordination, including surprise inspections from tax, fire, and health authorities. Fines and bribes could prove costlier than revenue lost from guests denied accommodation.

Orthodox Christianity has been Russia's principal faith ever since Prince Vladimir of Kiev adopted it from Byzantium in the tenth century. But for Russians, Orthodoxy is more than a religion; it is a pillar of identity. To be *russky* (ethnically Russian) as opposed to a *rossiyanin* (a Russian citizen) means not only speaking Russian as one's mother tongue but also, to a great extent, professing Russian Orthodoxy, or at least considering it one's native culture. This has been true for a thousand years, especially since the Great Schism of 1054 sundered Christendom into the domains of the Western (Rome-based) and Eastern (Constantinople-based) churches. Baptists have historically made up the majority of "Western" Christians in Russia, and, accordingly, have been seen as suspect, regarded as "less Russian"; as a result, they suffered much persecution during the Great Terror. Yakutsk, the "prison without locks or bars," received great numbers of them during the Stalin decades. I wanted to meet the Baptists of today, and resolved to find one of their churches.

The morning after our arrival, all traces of the Lena's cool and salubrious breezes vanished. It was *hot*, the air foul with exhaust fumes and bog rot. Beneath a white sun afire in a steamy sky, my taxi sped out of Yakutsk's refurbished pastel center to bounce and trundle over mud roads, past sagging hovels of unpainted larch, through a marshy cityscape that had to recall prerevolutionary Yakutsk. We eventually pulled up by an unmarked one-story house with an address matching that of the Association of Evangelical Christian Churches listed in my guide. I got out. The association was said to be staffed or funded by Americans, so I expected a warm reception.

I knocked. The door cracked open. A clean-shaven Yakut in his thirties peered at me and gave me the once-over with his narrow eyes.

"Yes?"

I introduced myself as an American writer interested in learning about Baptists. He listened with a deadpan expression, but then a certain furrowing of the brows gave me to think that I might as well have been asking to meet the resident pedophile preacher. He opened the door a bit more and looked me over. To my surprise, he stepped warily aside and motioned me in, introducing himself as Stanislav. "Who sent you to us?"

"No one. As I said, I'm a writer —"

"I doubt I can help you. You'll have to talk to the chief missionary. Oh, as luck would have it, he's away. On a trip."

"When will he be back?"

"In . . . ah, how long will you be here?"

"Four days."

"Oh, well, he'll be back in a couple of weeks. Sorry."

"I really don't need to talk to the chief. I was hoping to get an idea of how average Baptists live here."

Stanislav absorbed this information impassively. Finally he replied, "Maybe you'd like to talk to the Americans?"

"Okay, at least for now —"

"*If* they're in town. Let me see."

He called a man named Frank on the telephone, turned away and said a few words to him about me in English in a low voice, nodded, and handed me the receiver. Frank was polite and professed regret at being too tied up to meet me anytime soon. However, he enthusiastically recommended that I head a hundred miles upriver to the village of Namtsy and search out the American missionaries there. *If* they were there; they too might be "busy" or "away." I protested delicately, reminding him that we were both Americans, and that I meant no harm, and was there nothing more he could do? He then gave me the name and number of another pastor to call. Stanislav rang him too and explained who I was, but this pastor was "away" too, said the voice on the other end of the line.

He hung up and shrugged.

"Look," I said, "I understand your suspicion, but here's my passport. I really am an American. I have nothing to do with the Russian government or with whatever problems you've had here. I've come a long way just to meet Baptists. Won't you help me?"

He took my passport and held it up to the light. He then asked me to have a seat on an old dusty sofa in a plain living room of sorts.

"Well," he said, "what do you need to know about us? Our constitution guarantees all religions equality before the law, of course, but it recognizes Russian Orthodoxy's special role in the history of the country."

"I know. Are a lot of Yakuts Baptists?"

"No. Being a Yakut means being pagan. [This is not entirely true. Some Yakuts joined the Cossacks and adopted Christianity.] They have this animist religion called Ayi. Ayi are the so-called Enlightened Beings living in the so-called Upper World, unlike us humans, who are stuck in the Middle World. Evil spirits live in the Bottom World."

He suppressed a smirk. I thought of bringing up heaven, hell, and purgatory as the obvious counterparts. But I didn't want to alienate him.

"Anyway, our local government does a lot to promote these animist beliefs nowadays."

"When did Baptists first appear here?"

"In 1925 or so. We're now around four hundred, spread throughout three churches. Originally we were just a small group."

"Did the first ones survive Stalin's purges? He sent so many Baptists to the gulags."

He stiffened. "You'd have to research that. I can't answer. Say, wouldn't you rather to talk to that American in Namtsy?"

"No, actually I'd rather talk to you. Even Frank sounded reluctant to talk to me."

"That's not surprising. The government doesn't want to renew the Americans' registration here."

"So you *are* having problems with the authorities? There's still a conflict between Orthodoxy and the Evangelicals?"

He stood up. "Excuse me, do you have any documents proving who you are?"

I showed him my American passport again. He shook his head. "Fine, but this only tells me your nationality. I'd like to know what you'll write. Really, you'll have to see the chief."

I stood up. I had inconvenienced him long enough. Just then the front door slammed. A cheery, russet-haired young Russian in jeans and a pressed shirt walked in and straightaway came up and shook my hand. "I'm Sasha. Who are you?"

Sasha had a lisp and a genial smile that contrasted with his brawny build. Stanislav took him aside and whispered something to him. Sasha said, "So what?" and walked straight back over to me.

"Listen, I'll be happy to introduce you to one of our main Baptists. He converted after his crime."

"His crime?"

"He did his time for it. Anyway, he's been born again. Come with me."

Outside, as we walked through the swampy plots and crooked cabins, Sasha put his hand on my shoulder. "Don't worry about Stanislav. Yakuts are different from us. They're always more suspicious. It's their nature."

"So you're a Baptist?"

"Yes. My faith is the only thing that's kept me out of jail. I found God and He saved me from the chaos here."

Soon we were picking our way through junk-strewn, muddy yards, shooing away giant mosquitoes, shielding our eyes from the sun. We ended up in a just-built shed, its walls still sawdust fresh, where a tanned, bare-torsoed man in his early forties was sawing planks of wood and wiping his forehead with a rag. He was dark-haired but handsomely graying at the temples. As we entered, he raised his eyes, clear blue-green orbs set above an engaging smile.

"Oh-ho! A guest! I'm Viktor."

I introduced myself and told him what I was doing in Yakutsk. He didn't hesitate.

"Well, welcome to our clubhouse, to our *zasypukha!* We call it that because the walls are hollow, and we'll be filling them with sawdust for insulation. [*Zasypat'* means "to sprinkle in."] You see, out here the winters are ferocious. Would you like some tea and cookies?"

Viktor told me he was originally from Ryazan, near Moscow, and had worked as a boatman on the Oka before coming east in the 1980s to sail the rivers of the north. As he rummaged around in search of a pot for tea and a mislaid box of cookies, he expounded on the challenges of building in Sakha. "A yard beneath the surface here is permafrost, so we have to drill pillars nine yards down to set our buildings on, or they'd sink when heated in the winter. Many sink anyway. That's why you see so many lopsided houses around here."

"Stanislav gave him a hard time," interjected Sasha, who found the cookies and a baton of sausage and laid them out on a table.

"Ah," said Viktor. "Sorry about that. But you see, there's a reason for his attitude. We Russians have deceived the Yakuts a lot throughout the centuries, so they're suspicious. True, the Yakuts themselves arrived here as invaders and conquered the Evenks. Anyway, we got the Yakuts addicted to alcohol and ruined them. We Russians are a tough nation to contend with, you know? Because we're the biggest sinners. Sinners are always hard to beat."

"You're not worried about persecution now that Putin is in power? It seemed Stanislav was."

"No, because we're not a sect. Look." He showed me a small green card stating the Baptists' registration number with the Ministry of Religious Affairs. "If the authorities demand proof of who we are, we show this. Russians still see us as traitors who've sold out to the Americans and the Jews. Russians are so tied to Orthodoxy, they hear we're Baptists and think we can't be Russian. We've even had Orthodox priests come to our prayer meetings and demand we disperse, saying, 'You're a sect! Disperse!' But we're *not* a sect. And I tell the priests, who call themselves 'father,' 'You're no father to me. We have only one father, and He's in heaven. And all our papers are in order.'"

I appreciated his frankness, and enjoyed the tea and sausage. "Why do you think Baptists so bother the Orthodox?" I asked.

"For starters, in the early nineties the Russian masses were rediscovering religion, with perestroika and all. After seventy years without faith, our masses began repenting! It was beautiful. The Orthodox Church couldn't handle it, and many believers spilled over to us, which the Church didn't like. Most of all, though, being an Orthodox Christian means being a *ruler*, being the *boss*. That's why Orthodoxy is the basis of Russian nationalism. It gives Russians confidence that they're *superior* to other peoples."

He was indirectly referring to the Orthodox belief that, after Rome had slipped into "heretic" Catholic hands and Constantinople had fallen to the Turks in 1453, God blessed Moscow as the Third Rome (and a fourth there shall never be). Russians, according to this belief, were the Chosen People, gifted with a messianic mission to lead the world.

"You can hear Russians say, 'I'm an Orthodox atheist.' What nonsense! The point is, they're the bosses. And from worshiping an icon it's not such a leap to worshiping a portrait of Stalin."

Sasha cut in. "People now are hungering for a new Stalin; they want someone to lead them out of this chaos. They're really suffering from a spiritual hunger, but they don't know it."

"Yes," Viktor said, "but I'd say there's no longer a belief in anything — not in Stalin, not in communism. In some Russian provinces thirty percent of voters choose 'none of the above' on their ballots. But for others, patriotism and Orthodoxy are *everything*, hollow as they are."

"How can they be 'everything' if they're so hollow?" I asked.

"Patriotism for us is like putting on a suit: you wrap yourself in the flag," Sasha replied. "But how could anyone believe in Russia? You can't believe in chaos."

Viktor poured me another glass of tea and cut me more sausage. "You know the poet Tyuchev's line about Russia: 'In Russia, you can only believe.' Reason does no good here. With our volatile, unruly masses, he may have been right. Sin has shattered us; our society is rotten, and Moscow is a Babylon of sin. Everyone there says, 'I'm God! Give me everything!' Why do you think Russians accepted Darwin's theory of evolution? Because it abolished moral law. Without a creator, who does man answer to? To himself. The essence of communism was stealing, because there was no moral law."

Although I did not believe in God, I was comfortable with these two; their faith had made them almost as "foreign" in Russia as I was. I felt bold enough to ask Viktor about his crime.

He stood up and started planing a plank of pine. "A tragedy befell me. It happened in Belaya Gora on the Ingidirka River to the east, where I moved after leaving Ryazan. I was drinking vodka in those days, and so was my wife. We had two daughters, and I worshiped the youngest one more than anything on earth. Well, I found another woman to sin with, and kept on drinking vodka. My life got worse and worse; nothing was going right. I decided it must be the vodka, so I got an antialcohol injection to help me quit. My wife kept on drinking, though. She came home drunk one night and told me that she'd found another man and was going to take my daughters and live with him, and never let me see them again." His voice was steady. "That was too much for me. She got unruly with me, so I strangled her. The date was November fourteenth, 1994. The next day I went to the police and turned myself in. A couple of months later, another inmate gave me a Bible, and I started reading it. I started kneeling and asking God why my life was going so wrong. Then I read in the Bible that one can be cursed to the fourth generation."

"You think you were cursed?"

"Well, in Russia we have a lot of pagan rituals and rites. It's quite possible that someone put a curse on my grandmother that affected me."

"How did you know you were saved?"

"I heard no voices and saw no visions: faith saved me. I came to understand that evil spirits were working through my wife. And think about it. Can the spirits the Yakuts conjure up here be anything but evil?"

"How do you feel now about killing your wife? It must be terrible looking back."

"I won't say I don't have emotions about it, but I'm saved now, and I understand what happened to me. My daughters moved away and won't have anything to do with me. I've lost them, I think. When I speak to them I try to convince them to follow Christ, but they won't listen. I pray to Christ to save them.

"Anyway, I served only three years and eight months and was let out on good behavior. When they released me, they handed me a hundred and sixty rubles [about six dollars], and that was it. I went straight to church. I saw the Orthodox priests baptizing people and wanted to cry out, 'That won't save you! You need to find Christ *personally!*' Eventually, I ended up with the Baptists. Now I have a fantastic wife. She's a missionary."

"And you've never had any doubts."

"I *have* had doubts. But I'm saved nonetheless."

Years ago, fervent rationalist that I was, I might have argued the case for atheism, even to him. Back then, I thought it better to suffer in the glare of truth rather than seek solace in the darkness of faith. But the older I get, and the more I see of human suffering, the less dogmatic I feel. If faith worked for him, so be it.

When the time came, Viktor said he would arrange transport for us from the hotel to the river, which I greatly appreciated. After more tea and sausage, they walked me to the main road, said goodbye till then, and hailed me a taxi.

Around ten-thirty the next evening I wandered out of my hotel in search of a café where I could sit and enjoy the white night. The sky glowed ashen, with the hidden nocturnal sun bathing the renovated pastel-colored government buildings around Ordzhonokidze

Square in an impressionistic pallor. But it wasn't peaceful. Threesomes and foursomes of rowdy Yakut teens stumbled down the sidewalks, guffawing and tussling, passing around bottles of vodka. By a psychedelic fountain they upended giant cans of beer; at kiosks on side streets they formed unruly lines to replenish their booze, bending over to bark their orders through tiny, waist-high windows. Scuffles broke out, and there were shouts and screams. Small groups of Russians, taciturn and sober, diluted the mayhem, cathartic mayhem prompted here by light and warmth in a city where during the endless dark of winter temperatures average −55 degrees.

I decided to drop by a café near my hotel. As I entered, two Yakut women, their breath vodka-sour, shoved past me and careened into the arms of a massive Russian bouncer wearing a camouflage uniform and jackboots, his bald head all angles and knots.

"Ladies, there's a cover charge here."

"We want to drink!"

"Pay up or beat it. You know the rules."

"How rude you are!"

I slipped by, exempt from the cover charge as a guest of the hotel. But the argument continued, until the guard threatened to evict the pair. They showered him with curses and left, slamming the door and rejoining the crowds stumbling through the white night.

The lounge was paneled in brown, and décor was minimal, consisting of an illuminated row of vodka bottles lined up behind the bar and a disco ball spinning stars over a cracked linoleum dance floor next to a mess of Formica tables. The guard showed me to my seat, and I ordered a beer. Immediately I became aware of six or seven drunken teenage Yakuts at the next table. Shouting, yakking, shoving one other and singing, they almost drowned out the Russian pop blasting from two giant speakers. They jumped up and took to the dance floor, forming a haphazard circle. The guys leaped into the middle one by one to mimic gorillas, swinging their arms and raising their legs, screwing up their faces and bugging their eyes; they stomped like elephants; they jammed fingers in their nostrils and yelped; they dropped to the floor and bungled break dances; they patted their mouths and whooped like Apaches. The girls shrieked with laughter at their goofball heroes, themselves enacting loony jumps and loopy shimmies.

The song changed and they returned to their table and took to toasting and knocking back shots of vodka. The bartender came over and pulled a seat up to my table.

"You're not from here, are you?" he asked.

"No, I'm not."

"I must apologize for my countrymen. Every night now it's the same here. I feel ashamed at how they behave."

I took a good look at him. He was a tidy-looking Yakut youth, in a white smock and jeans, and his Russian was unaccented. He said his name was Ivan.

"You don't have to apologize for them. But why are they acting so ... so —"

"Idiotic? You see, Yakuts just don't know how to drink. We can't handle our alcohol — it's a medically proven fact." (Frequently Yakuts told me they lack a gene that helps protect them against alcoholism.) "Booze is destroying us. But as for these kids, well, they're from villages, so they don't know how to behave. They come to Yakutsk to try to get into schools and institutes. For them this is the big city."

Just then a hulking boy of eighteen, one of the shimmying gorillas, stepped over to my table. He reached around his belly to shake my hand, and he thrust his blunt face to mine. "You're not from around here?" he shouted with a waggly tongue.

The bartender stood up and began ushering him away, apparently delivering a grave message in Yakut, which he emphasized with shakes of the head. The hulk dropped puzzled eyes on me and turned, tripping over his comrade's outstretched leg. A round of guffaws erupted from his table.

Ivan sat back down again. "I told him I was from KGB and here to guard you, to keep him away. Or else he'd start bothering you. I'm ashamed, really ashamed."

Ivan and I chatted. He was eighteen, but his manners made him seem older. He told me he played a synthesizer at a nearby karaoke restaurant; he tended bar here on his off nights. For Yakuts who didn't drink, there was almost nowhere to go in town and nothing to do. When I told him how much improved the center looked compared what I had seen in years past, he scoffed.

"That's all our government has done, remodel the center. It's window dressing. This city is completely corrupt. Nothing good ever happens here. No one can ever understand Russia, and no one knows what is *really* going on, not even us. Our future is black."

The loudest partier at the nearby table was an obese girl. Each time one of her gang impersonated an orangutan or whinnied like a filly she emitted a laugh resembling the shrieking skirl of a maniacal monkey. She came over to me and stuck out her hand.

"Hello, I'm from Kyusyur but I now live in Tiksi! Who are you?"

Ivan stood up and began pushing her away, but she managed to pass me a note. It read, "Greetings to a stranger from the guys from Tiksi!"

I found this touching. But between songs I heard Ivan telling the kids that the KGB was filming their every move, and that they'd better leave me alone. Absurd, I thought. During his admonition they jumped up for another dance and recommenced their antics, knocking over a chair, bumping into a pair of Russian women nursing drinks nearby.

"Look," Ivan said, "things can get dangerous here about now. It's pretty late and they may lose control."

The waggly-tongued hulk hurled himself, sweating, off the dance floor and into the chair beside me. Again Ivan moved to shoo him away, but I stopped him. His name was Sasha. He asked my nationality and I told him.

"Wow! Give me a present from your country!"

"My country? What kind of present?"

"Anything! Here's a gift from *my* country." He handed me a made-in-China pen leaking ink. "Well, what do you have on you from America?"

I took his question too seriously, and it put me in a quandary. Everything on me I had bought abroad. But by the time I could explain this too him, he was squeezing my hand in his sweaty ham fist, grabbing my neck and proffering his best wishes to his foreign guest. Ivan stood ready to have him tossed out, but I signaled no. In this black-futured city I resolved to show compassion, and returned Sasha's wishes.

In my Russian guidebook I found an advert for a "traditional Yakut restaurant" that would suit "lovers of the exotic." What had I seen of "traditional" Sakha? In clothes, names, and architecture, Russian influence predominated. I decided to try it out.

I called the restaurant and spoke to the proprietor, a young woman named Alina with a birdlike voice and ungrammatical Russian.

"Oh, hi!" she said, as if greeting a friend. "We've set up a restaurant in our *balagan* [Yakut for "log cabin"] outside the city. Wanna eat with us? I'll come to your hotel and pick you up." Her chipper tone hinted at a homey affair, which seemed natural; after all, Yakuts probably had no restaurants before the Russians took over, and must have eaten all meals *en famille.*

The next evening Alina hurried into my hotel lobby, excusing herself for a few minutes' delay. In her midtwenties, she was short and plump, with high rounded cheeks and a full-lipped smile. Though she was a schoolteacher, her Russian was slipshod.

We hired a Volga taxi from Ordzhonokidze Square and soon were bouncing down dirt roads through a forest where bars of golden light beamed through short, widely spaced pines. Alina's *balagan,* like others around it, hunkered sturdy and weathered behind a freshly cut pine fence. Behind the cabin, a half-acre of land sloped down toward the forest — a farm plot cut with peat walkways between crops of cucumbers, potatoes, and onions. Sheltering tomatoes was a stove-heated greenhouse — sheets of translucent plastic tacked over a pine frame.

Inside, the *balagan* was immaculate, furnished with sturdy pine tables and chairs and benches that gave it a Scandinavian aspect. In the main room, where we would sit, there was a small fireplace.

Alina called from the door, "Aunt Yekaterina, we're here!"

"Just one second!" replied a trembling old voice. "I'm putting on my outfit!"

A Yakut grandma entered, tiny and stooped, wearing an embossed silver headband adorned with a pair of chains dangling snowflake-patterned silver bangles, a Chinese blue silk dress stitched with intricate raised patterns, and a red silk vest. To my surprise, she greeted me in fluent Russian. I had expected more traditional Yakuts to have undergone less education in Russians schools.

She took my arm and gently pulled me over to a spot in front of the fireplace. "Okay, let's do this right. You stand here. I'll perform the ritual."

"The ritual?"

"We have to appease the gods before dinner."

Had she uttered these words in Yakutian with Alina translating, they might not have struck me as odd. But in Russian they sounded comically inauthentic. In any case, Alina lit tinder and made a fire. Yekaterina jangled out of the room and returned with a small paperback in hand. Glancing at it, she began a rapid recitation, pausing to snatch blini from a tabletop tray and toss them into the fire. The blini flamed up, and she raised a cup of stinky white fluid and poured half into the fire.

She then handed me the cup. I moved to pour my share of the brew into the fire, but she stopped me.

"Not so fast. You're the guest here. Bottoms up."

I lifted the cup to my nose and caught a rancid whiff. "What exactly is this?"

"*Kumys!* [Fermented mare's milk] Drink up! Perform the ritual! Honor the fire spirit!"

I put the cup to my lips and sipped, my throat contracting in an embarrassingly audible gag, but the liquid lost some of its rancidity after the second gulp, and I downed it all.

Aunt Yekaterina ordered us to take seats. Without further ceremony we tucked in to a dinner of sausage, pelmeni, boiled potatoes dashed with dill, tomato and onion salad, and slivers of lightly salted fish, raw yet succulent, called chir. It looked delicious, but apart from the chir, all the dishes were Russian.

She noticed I liked the chir. "We hardly knew what chir was in my childhood. We had to ship it all to the Kremlin! Do you like the horse meat?"

"Horse —"

"Yes, that's horse-meat sausage there. The tenderest you'll taste, from a four-month-old foal."

We started talking. Her family belonged to a horse-breeding kolkhoz, and she had grown up in a *balagan* like this one ("built without a single nail . . . four families to a cabin, one corner per family"). Her youth fell during the Stalin years, in conditions approximating slave labor. The kolkhoz gave them no time to collect firewood, so the family had to head out at four in the morning to search for it; the house had to be heated continually or the frosts would overwhelm it. "The taiga is silent in the sixty-below frost. All you hear is the whispering of the stars" — the sound of breath crystallizing and tinkling as it falls to the ground. "Those were hungry years," she said, "war years, Stalin's time."

"Where did you learn your Russian?"

"I was a doctor, and most of my schooling was in Russian. I finished the medical institute in Blagoveshchensk. I met my husband on a field trip to Moscow. Wait a second."

She ambled out of the room, her bangles tinkling, and returned with a black-and-white photo of a distinguished-looking Yakut in a suit and tie. "Here he is. He . . . was . . . he was from a village near mine." Her voice caught. I glanced up and saw her eyes watering. "I still remember seeing him for the first time at the student party," she said, softly. She wiped away a tear. "He died not long ago. Suddenly, on the way to work, of a heart attack." *La belle mort,* the French would say — the easiest way to go for the deceased, and the toughest on all around him.

Alina cut in, telling me about her teaching job at an elementary school and giving Aunt Yekaterina a chance to compose herself.

"It seems very peaceful out here," I said. "You must prefer living here to Yakutsk."

"Oh, we only spend summers out here," said Yekaterina. "The youths bomb the village in the winter."

"Bomb?"

"I mean rob. They go wild, our youths. You see, the Russians came and taught us to drink and steal. In my day, we were so poor that there was nothing to steal, but now there is. Anyway, one learns bad habits more quickly than good. Stealing is in Russians' blood. They leave ruins wherever they go."

"Do Russians and Yakuts get along?"

"Actually, we get along better now than during the Soviet days. We have more rights, now that we have our own republic. [Sakha declared "state sovereignty" in 1990.] But we hear the Kremlin wants to abolish it and attach us to the other eastern oblasts. No one here will go for that. Our local leaders won't give up their power."

"So what will happen?"

"Russia as a country will disintegrate," she answered flatly. She stood up, her headband jingling. "The republics are used to their independence. Anyway, can I show you around?"

She led me outside for a tour. She opened the door of a shed and rummaged about on a cluttered shelf. "A Yakut thermos!" she said, holding a footlong cylinder made of birch bark slabs. "A spear for bear hunting!" she declared, brandishing a six-foot pole ending in a giant rusty blade. "One hunter scares the bear out of his lair, and the other stands with the spear, its butt lodged in the earth, blade up, and waits for the attack. The bear throws himself on the man, who falls back, leaving only the spear. You had to be courageous to hunt that way!" Next to the shack was "a Yakut refrigerator!" — a six-foot-deep hole in the permafrost a yard across, where produce would keep during the brief summer.

Back in the *balagan* we took our seats around the table for tea. Did she, a physician by training, educated during Communist times, really believe in spirits?

"Oh," she said, "the Soviets brought us up as atheists, so no, of course I don't. It's just a ritual."

Wheezing slightly, she lifted herself off her bench and waddled into the next room. After some fossicking around, she emerged with an ancient, dusty gramophone, which she placed on the bench next to me. She flicked a switch and the old motor cranked the grooved disk around and around. From a pocket on her vest she retrieved a 78 record and centered it on the disc, carefully positioning the stylus.

A waltz by Strauss flowed out, crackling and plaintive on the old machine.

"I met him at student ball fifty years ago, and he was so dashing, so dashing . . ." When the waltz finished she replaced the stylus at the record's edge, and it began anew. Did it matter what here was "traditionally Yakut" and what not? The human constants of birth, love, marriage, and death remain, in essence, the same, whether in Yakutsk or Yorkshire.

Alina and I agreed to meet the next day in front of my hotel so she could show me Yakutsk. She brought along another young Yakut schoolteacher named Tatyana. Tatyana was shapely and fair-skinned, with narrow eyes almost occluded by heavy lids that gave her a languid air. She was anything but languid, however. She possessed the vibrant poise of a leader, with a militant manner of asking questions that announced that she would settle for the truth and nothing but the truth. She exemplified a beauty and energy I would come to associate with Yakut women. If Yakut men had been laid low by alcohol, their women possessed a spirit Turkic and martial that harked back to eons on the steppes of Asia to the south, a spirit that made them conquerors here, both of indigenous peoples and some of the roughest terrain on the planet.

Soon after Alina introduced us, I said something about *Yakuty.* Tatyana snapped back, if smiling, "Excuse me, we don't like the Russian word for us. We are Sakha, and our republic is called Sakha Sire."

The sky threatened rain, so we started off at the National Art Museum, in a capacious modern hall. The Yakut painter Timofey Stepanov was exhibiting his work, most of it completed in the 1980s. His oeuvre radiated light: canary yellows and electric blues and flaming reds dominated wall-size canvasses featuring Yakut gods and mythical beasts, shamans and princesses and knights on horseback — figures from Ayi, Tatyana explained, roaming the three-tiered world that Stanislav had disparaged. His renditions, though artful, recalled illustrations for children's books — fantastic, lurid, and unbelievable.

Tatyana gazed into the paintings. "Our scenery is so gray, but here you see how much color we have inside us." She went on to talk as if the three-tiered world really existed.

"You don't believe all that, do you?" I asked.

"We *do.* We believe and we practice our religion. If we don't have a fireplace, we put our blini and *kumys* offerings in a corner for the fire god, or on the streets. We *believe.*"

"Who teaches you the religion?"

"We learn about it in a national culture class. Because of our Soviet past we couldn't learn it at home. Stalin killed off all but my grandmother on my mother's side of my family. She knew the rituals and all about Ayi, but she was afraid to teach them to us."

Her militancy had solid roots. She paused and gazed into the canvasses, examining details the same way I might peruse maps of the Lena, or Medieval churchgoers the frescoes of biblical scenes on cathedral walls. Her faith in Ayi *had* to derive from pride in her people's heritage. She affirmed her nationalism, telling me: "We're one of the most educated minorities in Russia. We take top prizes in national scholastic competitions. Not bad for a people that until just recently lived in *balagany!* When Moscow tries to take away our rights, we protest on the streets in fifty-below weather. We're not some people at the end of the earth; we've shown the world who we are, and we want our sovereignty. And faith in our religion, Ayi, is *good.* It's the basis of our character. Our national struggle continues!"

"What exactly is your national struggle about these days?"

"Right now, Moscow returns only three percent of the revenues it takes from Sakha. We want at least half."

To experience a ritual spiritual cleansing called *algys,* Tatyana and Alina next took me to an Ayi temple, the House of *Archy* (cleansing), situated beneath crumbling cement apartment complexes on the Lena. A multipeaked pyramidal palace of pine, the House of *Archy* resembled, on the inside, a modern conference hall decorated in Swedish style, all beige wood, with tastefully sparse furnishings like those found in an Ikea store.

A little old Yakut lady greeted us at the door and let us in. She looked adorable, with the finely featured face and hair bun of an Oriental doll, if an aged one. But as we walked by, she barked something at us in Yakut that provoked a row with Tatyana, and all at once both erupted in guttural remonstrations punctuated with the Russian for "Oh, really!" and "How dare you!"

The old lady hobbled away down the corridor, still ranting.

"What's wrong?" I asked.

"We must struggle against the commercialization of our religion!" Tatyana said. "She's demanding the entrance fee, plus five hundred rubles [about seventeen dollars] for the *algys!*" Then she whispered, "Maybe she's a black shaman."

"What's that?"

"A shaman who consorts with spirits of the nether realm."

I was inclined to pay, but before I could say anything a stout Yakut in knee-length chino shorts, a white tennis shirt, and new Top-Siders sloughed down the pine floor toward us, his shoes squeaking. Looking fresh from the yacht, he introduced himself as Arian Petrov, shaman and *algyshyt* (performer of the *algys*), and with a jovial smile explained the charges. "Down the street, the Russian Orthodox charge fifteen hundred rubles for a baptism, so if you ask me, five hundred is a bargain. Don't forget, we're building capitalism in this republic. Isn't that what you Americans wanted? Of course it's in our blood to show mercy to the unfortunate — we'd perform an *algys* gratis for a repentant criminal — but you as a rich man will have to pay. However, we won't charge you extra for being a foreigner. How's that?"

He extended his palm and I handed him the cash.

He led us into a hexagonal pine-paneled chamber with windows set in an airy apse high above. He then excused himself ("I've got to put on my *algyshyt* getup") and trotted off, reappearing a few minutes later in white tasseled robes and a white headband bearing a silver medallion and two ponytails of white horsehair. He was carrying a khomus (a metallic instrument the size of a tiny harmonica), a small pine mug sloshing with a malodorous fluid, a plate of butter, and a white horsehair wand he called a *delbir*.

"Please be seated." He put the cup of fluid — *kumys*, again — in my hands. "Don't worry, I'm not giving this to you to drink. I'm just showing you what I sacrifice to the spirits."

In front of a miniature sand hearth with a foot-high teepee of pine twigs in the middle, he seated us on wicker stools, urging us to turn our palms up and relax our legs, close our eyes. He stuck the khomus into his mouth and blew, cheeks bulging, producing an eerie *boing-bong-boing-bong* as he began circumambulating the room, rocking from leg to leg. He paused to pour *kumys* into the fire and then tossed in gobs of butter, waving his *delbir* and uttering soothing if guttural prayers in Yakut. For twenty more minutes he circled us, boinging and bonging, reciting prayers, boing-boing-boinging some more, and waving his whishing wand. The pine embers scented the air, and we drifted into pleasant somnolence.

I may have fallen asleep, in fact. Finally I became aware of his presence in front of me. He cleared his throat and switched to Russian, opening his arms. "May you find peace. May you succeed in your journey. May you tell other Americans about the House of *Archy*, soon to appear on the Internet at www.domarchy.ru! The end!"

13

"YES, SIR, THERE'S NO SAVIOR like the Lord!" shouted Viktor from the front seat, over the van engine's clank and roar, his smile beatific, his head cocked to the left, his eyes heavenward.

"You said it, Brother in Christ, you said it!" chimed in Sasha, the van's owner, as he wrestled with the wheel, turning off the tarmac onto a sandy road leading through a grove of alders out to the river, a turquoise presence glittering with the morning sun, through the leaves. Just ahead of us, bouncing along in a dust cloud, was Vadim in a Gazel flatbed truck carrying our raft, fuel, supplies, and heavier gear. "In my experience people always let you down. But the Lord — no way! He stays with you, doesn't he, Brother in Christ? I don't have a care in the world as long as I'm walking with the Lord!"

Viktor fixed me with his eyes, clear and blue and droopy with compassion. "You should give that some thought, Jeff. Where you're heading only God can help you. Walking with the Lord means comfort, and there's no comfort but God up north."

In fact, I *had* given it some thought, but in the past, fear — and how many times had I been afraid, in Siberia, on the Congo, crossing the Sahara! — had never shaken my atheism. It didn't now. I've never been able to grasp what the pious mean by "faith in God," or "walking with the Lord," or any variation thereof. What vision do they see that I can't? What words do they hear that are inaudible to my ears? And how can they trust their senses, their sanity? Nevertheless, I accepted Viktor's words as well-intentioned advice and let it go at that.

But as we rocked down the road toward the river, which, the closer we got, thrashed ever more loudly and shone ever more brightly through the trees, I did feel fear. Early the previous night, a northern gale had hit and dispersed the clouds, banishing the warm doldrums that had accompanied our arrival in town and bringing on an autumnal chill that drove the rowdy revelers from the sidewalks. Once packed, I looked for Vadim in the hotel, but he was out drinking with new friends he had made, tailors who sewed clothes from animal skins — people who might be useful for him to know. I returned to my room and lay awake in my bed listening to the wind barrel down the empty streets and rattle the windows; I tried to imagine the 1,058 miles of river ahead. All that came to mind, when I thought of the Arctic, were seals and ice floes and polar bears; I had scant idea what continental Arctic terrain might actually look like.

I took our maps out of my pack. From Yakutsk the Lena flowed north by northwest through a maze of islands, seven miles wide from bank to bank, augmented by lesser yet still mighty rivers, the Aldan and the Vilyuy, that surged out of little-explored *sopki* and bog to the east. Then it straightened out, crossed the Arctic Circle, and ran almost due north into the tundra, narrowing into the notorious Pipe before finally debouching through a vast delta into the Laptev Sea. From Yakutsk to Tiksi there were only a half-dozen real settlements, about which we could find no current information. The weather, Vadim had repeatedly reminded me, could betray us and pin us down: fickle August was only days away. Yet storm-occasioned delays would only increase our chance of catastrophe by ensuring a later entry into the turbulent waters of the Laptev Sea. If I ever needed to believe in a savior, it was now.

The gales shook my windows. I put the maps aside. I had lived forty-three years, and largely done what I had dreamed of; I would have few regrets if my time ended on the river. I lay down and surrendered to the spirit of nihilistic abandon I had known on other expeditions. I slept hardly at all, though, and rose eagerly when my alarm rang.

Now, we drove out of the alders and burst into the Lena's glare, suffering a blast of sand and river spray. Across the bay stood the rusted dock cranes and ruined ferry that had presided over our arrival four days earlier. We halted and got out. The wind compelled us to shout. Still smiling, turning his face to the sun, Viktor walked to the flatbed's rear and grabbed at the straps of the 180-pound red vinyl sack containing our deflated raft. He yanked and couldn't budge it.

A camouflage bandana tied around his sunburned head, his reddish beard tinged with gold, Vadim walked up and motioned Viktor aside, smiling as he often did to people he considered inferior. He ripped the sack off the deck with one hand and thrust his other through the straps, donning it as a backpack, and then grabbed two twenty-liter jerry cans of fuel. Thus encumbered, he stepped sprightly across beach to the water's edge, released his load, and came back for more.

"Lord be praised!" exclaimed Viktor. "Vadim is one serious fellow! You're in good hands, I'd say."

Viktor picked up a jerry can with his right hand, and, leaning hard left, took unsteady steps down the sand to deposit it by the raft. As we lugged our gear, I watched Vadim hoist, haul, and carry. Next to lesser mortals like us, he appeared almost Herculean. But for the first time since leaving Ust'-Kut he dropped his air of forced joviality and went grimly and intensely about his work.

As we got ready for departure, Viktor and Sasha put questions to Vadim about the raft, the mileage we got on our fuel, and how we intended to handle the weather. Giant barges traveled from Yakutsk to Tiksi, and even for them the trip was tough. Did we really think we could make it in such a small craft? Vadim explained the hydrodynamics of our boat: its V-shaped prow and narrow width were ideal for speed and rough waters, and its foreign-made motor would not fail us as a Russian model certainly would. Viktor nodded and declared that just such a craft would allow him to take the Word to the remotest reaches of Sakha, and Sasha praised the Lord.

Within an hour we were loaded. Our goodbyes were short — a few blessings and Godspeeds from our helpers, nothing more — and we jumped aboard. Vadim yanked the engine cord. We pulled out, swung around in the wind, and, after a last shout goodbye, breasted the rising waves and headed for the giant river stretching wide, wide to the north, beyond the reedy islands.

Around noon, as we chugged across a six-mile clear stretch of river toward more islands, the headwind strengthened.

"Damn it!" shouted Vadim, breaking his silence. "I'm never lucky. Of all the sailing I've done in the north, I've probably had only a day or two of tailwind."

The sky to the north was now split: above was brilliant azure; below, heading toward us, scudded clouds gravid with rain, blocking the sun and casting kaleidoscopic patterns of light and dark over the wind-ripped river. Soon waves started slopping over the bow and we began taking on water.

I grabbed a steel pitcher we had bought for such moments and began bailing. His left hand on the keel, Vadim stared straight ahead, ignoring the spray that flew up from the bow in sloppy arcs, passed over me, and splashed down into his face. He grabbed the binoculars and examined the islands — loaves of sand with reed and willow crowns — and glanced down at the squiggly ovals on the plastic-wrapped map on his knee.

"We've got to keep to the channel," he said. "Hold on . . . wait!"

The motor choked; the propeller launched out of the water and in again. Our bow, heavy with a full load of fuel, rose and dropped, cutting deep into the river. In an instant, waves broke loose and slashed and collided, hitting us from all sides.

"A *boltanka!*" shouted Vadim.

The *boltanka*, ever the enemy of sailors on Russia's northern waters, is an anarchy of breakers knocked laterally from one bank to another, combined with waves driven by longitudinal blasts of wind. The *boltanka* tossed our stern out of the water, leaving the propeller's pump gagging and blade spinning, just as our prow crashed back into the river. I bailed as fast as I could.

"We can't risk it now, not here, not so heavily loaded," shouted Vadim. Soaked and manic-eyed, he finally managed to pilot us out of the *boltanka* and onto a nearby island's sandy shore.

"Things are changing fast, now that we're beyond Yakutsk," I said.

"You haven't seen anything yet!"

Feeling newly vulnerable, shielding our eyes from blowing sand and watching the river rage under a canopy of iron cloud cut with turquoise rifts, we stretched out on the beach and awaited calmer waters. Three hours later the wind subsided, the river coursed glassy beneath an azure vault, and a celestial peace came to reign. We continued our journey.

Later, sailing north through an ancient panorama of shimmering blue-gilt river and flint grays, spruce greens, and larch browns, I leaned back against our load, relaxed and enthralled. Warmed by the sun shining anew over the southern horizon, I followed errant breezes as they dimpled the river. Clouds rising in tiers and arches from bogs to the west, from taiga in the east, coalesced into castles and abbeys, valleys and summits. Drowsy from a month's nights of shallow sleep, I fixed my gaze on the clouds and envisioned the jagged crags of Kurdistan, the ocherous chasms of the High Atlas.

My head lolled. On wind sighing through the reeds, I discerned notes and half-notes, breves and minims; I caught echoes of melodies that segued in my mind's ear into verses from songs almost forgotten. Often I found myself listening to voices from my past, voices I would never hear again: my mother on the porch of our beach house, calling us to dinner through the cool blue of a June evening; my grandmother Rosalie's boisterous laugh at the table; my grandfather growling out greetings as he marched barrel-chested down the hall from his study. We hanker after sounds artificially reproduced by the latest technology, but here, on this Siberian river, drifting toward the top of the world, I relished the company of loved ones departed yet revived by nature's invisible choir. "Where man hath never trod . . . Heard melodies are sweet, but those unheard / Are sweeter," wrote Keats. For the first time, I understood his words.

Later that pacific evening, we camped on a patch of white sand, beneath birches uprooted and knocked over by floes of spring ice. The sun shone low, bleeding red and orange into the Lena's powder blue expanses, the sky to the north a mat of cloud; somewhere ahead, a storm was breaking. After we unpacked, I watched Vadim prepare dinner and noted his newfound reticence, the urgency with which he checked and rechecked his maps, and the change in his dress.

Instead of rubber sandals, he now wore his black waist-high boots all the time. Beneath them, replacing his camouflage cotton trousers, were waterproof trousers. An all-weather black vest cut and slashed with zippered or buttoned pockets covered his torso. On his belt hung a sturdy hunter's knife, sheathed and sharp, a blade to gut and dress a bear with. A set of pliers on a long cord reposed in one pocket; in others hid bits of string, lengths of wire, ropes, hooks, and metallic clips; at various times of the day, especially when setting up camp or checking out the motor, he dipped into his pockets for one or another of these oddments. Elsewhere on his person he carried his compass, GSM module, and rounds of ammunition.

I had grown tanned and shaggy-haired, and had lost weight, but Vadim's features had evolved in a subtler way with the rigors of our expedition. His beard was now a rich russet brown, speckled with gold, his brows were sun-blond and bushy, his cheeks and eye sockets deeper. The black baseball cap he wore with the visor backwards gave him, with his beard, the air of a piratical Daniel Boone.

As a rainbow flushed its colors against the clouds and tinted the water, I watched Vadim move about camp. The north energized him. He was ever turning a screw, tightening a knot, cutting string, attaching something to something else. At first I wondered if he wasn't fidgeting to kill time, but eventually I would see that in fact he devoted every moment ashore to bettering the campsite or to preparations for the trials ahead, when we would have little energy for anything but survival.

I asked him why he couldn't just sit and rest.

"I will, but only after I've made our camp as comfortable as I can. Out here, you *have* to be as comfortable as possible. Always. It's not a luxury. If you're not resting thoroughly, fatigue builds and you end up getting sick. And if you catch a virus in the Arctic, you're done for."

A skilled *tayozhnik* (taiga dweller), he looked always to rectify the tiniest imperfections: the pot hanging crookedly on a chain over the fire; the fire burning askew, heating one kettle but not another; the inconvenient slope of his stone seat. But while he concerned himself with vital minutiae, he continued railing against my mission. "You waste all this time in villages talking to people. What's the use? How to survive in the taiga is what you *should* be learning."

Two days later, as solitary, widely spaced clouds dumped rain here and there across a boundless river vista, the Verkhoyansk Mountains reared above the taiga on the northern shore. Gloomy leaden irruptions, pitiless rock sentries of gulag toil and death, the Verkhoyansk, the remotest and most ill famed mountains of Russia! Beneath them is the mouth of the Aldan River, the circuitous course of which leads fourteen hundred miles away into the barrens of eastern Sakha and Kolyma, to its source, north of Manchuria. The Aldan supplies the Lena with a third of its water, and its name means "gold" in Evenk — apt, for it traverses land saturated with lodes of gold, plus, according to one gatherer of Siberian lore, "all the elements in Mendeleyev's table."

We stared at the Verkhoyansk in disbelief. How far we had come!

Yet, the sun emerged to warm our cheeks. Faced with the very landscape of doom for so many Russians, I asked myself, paradoxically, What more could I want than to be free and healthy, traveling down a great river, not knowing where I'll pass the night or what new people I'll meet? Our expedition was now in its sixth week. Its rigors were slowly transforming me, its rustic delights edging out urban pleasures. Our campfire of larch burned fragrant under a fiery midnight sky; the air chilled and invigorated; the silence soothed. I now craved tea laced with bagul'nik; I delighted in sprigs of black currant; I savored Vadim's lenok and nelma more than any sweetmeat. Under this torrent of primal sensations, my life in Moscow seemed pallid, unreal.

During such moments I felt inspiration flow from nature itself. *"Aux temps primitifs, quand l'homme s'éveille dans un monde qui vient de naître, la poésie s'éveille avec lui,"* Victor Hugo had written. ("In primitive times, when man awoke in a world newly born, poetry awoke with him.") We drift away from nature's bounty, and try to accustom ourselves to our own mediocre creations, seeking happiness in flawed worlds of our own making, when all along transcendence has lain in the wind and sun on our faces. Yes, escape to the wilds involves risk, but who evades death? For one who has *lived*, death comes not as defeat but as consummation, and his friends should not weep but dance on his grave!

The Verkhoyansk finally reached the Lena in bankless escarpments, in grim walls of granite. Late in the afternoon on our fourth day out of Yakutsk, as we crossed a five-mile-wide bay abutted by Baatyly, the mountain sheltering our next destination, the settlement of Sangar on its far slope, a terrible northeasterly wind arose, hitting us with diagonal waves that we could not safely endure.

"This isn't sailing for the weak-nerved. We can't take these waves sideways," Vadim shouted. He steered starboard to plow through each yard-high breaker and then straightened out again. "We're too heavy with fuel. We've got to make shore." Halting just shy of Sangar was frustrating, but Vadim was adamant that we avoid risks now as much as possible; later, we would have little choice but to run them. It was all he could do to weave and swerve among the waves to the nearest sandbar. There we jumped out and dragged our craft to the island attached to it. Lyaukiriy, the map read.

Lyaukiriy was a lump of sand topped with a crescent grove of alders that were home (tracks told us) to a fox and a hare, plus legions of fat mosquitoes that sallied forth to attack us any time the wind lessened, or whenever we happened to step on the lee side of a tree or dune. Looking out over miles of open river, of thrashing whitecaps between our bivouac and Baatyly, we dined on smoked lenok and buckwheat. I stood up, ready to turn in.

"Wait," said Vadim. He produced his bottle of spirits and poured us shots, mixing them with drafts of honey and river water.

Like the sun at midnight, it went down like liquid fire.

14

THE WINDS HAD MAROONED us on an unpromising island, but they soon lulled me to sleep with an Aeolian symphony produced in concert with the sealike churning of whitecaps, the distant, soothing crash of waves against the cliffs of Verkhoyansk, and the cadenced flapping of my tent walls. Dreams came to me, numerous and vivid, and then a deep dark slumber.

Toward midnight, silence. I awoke to find my tent walls stilled, lit with the gloam. I sat up. Outside mosquitoes whined, and from somewhere afar on the shoals, a sandpiper cried out *wee-wee-wee*. Then, with a whooshing roar, a mighty wind from the south blew upon us, warm and humid. My tent, set up for a northeaster, flapped and rattled, bent double, and almost collapsed over me, so I jumped out to reposition it. The sky in the west was a mass of lava clouds roiling against a golden vault.

On arising, we found that the southern wind had died in doldrums and heat. But fearing that another meteorological caprice could delay us further in reaching Sangar, we breakfasted and got going early, pulling out around the shoal, cutting across the bay beneath the Verkhoyansk, and circumventing Baatyly's cape. An effulgent sun bore down on Baatyly's thinning larches and slopes of shale, striking, near the water, the skeletons of derelict shacks with smashed-in windows and missing doors. Farther ahead, smokestacks rose in crooked dominion over a looted factory; an overturned wreck of a bus sheltered a pair of hawks that bounded into flight as we passed; and all over the shore were scattered the hacked-up remains of cutters and rowboats. The bank, as far as we could tell, was more an amalgam of rust and rotted wood and wire than sand or rock. Vadim and I exchanged distraught glances. If this was Sangar, it looked dead.

But then we rounded another smaller cape and saw, on Baatyly's north slope, central Sangar (the ruined neighborhood on the first cape having been just a suburb) — hodgepodges of two- and three-story larch tenements, coffee brown or raw gray, and a mess of shanties sunk amid overgrown bushes and wild grass. Beneath them spread a crescent-shaped sandy harbor on which old boats, many with holes in their hulls, lay beached. On the main street people were out and about — and staggering.

Sangar was born of the Soviet Union's earliest plans to exploit Siberia's resources. In 1928 twenty Russian geologists set out on horseback from Yakutsk, arriving a month later at Baatyly, where they founded the settlement and begin mining the mountain's coal. Coal aside, it was not a propitious spot: *Sangar* meant "lowland" in Evenk, and swamps stretched into the village from the north. Development nevertheless proceeded apace. By the early 1980s, Sangar had nine thousand inhabitants and supplied much of Yakutsk's coal. Even now it is the most populous outpost from Yakutsk to Tiksi. We planned to buy bread and vegetables, pass the night, and move on.

Vadim shook his head as we pulled into the harbor. "Just *look* at this dump. Everyone on shore's drunk." He squirmed in his seat. "I have a *bad* feeling about this place. Don't stay long."

We drew up to the bank and I jumped ashore. Vadim quickly pulled out to find a campsite on Khodusa Yuyesyun-Arylara Island, a mile or two opposite. The sun doused Sangar in desolating glare and brought to mind Africa; the ramshackle cabins, with their tin pens and chickens and dusty yards, also recalled that continent. I walked up the beach, sidestepping nail-studded boards and crushed gin-and-tonic cans, and passed a pair of glassy-eyed Russians loitering over a half-empty bottle of Chinese vodka. I needed to find a store, and I considered whom I might ask for directions. Then it occurred to me: it was Sunday. What would be open? And who would be sober on the outback's traditional drunk day?

From just beneath a tenement, two deadpan, flinty eyes followed me. A middle-aged woman in old blue sweatpants and a frayed T-shirt was sitting on a knocked-down telephone pole, rocking an infant in her pale flaccid arms. The baby's presence suggested sobriety, so I walked over to her.

"*Zdrasst'ye!*" I said. "Can you tell me where I might find an open store?"

"*Zdorovo!*" she answered, clearing her throat, her voice hoarse with phlegm, as though she hadn't spoken for hours. "The store's up that way." She gave me a once-over with her hard eyes. "But you probably won't find it if you're not from here." She patted the baby's back. "Where you from?"

I told her. Expressing no surprise, she told me that if I'd accompany her, she'd put her grandson in his crib up in her daughter's house nearby and take me to the store herself. We set out on a gravel road that wound up around the harbor's tenements into the settlement. She addressed me with the familiar *ty* form (like *tu* in Spanish and French), as she might a friend or a child. Maybe such was the custom out here, but I found this as affectionate as it was oddly portentous, and I took a closer look at her. She had thinning hennaed orange hair with gray roots; her face was sallow and crinkled like parchment. Yet she maintained a steady gait, and her tone of speech was domineering, even masculine. She had the look of an alcoholic, but she didn't act like one.

"My name's Olga. You gotta be careful here. It's not good to wander around alone."

"Oh, I've been all over Russia. I think I —"

From around a fence a German shepherd lunged, barking at me, his yellow fangs bared. Olga reached down and hurled a rock at the mangy assailant, which sent him scurrying back a few paces.

"They'll rip your nuts off, these damn strays, and they're all over the settlement. Keep your eyes open, young man."

The dog trailed us for a while, but he kept his distance. I picked up a stick, just in case. Our steps kicked up ashen dust, and soon my sandaled feet were caked with it. We reached a two-story larch tenement, one of many on the main street, and Olga walked in with the baby, leaving me outside for a minute.

I bought bread in the store. We could find vegetables in a shop a few blocks away, Olga said. As we walked back outside, I decided that in this rough-and-tumble settlement, street-smart Olga would make a suitable guide, so I asked her if she wouldn't mind showing me Sangar.

"Sure," she said. "You'll need me here, anyway. Or they'll rip your guts open, the bastards."

"The dogs?"

"That's what I call 'em too. C'mon. First I'll show you the monument to the plane that crashed here."

"What plane was that?"

"What, you don't know? The pilot's name was Kalvitsa. A Soviet explorer. See, pilots out here are heroes. They get killed all the time, with our weather. The monument is right up there."

With the sun pressing hot on our shoulders and bare heads, we started climbing a footpath circling around a promontory above the river, built up with shacks, checkered with tiny vegetable garden plots. I stepped with care, hardly able to raise my eyes for all the broken glass, nail-studded boards, chunks of metal, and old wires cluttering the path.

Ahead of us teetered a bone-thin man in his forties, his black hair long and greasy, his trousers soiled fore and aft. He hesitated before a log in the path, raised his foot to step over it, and lost his balance. He keeled over, his lower back hitting a stout pipe jutting vertically out of the ground. If it had been thinner, it would have impaled him.

"Ooooaaah! Oooaaaah aah aah!" he groaned, and rolled around, clutching his side, his face nuzzling the dust. As he moaned his breath puffed dust, and dust covered his tongue, and he coughed and puffed more dust.

Without slowing, Olga stepped over him. He reeked of piss and more, so I did the same.

"Nothing but *bich'yo* here!" she said. (*Bich'yo*, a collective noun, comes from *BICH*, a humorous Russian acronym for *byvshy intelligentny chelovek* — "formerly cultured person.") She went on. "Look at how low you can sink. You start off an *intelligent*, and degrade into devil knows what."

"Why are there so many *bichi* here?"

"Sangar's croaking all around us, can't you tell? Perestroika killed it. When I arrived here thirty-five years ago, we were nine thousand people who had come here for a purpose: to build socialism and help the Motherland. Now we're half that in number and we have nothing left to work for. We used to produce so much coal, but now the mines are all closed down, all but one, that is, and it's on fire. Our fish-processing plant shut, and so did our oil-prospecting mission. The people left here now have nowhere to go, no jobs, nothing to live for. So they start boozing."

"Where do you work, if I might ask?"

"I was a doctor, but I'm retired now. Anyway, I'd never turn down a shot of vodka, but you won't find me lying in the mud like the *bichi*."

Doctors in Russia were paid little, and their skill levels were often low. So it didn't surprise me that a woman with Olga's manners could have practiced medicine.

The path abruptly ended at an eroded mud cliff.

"Oh, damn," she said, putting her hands on her hips. The monument turned out to be somewhere on the other side of the small ravine. She wanted to find a way to reach it, but I asked her if we might forgo the visit for now, at least; across the ravine were more dogs and trash-strewn paths, plus a maze of huts that we would find it difficult to cross through, and the sun was wearying.

She said yes, adding, "Anyway, I'd rather show you the miners' monument. So let's go there."

As she passed me, she grabbed my camera bag and shouldered it — a heavy load. I tried to take it back.

"Look," she said, pushing me away, "we northern women are stronger than you men, because we don't drink so much. I'll carry your pack for you."

"But really," I said, still trying to retrieve it, "that's not nec —"

"Back off!" She glared at me. "You're my guest, dammit."

With horseflies now in hot pursuit and mosquitoes pricking at our exposed ankles, we picked our way down into the ravine and followed the track, muddy with some sort of drainage, toward an agglomeration of houses and cabins. Once there, we ducked to avoid five-foot-high *teplotrassy* — foot-wide heating pipes wrapped in decaying insulation fiber — that crisscrossed open fields and ran along the streets. Because of the permafrost, Sangar's pipes have to run aboveground.

The miners' monument was a steel pillar some fifteen feet tall, with twenty-two names inscribed in red. Olga stopped and looked wistfully at it.

"Back in the eighties methane gas built up in the mine and it exploded. Killed all those guys. I knew 'em; I treated them at the hospital. Some were my friends." She turned to me. "You know, I come here and remember when they were alive, when I arrived from the *materik*, full of enthusiasm for this town! There were hardly any decent buildings back then — none of this modern stuff you see around you existed — but we didn't care. Now, everyone's searching for a way out. Anyway, we come here on Miners' Day with our vodka to drink in their memory. We'll never forget them."

We didn't linger but took a path to the gravel-topped main street, which ran straight between larch tenements. At a square we saw a steel bust of Lenin in front of the municipal building.

"There used to be a whole statue of Lenin here," Olga said. "In 1991, with democracy and all, some fuckers got all excited and knocked off his head. How uncultured. But the people here wanted their Lenin, so they just put the head back on the pedestal." Farther on was an empty field. "Used to be a workers' dorm here. But drunks burned it down. Seven or eight died in the fire. Enjoying the tour?" Her voice carried no hint of levity.

Five Yakut teens with shaved heads were walking by, swaggering and swearing. Olga watched them pass. "The little fuckers," she said a minute later under her breath. "All they do is rape and rob. Oh, don't think I can't handle them. They've never managed to rob *me*. If asswipes like them threaten me, I just tell 'em, 'Look, you, I can give it as well as take it, and better than you! You scum, if I blew through your assholes your heads would pop off!'"

"Ha oo-*aghghgh* m-m-m, Olya . . ." A Russian man in his fifties tottered along, taking higgledy-piggley steps toward us, and made as if tipping his hat in salutation. But he had no hat. He was graying and oddly distinguished, if sloggered — a *bich*, to be sure.

Olga returned his greetings. "Oh, good ol' Yura. Was the pride of our settlement, with his accordion. Now he's drinking himself to death."

All at once this phantasmagoria of post-Soviet perdition got to me and I felt pangs of pity for the drunks around me. And for Olga. She had a grandson! A generation would grow up here, never having known the élan of the boom years, learning about life from these stumbling souls. What future awaited them — and so many countless millions across Russia? What sort of politics would they espouse? Repression, revolt, and poverty came to mind — Russia's eternal banes.

Olga was crude, but I trusted her; I resolved to stick with her that day and learn all I could about her world. For now, I was tired of touring and wanted to do something to help her and her family. Hoping

I would not offend her pride as my host, I asked if I might treat her grandson to yogurt and fruit.

"Why yes, that would be nice. He should eat more yogurt than he does. So let's hit the store again."

We turned around and walked back up the block. By the store, another shack-shop, a limping bum with glazed eyes stuck a fingerless hand-stump in Olga's face. "Mama, give me a few rubles . . . I need to top off the tank."

She pushed past him and we walked inside. She asked for two four-packs of yogurt. As I bought vegetables and fruit, I decided to treat her to a full load of groceries. So we added bread, sausage, and slices of melon, plus cheese and a few other things. I then offered to buy us a couple of beers.

"I'd prefer vodka."

I was leery of vodka in places like this. Drunk the Russian way — straight hundred-gram shot after shot, knocked back on the host's command — the effect is violently unpredictable, which I don't like, but also, out in Siberia, fatal cases of poisoning are common. Chemically brewed moonshine, often imported illegally from China, took lives every year.

"Oh," I said, "I'd rather stick to beer, if you don't mind."

"As you wish." She asked the shopkeeper for six half-liter bottles of beer marked KREPKOYE — "strong" — for its 12 percent alcohol content.

Back out on the street under the withering sun again, we set out for Olga's tenement, where we would eat and drink in the kitchen. I told her how distressing I had found her tour of Sangar. Why did she stay on?

"I'll never leave," she replied. "Sangar's a place to grow old in. You can rely on people here; you need them as much as they need you. Mutual support is how you make it through life, young man. Anyway, I like the way people relate to one another out here." This she said without irony.

At her tenement's main door a bum sat sunning himself on a bench. A radiator had been sunk horizontally in the dirt as a doormat, possibly to give residents one last solid foothold before setting out into the mud or ice, depending on the season. The door itself had been knocked off its hinges, so we walked right in and mounted creaking stairs, inhaling rancid odors. The walls were sticky, our eyes not yet adjusted to the dark.

Her apartment was next to the stairwell on the second floor. She turned the handle and leaned into the door, but it wouldn't budge. She knocked and waited. Nothing. Then she pounded. No response.

"Oh, Christ, that bitch! It looks like my damned daughter's taken off with the key. Just like her. She'll hear from me on *that* account!"

She leaned over the stairs and shouted down to the drunk outside. "Kolya, where'd my daughter take off to?"

"Don't know, Olya, but she had a sack of beer bottles, so she won't be back soon."

"The little *bitch*," she said. "Sorry about my language. Say, let's try Katya's. Maybe we can drink our beer with her."

Katya lived across the hall. Olga pounded on her door and it edged open. A young brunette in a blue tracksuit stood clipping a dress to a laundry cord hung with wet clothes. Her arms were raised and her round breasts strained against her T-shirt; her slender waist sloped down to balloon into oversize buttocks.

She finished with the dress and turned to us, arms akimbo. "C'mon in," she said. She gave me a wary smile. Straightaway I noticed her clear pale skin, her penetrating green eyes. In the corner sat a girl of eleven or twelve, fine-boned, with long chestnut ponytails streaked with sun, her smile of straight white teeth shy and endearing. Her eyes were green too, with blond lashes.

We took off our shoes at the door, as is customary in muddy Russia, even in summer. Olga's feet had fat stubby toes and corns and red heels.

"My bitch of a daughter took off to booze and locked me out," she said. "I was thinking we might drop in on you for a little while. We'd like to treat you to beer and melon."

"Okay. Have a seat," Katya said. I introduced myself, as did she. She told me she worked at the local heating plant. The girl's name was Vera.

Katya's apartment was warm, stuffy, and damp; all the windows were closed to keep drafts away from her baby boy, who lay crying in a crib in the large, messy living room of which the kitchen formed a corner. Floral patterned wallpaper sagged and bulged; the woof of hanging wool tapestries had wilted. A Chinese clock ticked loudly, its second hand lurching around the dial. From outside a generator's determined chug could be heard.

Olga griped about the "bottom-feeding Yakuts" we had seen out looking for trouble earlier. Katya cleared the table of dirty dishes in preparation for our feast. "In fact," Katya said to me, "those probably weren't Yakuts but *Sakhalyary.*"

"*Sakhalyary?*"

"Half-breeds, those with Slavic and Yakut [Sakha] parents. There're a lot of 'em here. They come into town from the villages and raise hell. A decent girl can hardly walk around this town anymore without risking robbery or worse."

As Olga swore about *Sakhalyary* and her inconsiderate daughter, letting fly expletives that would have shamed a stevedore, I looked over at Vera, who sat primly with her eyes on her hands.

Katya turned to her. "Cover your ears when Aunt Olga is around!"

Vera's presence at an adult drinkfest was nothing exceptional in Russia, where poverty and cramped apartments have always exposed children to behavior and language for which Western kids might have to search XXX sites on the Internet. Yet I still found Olga's foul language excessive in front of the prim preteen.

"Is she your daughter?" I asked Katya.

"No, her parents aren't too well off, so they send her over to me. I keep her busy. She takes care of my son and does chores. I'm trying to teach her to be responsible." She popped open a can of beer and foamed spewed out. "*Za vstrechu!*" (To our meeting!)

We took gulps of beer. I handed Vera a yogurt. Accepting it, she smiled demurely, but then coughed hard and deep in wrenching, cacophonous spasms.

As the beer went down, Olga closed her eyes. She smiled and shook her head, turning to me. "So, like I was saying, the little fuckers, the Yakuts in from the villages — okay, Katya, the *Sakhalyary,* to be exact — they have the nerve to tell us Russians to get out of 'their republic.' I tell them, 'You'll be nothing but a mud smear when I'm done with you! We taught you to bathe and use forks and knives, and now *you're* telling *us* to get out? Go to hell!'"

Katya nodded in agreement but looked at Vera. "Close your ears, my joy!"

The son emitted a feeble cry from his crib.

"Where's his father?" I asked, immediately regretting my words.

"We don't ask questions like that in Russia," Olga said. "We don't ask women where their men are. Because we all know the answer."

"What use would a husband be?" asked Katya. "I don't need a man lying on my sofa, beating me, getting drunk. Anyway, here in Sangar girls begin having babies at fourteen or fifteen. Husbands aren't necessary. Say, you're not a preacher, are you?"

"No. Why?"

"We had some German preachers come through here once. I think they baptized me, but I can't remember. I don't really know what the word means. At least they were better than that Russian religious lady who came through."

"What did she do?" I asked.

"Oh, she spread the *porcha*" — a folk term for a supposed wasting disease. "One kid after his baptism developed this pimple on his nose. It just grew and grew, getting all red and puffy and pus-filled, till it blew up. Another boy she baptized drowned a week later. She was really a black *shamanka*, that baptizer!"

Olga too had a brush with the godly. "That slut baptized me too! I had to cure myself with an ultraviolet light for a week afterward!"

Katya brought her son from the living room and set him on her knee. He was thin and dazed-looking; a rectangle of adhesive tape covered his belly button. I asked what it was for.

"I don't have time to take him to the hospital," answered Katya. "So I take him to the grandmas who put spells on him to cure him." The tape was part of the "cure."

"What's wrong with him?"

There was a knock on the door. Right away Olga and Katya stashed all the beer cans under the table and pressed their forefingers to their lips as a warning that I keep silent. Katya put her son in Olga's arms and got up to answer.

A fierce-eyed woman about my age stood in the doorway. She had short hair and the same eyes as Katya, the same cheeks. She marched in and looked at the baby's navel tape.

"All right, dammit, take that baby to the hospital!" she commanded. "He's been sick long enough!" She put her hand on his chest. "Why, he's burning up!"

Katya yanked him out of Olga's arms and plopped him into her lap.

He dribbled pee onto her thigh. She patted the stain with a rag. "Mom, I don't need the hospital. I'm treating him myself. Don't you see the tape? And don't be rude: meet our guest from America."

Mom kept her eyes on Katya. "I want to know why you're not taking care of your son! You should be taking him to the hospital and not looking to get your ass in trouble with some American. Let the authorities deal with him."

"Olga brought him here," said Katya. "He's very polite."

"Oh, did she?" She turned her eyes on Olga.

"Well, he asked me *politely* to show him to the store," Olga said in a steady voice. "He didn't start swearing at me like some kind of asshole. And look, you don't need me as an enemy in this town. So watch how you talk to me."

Out of nowhere Katya started begging Mom for money, touching her cheeks and speaking in a little-girl voice. Mom resisted, pushing her away, with tears brimming in her eyes. Finally she slipped her a hundred-ruble note.

"That's a good mother," said Olga. "Gotta help the children. Children're our future."

"I wish you'd stay away and not come over here corrupting my daughter."

"My own daughter locked *me* out. What d'ya want me to do? Treat our guest to beer in the hallway? It's not *my* fault. When my daughter gets home, she'll need to be treated for the rubber."

"For the rubber?" I asked.

"For the rubber hose I'll whip her with! Better that the little bitch had never been born than to lock out her mama!"

Mom marched back to the door and turned around. "Take that damn kid to the hospital. That's all I have to say." She walked out and slammed the door.

Olga explained that Mom was really quite kind ("she pities her daughter and tosses her a hundred rubles now and then"), but that she was just "too nervous, and not very fun-loving. Uh-oh, we're running out of beer here!"

"Maybe we *should* take the baby to the hospital," I said. But again I regretted my words; staffed with doctors like Olga, hospitals often did more harm than good.

"What, are you kidding?" Katya snapped. "He's better off with the grannies and bellybutton tape!"

She had a point: at least folk cures were generally benign. Olga mentioned the dwindling supply of beer again, so I handed her two hundred rubles. She turned around and asked Vera to run down to the store and buy us booze.

"Excuse me, they'll sell alcohol to her?" I asked. "At her age?"

"No, but I'm going to write a prescription." Doctor Olga scribbled out a note ordering the shopkeeper, Lena, to sell the girl beer, and handed it to her. "Don't let that whore rip you off this time. Bring me a receipt."

"Please, Vera," I said, after giving her some rubles, "buy something for yourself. Whatever you'd like."

She smiled bashfully and skipped out, but as she was shutting the front door an old lady peeped in, singing to herself, wearing a besotted smile. Katya lit into her.

"Get lost, old bitch! I've had enough of you!" She got up and slammed the door on her. "Crazy old bitch's lost her mind. Goes around knocking on doors all day and babbling nonsense and singing. Hey, we need some music." She flicked on a boom box and Russian pop blared out. Katya began swaying to the music but promptly took her seat again when Vera came running back inside with more beer and a pair of stiff salted okun'. She had bought nothing for herself and turned away, smiling shyly, when I asked her why not. I thought, *How long will she have until she coarsens and degenerates in this dying settlement?*

We ate and drank. They began telling me that tomorrow they would show me the town in style; we could hire the local taxi and see all the sites: the town dump, the boiler plant, the sludge-filled pond. They weren't joking.

"If you're here to see how we really live out here," Olga said, "we won't spare you anything."

We spent the next hours chatting. Both were polite to me; Olga never swore in addressing me. I had landed in an average Sangar home, and if life there wasn't exactly sweet, it seemed bearable. Neither mentioned leaving, and both apparently had enough money to live without distress; neither drank too much.

Outside, the sun lowered and the light was finally softening. It was already six in the evening.

"Let's do the town!" said Katya. She slipped behind a partition and changed from her blue tracksuit into a shiny white sateen one. She then wrapped the baby in a blanket and put him in a carriage. Vera would take him to Oksana's, the babysitter next door. Ready for action, we walked out, passed the drunk on the bench, and joined a stream of young people, mostly female and already intoxicated, and well turned out in tight jeans and sheer blouses, with high heels despite the dirt, strolling down the road toward the port. The air was cooling, and Sangar, without the sharp midday sun, looked more appealing than it had when I arrived.

"There are so many beautiful girls in Sangar," I said.

"They're pretty now, when they're young," Olga replied. "But then they start living. Living wears us out here."

Katya walked like a trailer park queen, turning up her nose and swinging her fleshy hips. The dreaded *Sakhalyary* were not out, and to my surprise Olga greeted Russians we met along the way warmly, even several drunks, men with fine features in suits much abraded whose speech was correct, if slurred — in short, *bichi* who but for the grace of God might be any one of us.

We stopped at the town restaurant — a flat cement building with a fresh coat of paint and dirty windows.

"We don't usually have the money to go out like this. It's really nice of you to treat us!" said Katya.

"My pleasure."

This was an establishment surely *sans pareil* from here to the North Pole. Neat tables set with elaborate rows of silverware and glasses of varied heights — for wine, champagne, shots, and water — stood around a tiled dance floor with a disco ball in the middle. At one table sat the restaurant's only guests: two platinum blondes with their thug dates, who wore black jackets and no ties; their fat jowls spilled over their collars, their paunches over their belts.

A black-clad giant rose from the back of the hall and took menacing steps toward us. His head was the size of a basketball.

"Oh-ho! The prison warden!" whispered Katya.

"What you want?" he demanded.

"What," said Katya, "do you think? We'd like to eat."

"Not dressed like that, not in here."

He had a point, I had to admit. I was in sandals, a T-shirt, and baggy gray slacks — hardly evening attire. Both Olga and Katya wore tracksuits.

But Katya didn't like his tone. "Who are you to refuse us?"

"Look, miss, we have our standards."

I quietly urged leaving. "No way," retorted Katya in a voice far too harsh considering the maitre d's bulk. "I'll pay my money and eat wherever the hell I want! That's what democracy means, no? We have democracy here these days."

"Out!" barked the giant.

I pulled them back onto the street. There was one other place we could try, Katya said.

The sun hung just above the bogs across the river; a breeze huffed ripples over the water. At the port we left the road and walked onto the beach. We slogged across the sands to Na Kamushkakh (On the Pebbles) — an outdoor café at the harbor's southern end. Behind a waist-high wooden fence, on an unpainted plank dance floor sheltered by an aluminum-siding roof, a drunk crowd of mostly women and teenage girls — perhaps three females to a male — gyrated wildly to Russian pop. Other partiers, also in the advanced stages of inebriation, crowded around beer-splotched wooden tables. From an adjacent tin shack, through a little window, a woman was selling bottled vodka and cans of beer and gin-and-tonic, plus peanuts and salted fish, tails and fins attached, to a succession of clients who staggered flat-footed back to their seats, trying not to drop or spill their armfuls of food and liquor. With the teens, despite the age difference, were quite a few *bichi* — the same sort of folk Olga had greeted warmly earlier in the day. Here everyone partied in the same place. There was no choice.

We made for the table in the rear, where a beautiful *fausse* blonde sat cuddling a baby on her lap and sipping a can of 12 percent beer. Across from her was a younger teen, maybe her sister, whose greasy hair was pulled into a ponytail and whose bulging cheeks looked to be stuffed with nuts. They turned and smiled at us, and urged us to sit.

Olga said a warm hello to the blonde but pointed a pale stubby finger at the teen. "You've got some explaining to do! And you know what about!"

The teen's cheeks deflated and she looked down. This was after all a small town, and people were close, probably too close for comfort.

I got up and visited the shack. I ordered a round of beers for my table. I set a can in front of the teen, but Olga snatched it. "Don't give her anything. She's the kind of slut who returns a favor with treachery." When Olga looked away, I slid the beer back to the reprobate.

Olga and Katya talked more about what they wanted to show me the following day, and the blonde joined in, but Olga wouldn't let the teen speak. Soon a drunken, unshaven fellow in a baseball cap appeared at the end of the table, standing over Katya. He bent down and pursed his lips for a kiss. She socked him in the cheek, and, recoiling, he punched her back, nearly knocking her from her seat. Both had bright red fist imprints on their jaws.

"Meet my brother," Katya said, massaging her cheek. "Just fooling around."

Holding his jaw, he took a seat beside the teen and shook my hand. He put his arm around the teen's neck and began leaning into her face to kiss her. At first she pulled away, but her neck was lodged in the crook of his arm. He dug his flexed thumb knuckle into her jugular, and she gasped and turned red and relented, opening her mouth. He thrust his tongue between her lips.

When he finished, she looked at me. "Meet my boyfriend."

The partying proceeded apace; Sunday's drinking was often the hardest of the week, as people tried to forget about Monday. The blonde smiled and drank her beer, patting her baby's belly; the love-birds across from me horsed around, necking and sparring. A woman in her forties, her hair pinned up behind but coming down in sensuous loops on the sides, tottered over to me and asked me groggily to dance, extending a delicate but soiled hand with painted nails. Olga jumped up and pushed her away, sending her rebounding off the outer railing onto the dance floor, where she collapsed.

"You don't need the disgrace she'd bring you!" Olga said.

She was probably right. As Olga turned to argue with the teen, and Katya and her brother fought another round of fisticuffs, I sat back and reflected. Sangar was a purely Soviet creation, and Olga's words about its heady early days rang true. The corruption, as she would have it, came from the collapse of the Soviet Union, from the obliteration of the dreams and national ideals that ordered people's lives. Yet those dreams and ideals — the triumph of communism according to Marxism, the ascendancy of the working class promised by Lenin — were themselves deceits. Everything here was a lie, and much in the Soviet past, even now, remains unknown; the crimes were great, and the population was largely complicit. How could anyone acknowledge these facts? And would doing so make the future any more prosperous? Yes, I thought, it might. But it was easiest to drink and forget.

The sun burned lower and lower, touching the top of the bogs. Soon an SUV with tinted windows roared down the beach and scrunched to a stop, showering us in sand. Three fat guys in Speedo bathing suits — the *mafiya?* The bar's owners? — stumbled out and took heavy steps to the shack to order vodka. Something close to anarchy came to reign at Na Kamushkakh: men's voices grew louder, fighting words were in the air, another woman collapsed on the dance floor. Across Russia, especially rural Russia, this scene would now be repeating itself; the Sunday debauch offered the only escape from the present, the only way to forget the past.

"You know," Olga said to me, before I got up to say goodbye, "nothing is simpler than life in Russia — or tougher to bear."

15

MORNING ON KHODUSA Yuyesyun-Arylara Island. My tongue felt like a slug that had crawled inside my mouth and died, my head a log of larch. I cracked open my eyes and pained to focus on jumbo-size mosquitoes with blood-engorged bellies stretching their legs on the inside of my tent walls. As I became aware of their burning bites on my arms and legs, Olga, Katya, and Na Kamushkakh flitted before my mind's eye, followed by kissy goodbyes and a sprint across the sand to meet Vadim, who pulled into port backlit by an apocalyptic sunset of flaming clouds, true chariots of fire . . . I wondered what toxins went into brewing that 12 percent beer.

Alarmed, I sat up and rummaged around for the notes I had scribbled in Sangar on a tiny pad during quiet moments or on supposed visits to the loo. I found them in my trousers' front pocket. Opening the pages, I lit upon expletives, and found myself disinclined to read on, to remember what I had seen. How often had I felt this way in Russia, land of the eternal debauch!

The weather was balmy, the Lena flowing silken, glossy, and gray. Vadim stood at water's edge, just down the bank, binoculars raised, and studied the sky to the south. There, clouds of menacing iron were forming and billowing toward us, subsuming the grim summits of the Verkhoyansk. We had 480 miles to cover to Zhigansk, above the Arctic Circle, and it looked like a bad day to set out. But we would; I had already canceled my sightseeing tour of Sangar, feeling the need to get moving.

"You're up?" he said, looking my way. He lowered the binoculars and shook his head. "We'll have a tough time if we can't outrun this storm. You've got to prepare yourself for what's coming. Heard any weather reports?"

"I listen to *Golos Rossii* [the Voice of Russia]," I replied, my voice cracking, now as hoarse as Olga's, "but they never give forecasts for anywhere out here."

"Why should they? No one cares on the *materik*. Everywhere here and ahead is nowhere."

As we loaded up, I ran through some rough calculations aloud and suggested that we'd reach Zhigansk in five days.

"You shouldn't think numbers out here," said Vadim. "Nature will decide and we'll obey."

"I was just estimating."

"Numbers are no good out here. This is the north."

"Who said it wasn't? But we have *made* estimates. How else would we know how much fuel and food to buy?"

My rhetorical question elicited a tirade against disrespect for the Laws of the North, laws that superseded all human priorities, vitiated all mortal plans, trumped all numbers. At first I took Vadim's words as subtle affirmation of his own abilities, he being the only one who could get me safely through the hell to come, but I listened more closely. He was in fact declaiming his own powerlessness before the Supreme Power, and enjoining me to do the same. We faced a redoubtable sovereign, *Sever*, the North, and we should not try to second-guess Him.

Soon we pulled away from the island and steered a course north, the Verkhoyansk massif jutting above the taiga in front of us, splashed with sun. Sangar slipped behind the trees of the curving shore, and we maintained full speed to keep ahead of the storm. Now and again we spotted a circling hawk, we listened to the quack of a lone eider duck hurrying south.

Our maps told us that every island we passed out here had a name. And what names! Achchygyi Baryya, Kuchuguran, Arylakh-Kumaga, Khatyng-Ary, Kyuide, Khatyngnakh . . . bizarre Yakut and Evenk agglutinations that sounded like incantations concocted by shamans to rouse the spirits of this drowsy ancient land. The names' length and complexity seemed to increase the more the reedy, sandy outcroppings they designated came to resemble one another.

· · ·

We swept past the mouth of the Lena's mightiest tributary, the Vilyuy, a 1,647-mile-long river born in Krasnoyarsk Krai to the west. Near Vilyuy's source, amid boggy forest, stands the settlement of Vilyuysk, founded originally as Olensk by the Cossacks of Ivan Shakhov. For its isolation, the tsars chose Olensk as a place of exile for some of their worst enemies, most notably the partisans of the Cossack Yemelyan Pugachev. In 1773–74, during Catherine the Great's rule, Pugachev led one of the fiercest rebellions against serfdom and autocracy in Russia's history. As chaotic as it was lethal, the rebellion raged across the Volga and Ural regions and eventually threatened Moscow. Mobs of serfs slit the throats of landlords and state officials and burned down manor houses and government buildings, and ethnic minorities seething under the Russian imperial yoke joined in the slaughter. Until the violence, Catherine had dallied with Enlightenment notions of liberty and human rights, but Pugachev's uprising sobered her, prompting her to enact reforms that would strengthen autocracy and worsen the masses' lot. Once the rebellion had been suppressed, she had Pugachev himself brought to Moscow in a cage, where he was beheaded and dismembered, his limbs displayed about town. Those of his followers to whom she showed mercy finished their days in Olensk.

The Russian countryside has always been a sea of desperation. In tsarist times as now, away from the capital, across the hinterland of mud, taiga, and swamp, distrust of the Kremlin simmers. But there has been one improvement in recent decades: in the outback, the government, so onerous under both the tsars and the Soviets, has largely left people to fend for themselves in something like a state of nature. Outside Ust'-Kut and Yakutsk, I had not seen a single officer of the law.

Late in the afternoon we lost our race with the storm. In the northwest, where we were headed, the sky still gleamed bright blue, but from the southeast black clouds swept upon us, dragging curtains of rain, obscuring the upper slopes of the Verkhoyansk. The wind hit us in a succession of warm blasts, kicking up whitecaps and bending the larches on shore.

"Ah-ha!" shouted Vadim. "Finally, a tailwind!" The blasts were raising waves to our stern and powering us smoothly from swell to trough to breaking swell. Our speed jumped from fifteen kilometers an hour to twenty, and we shot along, whooshed ahead by breaker and gale, without a drop of water breaching our pontoon gunwales.

As excited as Vadim by the wind's shift, I exulted in our newfound speed. But not for long. I turned astern to watch swells behind us rise to three feet, and then, distressingly, to four and five feet; they lifted our stern and plunged our bow down at increasingly perilous angles. Our load, still heavy with fuel, made this dangerous sailing.

Vadim looked over his shoulder. "That's it!" he shouted. "No more! We've got to get ashore or we'll be swamped! We've got to cross these waves sideways!"

"Sideways? I thought we couldn't do that!"

He grabbed his binoculars and began scouring the shore. "There! See that finger of land jutting out? There's a cove just behind it." A wave foamed up and teetered over our motor, and we slipped ahead of it as it broke just behind us. "We're going to have to make a landing on the run. You're going to have to jump out near shore and grab the rope and drag us onto the bank. With these waves, we'll have no second chances!"

Like a matador evading charging bulls, Vadim steered us from swell to swell. The clouds lowered; the wind showered us in spray and rain. The finger of land, a stony crescent, was now approaching. Three yards away from it, Vadim swung hard starboard. Just after we slipped through the trough between two unruly waves, I jumped out into thigh-deep water. As our hull skidded and bumped against the bank, I lunged for the bow rope, barely catching it. The waves pushed the craft ahead, almost tearing the rope from my grasp. Then Vadim leaped out and grabbed the rope too. We wrestled the boat around the finger of land into an eddy and finally dragged it ashore.

We set up our tents and made a fire. The river frothed like the sea, and the wind howled off the *sopki*'s barren slopes.

Throughout the white night the wind lashed our tents and rain pummeled down. Now and then an animal screeched from the grove of charred pines and larches behind our camp. A fox? A wolf cub? I couldn't tell.

There was no perceptible dawn. I awoke to an invasive damp, a temperature of 50 degrees, a loudening roar of waves. Chilled, my breath puffing white, I peeked out of my tent to set eyes on an angry river. The world was now a drear chiaroscuro of low cloud and fog, wet sand and gravel, a sodden forest of blackened trees, and rising whitecaps, with the Verkhoyansk lost in mizzle somewhere above. Still, I was pleased: how quickly that tailwind had moved us along! The speed it afforded us would compensate for the discomfort brought by the rain.

But then I examined the waves and my spirit sank: they were rolling out of the northwest. They would hit us head-on.

Vadim unzipped his tent and stepped out in his camouflage poncho; rain pattered off its folds. He surveyed the scene.

"Well, this looks bad. From all that fog to the north I'd say we're in for a *long* stretch of bad weather. Just like the north: when we didn't need good weather, we had it. Now when we need calm, we get a storm. I told you so." He shook his head.

"Well, it's only July twenty-seventh," I said. "According to the weather charts, it should clear up."

"Let's hope so. But autumn is reminding us she's on her way. I doubt the warm weather is over for good. Or maybe, maybe this is an early fall, a freak year."

"What would that mean for us?"

"It's hard to say. But we'd better get moving. We've got to cross a ten-mile stretch of open water south of Yurta by evening: if we misjudge, we could be in trouble out there."

I donned my waterproof kit, all of it, and stuffed the rest of my gear deep in my hermetic sack.

An hour later we were crashing through breakers six feet high, hanging on for our lives, soaked to the skin, shivering, straining to catch glimpses of barren-sloped *sopki* through rents in the fog. Cramps burned my legs as I squatted, facing the stern, to bail out water splashing over my back, pouring in over our gunwales; Vadim held his plastic-wrapped maps under his poncho, close to his chest, taking spray in the face from wave after breaking wave. The Lena now stretched twelve miles from bank to bank, but in places islands covered with runt pines split the river into a maze of channels. Amid them, we were at once on the river and in the taiga, sheltered from the worst of the gales. But always the islands ended in another white-capped sea, and we pitched and yawed and crashed, the banks distant again, lost in fog.

When noon arrived the storm grew unmanageable, and we had not even reached the ten-mile open stretch. But we lucked out, pulling up to sandbar shallows by an island of dunes tufted with alders. A pair of gulls swooped down at us, screaming, defending a nest somewhere. The wind would soon drive them aground.

A half-hour later, sheltered by alders and high dunes, we ate a lunch of sausage and bread and drank tea. The rain had stopped. Out of the wind, we began thawing out, drying off, and even relaxing. I took off my rain gear, sweater, and Windbreaker and spread them out to dry. The temperature on my pocket thermometer read 50 degrees — bearable when sheltered, but how cold this felt when soaked and riding through spray-splattering winds.

Vadim finished his tea and leaned back on the sand. "You know, I don't know a single person who finds anything positive about the collapse of the Soviet Union. The Soviet state gave us free health care, free education, and guaranteed jobs. True, they could arrest you for *tuneyadstvo* ["parasitism"; it was a crime not to work], so back then I couldn't have made this trip or done the things I like to do now on my own."

"Were you happier then?"

"Well, let's just say under the Soviet system, there was no sense of injustice. Sure, the Communist Party officials lived better than we did, but we hardly noticed, because pretty much most of us were equal. Now we have a few billionaires and a huge state machine run by corrupt security services. The Russian people can't work hard enough to provide all the luxuries these bureaucrats want. It's always the same in Russia. The state uses the security services to protect itself from the people."

"On the whole, would you rather have the old system back?" I asked.

"Well, what is communism supposed to be? Communism is when everyone is equal and has a full belly. That's a utopia. It can't exist. So no, I really wouldn't. Look, what upsets me now is that we have absolutely no sense of community, no patriotism left in this country. Today a melon trader would sooner see his melons rot than sell them at a discount when they're getting too ripe. He would never give them to the poor. In the past people had a sense of duty to their fellows. So what's the point of all these reforms? To make us hate one another and live poor?"

For Vadim, just as for the residents of Sangar, the end of the USSR was the beginning of misery and uncertainty. But he was sophisticated enough to recognize Soviet ideals as unrealizable.

Just after three in the afternoon the sky lightened, and our hectoring seagulls took to the air again, circling us and berating us with their cranky cries. They woke Vadim from his nap. He grabbed his binoculars.

"I'll go take a look at the river."

He slogged off across soggy sand toward the island's northern tip. Twenty minutes later he slogged back. A ray of sun auguring a clement spell now beamed through clouds to the north.

"Let's give it a shot."

The calm lasted only long enough for us to reach midchannel, where once again we found ourselves besieged by violent headwinds and breakers. On a river now ten miles wide, now twelve, we were navigating amid oblong shoals and pine-covered sandbank islands that, in their profusion, confounded the taking of exact bearings.

As I knelt in cold sloshing water and bailed, heeding Vadim's calls to hang on as one or another breaker coiled up and rolled down upon us, I tried to imagine what sort of *human* barrens it would take to generate a passion in him for this wilderness. The landscape through which we were sailing, all sodden forest and mist and gray river, was a *terre d'abandon* where most of those who preceded us had parted with hope and faced death from exhaustion, cold, and hunger. In more than two decades of travel, I had never seen such nullifying wilds, never hit this nadir of gloom.

Vadim sat facing the wind, and took drenching after chill drenching without flinching; I kneeled, too cold and numb to fear, and bailed, submitting, as he said I would, to the north. Submission! Submission *was* life in Russia. One submitted to the bureaucrat demanding a "fee" for a free service, to the *mafiya* extorting tribute, to the doctor's request for a bribe, to the traffic cop who needs a sweetener to release your car (when you have committed no infraction), to the beat-walking militiaman who seizes your passport for a "document check." Submission, nowadays, meant mostly giving money. But in the Soviet past, it meant signing over your land and livestock to the collective farm, surrendering half the rooms in your apartment to alcoholic proles, suffering through interminable queues for bread and sausage, for train tickets and shoes and books. During especially horrific times, submission meant confessing, for the "good of the Party," to crimes against Stalin that one never committed; it meant facing, with calm, the executioner's bullet or exile to the gulag. It meant watching thugs destroy one's loved ones and not fighting back. It meant obeying the *Vozhd'* — leader — supposedly as brutal as he was "just," but whose "justice" repeatedly turned out to be brutality alone.

For four hours more we lurched north, soaked and bailing and dodging waves. Like a galley slave I bailed and shivered, bailed and grabbed the crossbeam, bailed and shivered, my mind blank, my consciousness disappearing into cold and wet and rote labor.

"There!" shouted Vadim. "Finally! The ten-mile stretch!"

I ceased bailing and raised my head. "What? We haven't got there yet? How can this be?"

At that moment the *boltanka* hit: waves crashed into each other and over our gunwales from every side. Every few seconds the propeller jumped free of the water to gag and gasp and spin.

"We're going to be swept overboard!" Vadim shouted. "That's it. We can't make Yurta today. Get ready for an emergency landing!"

"Where?"

"That island, there!"

Through the spray and wind-whipped fog, a mere twenty yards away, loomed the hazy outlines of alder bushes on a flat piece of land overblown by sand — the sort of terrain where mosquitoes abounded, firewood was scarce, and shelter would be limited.

"No choice!"

I positioned myself for another jump into the water. But we jolted through the *boltanka* and final breakers to hit the shore full speed, at a right angle. We tumbled out into waist-deep water, which poured frigid into our hip boots. I clambered, numb and clumsy, onto the sandy bank and tried to drag the boat ashore, but it was too heavy.

"The fuel! Unload the fuel cans first!" ordered Vadim. "Quick!"

That we did, and we dragged the much-lightened craft almost fully ashore, and then quickly reloaded the cans to anchor the boat in case a wave should hit. Vadim took the bow rope up the beach and tied it to the trunk of a pine uprooted by ice floes. The sun appeared, the clouds began passing. I stood in the wind frozen and dizzy, detached, my eyes senselessly focused on Vadim.

He looked at me. "You cold?"

"A little."

"'A little.' Right. Wait a second." He ripped open his big blue food sack and pulled out a bottle of pepper-flavored Nemiroff vodka. "Drink, right away! To warm up!"

I had read that it was a myth that drinking alcohol warmed you up. But I obeyed, falling to my knees and facing away from the wind, and upending the bottle for a brief, hot gulp. The liquor burned pleasantly down my esophagus and heated my innards with a tingling fire. It revived me instantly. I opened my eyes just as the wind blew away the last of the mists and the sun shone from a clear sky. There was no way we could move on, though: the river still raged.

We set up camp by the alders; they broke the gales and created a haven of heat. I disrobed, peeling off layer after layer of soaked clothing. Standing in the windless shelter of the bushes, with the sun hitting me, 50 degrees didn't feel cold; in fact, I was warm. I dug to the bottom of my hermetic pack and extracted my camouflage thermal suit and socks, which I hadn't expected to need until we were above the Arctic Circle, and put them on. Now thoroughly dry and warm, I hung my trousers, long-sleeved shirt, T-shirt, socks, woolen sweater, and "waterproof suit" (ha!) to dry on alder branches; even my leather belt was soggy and cold, and I draped it over a branch. Vadim did the same with his kit.

The bellowing winds hindered conversation, but we were too enchanted with the warmth to talk. On the bank opposite, some three miles away, a low band of spiked taiga appeared to rise from an angry sea. We looked to the north, out across the ten-mile stretch of open water — a heaving ocean of spindrift and breakers spreading far, far to the horizon and melting blue into the blue sky. Somewhere beyond the spray was Yurta.

During the pallid interval that passed for night, the gales strengthened, battering our tents with a barrage of sand. In the morning I found that Vadim had set up his three-stick teepee for pots over the fire, dragged logs up from the beach for seats, and secured the boat higher up on the bank. The sun was out but the winds had shifted, driving sandstorms down the banks. To the north the river still thrashed a limitless *boltanka* of blue and frothy white.

Facing away from the blowing sand, Vadim sat on a log, sipping tea. He confirmed my suspicion that we were going nowhere. "These waves could tear our motor off. We'd be left with just our oars in the middle of the river. We can't risk it. If we left this island now, it might well be the last thing we'd ever do."

"So, we could be here for a while."

"We could be here for days. Nature dictates her own conditions. We have no choice but to submit. Think of it this way," he said. "If we'd been hiking out here in the winter, on the ice, and a blizzard hit, the snow would fall so thick you couldn't see. The frosts would be so fierce we'd have to sit in the tent in our sleeping bags or die of cold. Now at least you can walk around and explore." He stood up. "Maybe you can get a weather forecast for Zhigansk on your short-wave. There's supposed to be a meteorological station up there. I'm going to take a look around this island and see what's here." He grabbed his gun and stepped off into blowing, sun-bright sand and was gone.

After breakfasting on bread and jam, I climbed back into my tent and turned on my radio. I caught snippets of weather reports for Anadyr', to the east, and garbled words about unseasonable cold and wind somewhere — but where? Whenever the frequency began coming in more clearly, broadcasts in Chinese would crackle in and overpower it.

A few hours later, Vadim returned disappointed. He had found nothing except moose tracks. The winds roared on.

For two days we sat marooned on the island, the weather unrelenting. It was getting perceptibly colder. Spindrift swirled into clouds of spray that often hid the taiga on the opposite bank; the river fomented, a violent expanse of aquamarine blue and whitecaps and surf crashing against the shore, which several times prompted us to drag our craft higher. I tuned in to Radio Russia on the hour but still heard nothing about the weather in Zhigansk. Finally the broadcasts faded into static and I was left listening to the wind and waves and hissing sand.

Shortly after noon on our third stranded day, a tern flapped up to hover in the wind and fish over a spot of river near our boat. The gales had weakened. I called to Vadim in his tent.

He put down his volume of Fedoseyev and climbed out. Through his binoculars he studied the ten-mile stretch ahead. It appeared calmer than before, I ventured.

"It might be," he said. "I can't really say."

"You know," I answered, "even if it's still blowing hard, maybe we should move on. What if it gets worse? What about all the tough sailing ahead? Won't it be harder up in the Arctic the longer we wait?"

"Maybe." He chuckled. "Anyway, does it really matter how we die? From a bear, a gunshot, or drowning out there? It's all the same to me!" His voice quickened with enthusiasm. "So let's take a shot at the river. Who knows? We might get lucky!"

Wondering just what he meant by "lucky" but dearly sick of our island and eager to move on, I packed my gear and suited up.

Twenty minutes later, after we had loaded the boat and as we were emptying a can of fuel into our tank, the gale resumed, changing direction slightly. In the north the sky was filling with low gunmetal clouds and the river darkened into expanses of corrugated iron cut with foaming breakers.

With the wind, Vadim and I again found we had to shout.

"We'll have one chance to launch now," Vadim said, tossing aboard the can. "Follow my orders!"

His shouted commands — *"Davaaay! Tyaniii! Tolkaaay! Derzhiii!"* [Come on! Pull! Push! Hold steady!] — rang out, charged with a martial fervor. I felt a surge of adrenaline, combined with pride in Vadim. He knew his every move; he was brutish in strength, gimlet-eyed, a born commander. Though the weather was obviously spoiling again, he did not flinch.

"Jump in!" he shouted.

I clambered aboard just as he shoved the boat fully into the river. Blasts of northerly wind knocked us upstream, against the current, showering us in spray. Vadim leaped aboard and grabbed the ignition cord and yanked and yanked; the engine was cold after days of rest. But it finally chugged alive and we pulled out, lurching through spray for the open water.

For an hour or so we moved with surprising speed. The more fuel we used and the more food we ate, the lighter our load became. But when we hit midriver, several miles from either bank, the waves changed pattern and began battering us in groups of three and four, six to seven feet high followed by successions of four- and five-footers — a roller coaster of dizzying ascents and slippery slides. I grabbed the pitcher and began bailing.

The sky blackened from horizon to horizon, and rain, now frigid, drenched us, falling in showers so dense that we lost sight of the shores. This time, however, dressed in almost everything I owned, including a special synthetic sweater that retained body heat when wet, I suffered less from the cold than on previous days. Warm or not, with the rain and waves, we began taking on too much water for me to handle. I reached for my life jacket.

"Ha! That won't do you any good out here!" shouted Vadim. "Even if you're a champion swimmer, this water's forty-nine degrees, and the cold would numb you and the waves would push you away from shore." His eyes widened. Breakers for the first time broke over the bow, pouring along each side of the tarp, which deflected most of the water back into the river. Our gear rattled and banged. His voice hardened. "That's it! We've reached our limit. One wrong move and we're swept overboard. And these waves are going to rip off our motor. We're quitting *now!*"

His tone gave me to think that I had pressured him into leaving the island before he was comfortable in doing so. But we had crossed the open stretch. Yurta lay dead ahead through the rain, beyond the waves.

In a downpour and 42-degree cold, we set up camp on Yurta's rocky shore, beneath a fifty-foot-high windbreak embankment covered in stunted larches, with the escarpments of the Verkhoyansk massif somewhere to the east behind us, hidden in the fog. Despite the name, there was no yurt or cabin or habitation of any kind here, though Vadim guessed there must have been at one time, given the spot's natural shelter. Our world once again was low gray sky and cold, rain, and fog, with the only sounds the wail of the gale, the roar of the river.

For the first time, Vadim went about his chores in morose silence; he blamed me for having persuaded him to depart. "We won't be taking any more risks like that one," he said as he held matches to dry wood shavings from the inside of a log.

Yurta was opposite a sandbar and an uninhabited isle called Ulakhan-Kistyakh. I set off and hiked downriver for a few miles to reconnoiter. Along the way, I came upon a sign at the top of the bank reading "1155" — the distance in kilometers left to Tiksi, I assumed. (1717 miles.) Almost twelve hundred kilometers left! I walked back to camp dispirited, soaked, and hungry, suffering a despairing presentiment that we would not make it. The weather in late July was not supposed to be like this. Our craft was too small and our load too heavy, our motor too weak.

How had the Cossacks sailed into the north for years, not knowing where they were, what awaited them, or whether they would make it back? No doubt faith sustained them. They had completed an odyssey, yet without the temptation of the Sirens, the lures of the Lotus-eaters, the warmth of the Mediterranean. In the summer they endured heat and cold, waves and wind. And then, during nine months of winter and polar nights, they suffered snow and isolation and dark, cabin fever and frosts, hunger and scurvy, the musty confines of a *zimov'ye* or some lonely larch fortress. I would not like to have been among them. In view of what they went through, maybe things out here weren't so bad for us after all.

Back at camp, Vadim had just returned from setting out fishing nets at the mouth of the Delingde, a stream flowing into the Lena just to the south of camp. He was frowning, still angry.

"We'll have no more adventures like that one. That was an unjustifiable risk. If you weren't afraid out there, you were stupid. Only a novice or an idiot doesn't fear waves that big. We simply cannot and will not set sail in such weather again. If we'd been tossed overboard, we'd never have made it ashore."

He then went silent, and kindled the fire for dinner.

Around nine in the evening, the rain ceased. The taiga at our backs was silent. There was only the crashing river and the droning of fat mosquitoes, out hunting for a meal even in the cold. I had changed into my dry camp clothes and hung my wet garments by the fire. I noticed that my hands were cracked and chafed.

We dug in to a meal of buckwheat and canned meat, and for dessert munched on salty crackers.

"Someone isn't drinking for us," said Vadim glumly.

"How's that?"

"If someone were sitting at a table at home and drinking for us, we'd not be running into these storms. The end of July is too early — it *has* to be too early — for autumn. I hiked up into the taiga. There're no mushrooms, no berries up here, and there haven't been yet. Grave omens."

"Omens?"

"This will be a famine year. Animals will starve. There will be a lot of *shatuny*"— bears that, having failed to eat enough to hibernate, wander the winter woods, at times attacking villagers. Vadim's voice, so often hard, sounded close to breaking. "This freak cold won't let anything grow. Look, in Zhigansk, talk to the weather station people. Find out if they can tell us what to expect." He pulled out his bottle of pepper-flavored Nemiroff. "Well, should we have a drop?"

"Sure."

He poured two shots into his film canister cups. "To the river spirit!" he said.

We drank. He refilled the cups and we drank again. I had not seen him depressed before; neither had he drunk more than a thimbleful of alcohol thus far.

No semblance of night ever came. We soon tired from the vodka and climbed into our tents under the lurid sky. I clicked on my short-wave radio and got nothing but static and faint snippets of Chinese.

Seven hours later I awoke shivering, my breath puffing white, with one arm and part of my back soaked and numb with cold. It was 39 degrees and drizzling hard, and gusts had sent rain through the open quarter of my tent's window to fall on my sleeping bag. I remembered Vadim's oft-repeated admonition: Never let your sleeping bag get wet!

But it was quiet outside. I sat up and stared out at the river. Before my eyes a breeze became a wind, and the wind, gale-force gusts. The leaden river rose into whitecaps and surf started striking the shore, and then I heard an odd sloshing. I craned my neck: our boat was bobbing on the higher currents and had broken free! I unzipped the door and stumbled barefoot down the rocks to grab the bow rope and pull the craft ashore. I tied the rope to a log-rock assemblage Vadim had built and went back to my soaked bedding, where I lay down and shivered. My feet were cut and bruised from the rocks.

Vadim got up late and motored upriver to check his nets by the stream. He pulled them in — empty! Apparently losing his cool for the first time on our voyage, he threw them back in the water and cast stones into the stream. Then he hauled them in again; they were laden with okun' that had fled the ruckus of the stones straight into the nets. He fried them for a late breakfast.

That afternoon found us creeping ahead at half-speed through wind-whipped mizzle, fearful of moving out into open water. We hugged the shore, passing stands of larch, their trunks and branches gnarled skeletons in the fog, their sparse tufts of needlelike leaves already autumnal gold and glinting like streaks of lantern light in the boreal gloom. There was nothing that caught one's gaze, nothing to relieve the bleakness. I remembered that nine years ago on this day in late July I was riding a barge up the coffee-colored Congo, a river clogged with green hyacinth, passing riotous jungles of green, watching crocodiles and cobras cut the water, listening to tinny-sounding Congo pop, admiring muscular Zaireans paddling dugout canoes brimming with giant catfish and bush meat. I recalled feeling alternating surges of fear and zest, an insatiable desire to risk everything and remake my life, to jump-start my failing career as a writer, to prove myself. Well, in many ways I had succeeded, and this cold and taiga were my rewards.

"A settlement," said Vadim quietly.

I snapped out of my ruminations. We drew up on a birch grove with an oval-shaped clearing near the water. On the bank stood a lone bench facing the river. But as we reached it, we saw that all of the houses behind it had been hacked down; only their foundations and a wall here and there remained.

"You know," he said, smiling, as if pleased to discover no odious humans around, "the dumbest question people ask me back home is why I love the north. What needs to be explained? Look around you. It's so obvious, and if they're too stupid to understand they don't deserve to know. So I don't even tell them. They're so stupid, back in the cities, taking vacations on the beach with booze and sun and women."

I lacked the energy to respond, and could only think, wistfully, *Beaches, women, warmth.*

"Money, money. That's their curse. They don't know what they really want, so they want to make money and have kids — and kids are the *lamest* excuse of all for living. They should decide what they really want and sacrifice to get it. What we're doing *is* worth sacrificing for." He shifted in his seat. "How can you explain your love of such adventures? If you can explain it, you're either not telling the truth or you don't *really* love it. After all, can you honestly name all the reasons why you love another person? If you can, it's not love. Love just *is*."

Mists closed over the dead settlement behind us. A black-headed brent goose soared forth on short wings from the taiga, honking out his loneliness.

16

AFTER TWO MORE DAYS of soak-and-bail crashing through frothy swells on a cobalt river, and two more nights of bivouacking on gale-battered isles of blowing sand and silver-leaved alders, early in the afternoon of August the first we crossed the Arctic Circle in the company of a lone polar goose honking and circling above us in the frigid blue ether. The taiga now consisted of dwarf pines and mini-larches scarcely taller than a man and spaced out over rumpled mats of yellow-green lichen and patches of slatey earth. The slate glinted in the sun, sun ever more oblique yet newly strong, as if striking the land unhindered by an atmosphere. The tiny forest made the sky seem bigger, nearer; and the earth, more exposed than ever to the celestial cold of outer space. It did indeed seem as though we were nearing the top of the world.

That evening, after running a ten-mile gauntlet of pink limestone cliffs striated horizontally with glossy black veins of coal, the winds died and we spotted Zhigansk — shacks and tenements hunkering to a high curving bank, studded with crudely segmented smokestacks. It being already too late to visit, we pitched camp on Iosif Island, two and a half miles opposite the settlement.

As the sun sank at midnight, setting aflame both the sky's occidental bourns and the great, now glassy river that reflected them, I felt elated at having finally made it to the Arctic. Though strictly speaking the Arctic Circle is just a line on maps indicating the point (latitude 66°30' N) above which at the summer solstice the sun for at least one day a year doesn't set, or at the winter solstice doesn't rise, there began a part of the globe totally unfamiliar to me, a zone of novelty. Before arriving in the Arctic, despite all I had read and heard of the region,

I didn't know, and couldn't have imagined, that the air here smelled so fresh that it seemed to singe the lungs; and that the summer sky's endless luminosity could haunt the forest and give rise to notions of spirits and specters more effectively than the blackness of any equatorial night. I found these minor discoveries exciting, and they justified the misery that preceded them. Novelty rejuvenates like gulps from the Fountain of Youth. To stay young, we need its tonic in regular doses.

Facing Zhigansk, now dark across the waters, we set up camp on the sand, just beneath a tier of brushy bank ravaged by ice floes. Stars glittered dimly in the pastel pink and blue sky, mirrored in the shallows. I gazed at these points of light with something like amazement: owing to the white nights, I hadn't seen stars (except for the North Star) since arriving in Ust'-Kut.

Vadim was newly garrulous, buoyed by his success in getting us here — no small feat.

"So, now you know what the north is," he declared. "You're learning what clothes to wear to keep dry and warm in the Arctic. A real man knows how to survive in *any* conditions. Survival — that's the key skill. Nothing else matters — if you can't survive you can't do anything else. Of course one needs to know how to survive in cities too. But surviving in the taiga is completely different. Now don't you agree?"

"Yes, of course."

His didactic tone grated on me and disinclined me to answer more expressively.

He looked out over the Lena. "The taiga and the north are so rich that you spend a month here and you feel as though you've lived an entire life. I've seen things in the north — say, the frozen waterfalls of Taymyr — that are so stunning I've cried from joy. I . . ." His voice cracked, and he took a deep breath. "I can live a long time off the beauty of the north."

He stopped talking, and we enjoyed a moment of contemplation. Over the sparse taiga on the far bank just north of Zhigansk, silhouetted against a sapphire sky, a wedge of geese was flying south, honking farewells to the cold, lonesome land and river below.

It had taken us eleven days to reach Zhigansk from Yakutsk, and that seemed like a long time. Yet in 1632 the Cossack division of Aleksey Arkhipov and Luka Yakovlev spent an entire summer covering the same distance in their *kochi.* They established a *zimov'ye* here, on a spot favored by local Evenk hunters. (The Yakuts, who generally preferred the more southerly taiga, were still newcomers to the Arctic and had begun trekking this far north just a few years earlier.) The name the Cossacks would give their winter station, *Zhigansk,* had, it turned out, nothing to do with *zhigan* (slang in Russian for "thief"), as Vadim had once suggested, but derived from the Evenk noun *elti-geen* — "inhabitant of the lower part of the river." But the Cossacks were in fact thieves of a sort: they requisitioned *yasak* from the Evenks in the form of walrus and mammoth tusks (the dentine was as popular in Europe then as ivory was to become later) and, of course, furs — Arctic fox, sable, ermine, wolverine, bear, and squirrel, imposing an onerous burden on the few natives they encountered: in 1792, throughout the entire Zhigansk region, locals, who were mostly reindeer herders, numbered only 1,402.

The first political exiles to arrive in Zhigansk were illustrious ones, Grigory Pisarev and Anton de Veer, disgraced members of Peter the Great's court. Following them were Decembrists and Polish nobles. Runaway convicts sacked Zhigansk in 1805 and sent the settlement into a decline that would end only in the 1930s, when it became an advance post for Stalin's project to tame the Arctic. During that decade, Zhigansk acquired a few trappings of Soviet modernity: a dock, a radio transmission tower, and a ship repair facility, plus, of course, a concentration camp. These days Zhigansk hosts some thirty-five hundred souls.

The next morning broke windy and gray. As Vadim was running me across the water to the Zhigansk beach, I saw, behind him on the eastern bank beyond a fringe of taiga, the stone hulks of the Verkhoyansk, arrayed north along the river as if guiding a Russian River Styx to a boreal Land of Shades. (In fact, legends among certain peoples of the north posit the Arctic as the location of the netherworld.) I turned away from this panorama of gloom. But the view of Zhigansk also filled me with melancholy. Giant metallic fuel cisterns stood on the settlement's northernmost promontory, where once glistened the gilt onion domes of the Church of Saint Nikolai the Miracle-Worker, the patron saint of Slavs and travelers, and Santa Claus to Westerners. The Soviets turned the church into a village club and then an office building before tearing it down in 1960.

Vadim left me at the harbor beach. Guarding my eyes against blowing sand, I hiked past the boats dragged ashore ("Tubs that would sink with the first big wave," said Vadim on seeing them) and up the bank to the settlement, a disappointing spread of bleak wooden hovels set far apart from each other on ashen earth. Middle-aged Yakuts and Evenks, grizzled and stout in parkas, trudged about, few in number amid the many cabin shops, lugging old plastic bags and net sacks filled with produce, talking in guttural Yakut. Drunken, pimpled youths with sallow skin and shaved heads stumbled along in old blue jeans, river boots, and floppy-eared fur hats. There were some young women about; most had dyed their black hair an agent-orange blond. Roadside rows of dwarf larches offered some protection from the dust squalls raised by the occasional passage of giant-wheeled trucks — almost the only traffic. Zhigansk looked like a present-day reincarnation of the open prison settlement it had been in tsarist times.

As luck would have it, I arrived just as stores were closing for the one-to-two-hour midday break. But Zhigansk was a regional capital; surely there would be a restaurant. I asked around and was directed to a larch-shack greasy spoon. There, as I munched on slimy macaroni and gelatinous meatballs, the melancholy Russian proprietor told me that there was no restaurant here; Zhigansk was not, he added, "a tinsel town like Sangar." He corrected himself: Zhigansk *did* once have a café, but it had been "torn apart by drunken locals." I tried to chat more with him but he answered lackadaisically, and his eyes were hazy — maybe he was hung-over. I paid up and moved on. Later, as I toured the shops in search of bread and onions, in one establishment I walked in on a young female Russian cashier, a brown-haired beauty with a delicate nose and florid lips, sitting with her chin on her palms, staring at the floor with a look of utter despair in her hazel eyes, as if her sentence here would never end. All at once I felt homesick for Moscow, and Zhigansk and my expedition became hateful to me. I was sick of the north.

On the main dust track, I came across an elaborate cabin, the gable-roofed local museum, and walked in. A plump indigenous woman in her sixties was passing from one office to another. She stopped and stared at me.

"Yes?"

I introduced myself and asked if I might have a look. She was Maria Shchadrina, the museum's scholar.

"You're traveling on the Lena in a small boat? That's dangerous, really dangerous," she said. "People die all the time out there. You see, the climate has changed in recent years. This summer we had frosts in July that killed our potato crops. Normally the temperatures should have been in the eighties then. And this northern wind blew all month. It's been terrible, and we just don't know what to expect."

The museum was closed for renovations, so Maria invited me into her office for a chat. She was tiny, with a button nose and high flat cheeks, half Yakut and half Evenk. She told me about her two peoples' roots. Evenks had mostly assimilated with Yakut settlers and had even adopted their language. Their contact with Russians left them with a mixed heritage.

"We're grateful for the advances the Russians brought us," she said, pushing her glasses up her nose, "but it came with a price." Cossack bands, she said, usually fifteen to thirty armed men, forced locals to hand over the *yasak,* but also demanded "gifts" for themselves — as much as five times the furs the state required — taking hostage women and daughters if men couldn't or wouldn't pay. Russian merchants scoured the land for mammoth tusks, a pair of which could weigh 212 to 250 pounds and fetch fifteen or sixteen rubles here but ten times that in Yakutsk; in 1821 alone one merchant exported twenty thousand tons of the valuable dentine.

Native Americans and their exploitation and extermination by European settlers in my own country came to my mind. But there was a crucial difference: Russians had not killed off Yakuts and Evenks, of whom there were more now than ever before.

Yet Maria grieved for another kind of death. "We had lived as hunters, reindeer herders, and fishermen since Neolithic times. We were nomads, summering by the Arctic Ocean, wintering here. We lived so close to nature that we left almost nothing behind. We used bone for tools, birch bark for pots, horsehair for fishnets; we even made underwear out of suede! The Russians considered us the aristocrats of the north! In short, we produced everything we needed from nature, everything. And everything reverted to nature after use. The first Russians to arrive here were amazed by our decorations, our jewelry, our needlework, and the tattoos our women wore. But we lost our positive qualities, our culture, really, once the Russians introduced civilization. Then the Soviets forced us to settle, which accustomed us to village life and weakened our survival traditions. Perestroika all but finished off our reindeer herds. We once had seventeen thousand reindeer in our herds. Now we've got two thousand. But anyway, what normal young man wants to herd reindeer, living in the taiga and coming into Zhigansk once a year to get drunk? How can he meet girls out there?" Two-thirds of the Yakuts now live in cities.

"We were so freedom-loving, we had our own way with nature. Think of it: we were pagans. We had shamans. I still don't think anyone has proved that shamans did any harm. They contacted other worlds, they found lost animals and people. What's wrong with that? What's so bad about worshiping nature? If we had stayed pagan and lived the way we traditionally lived, nature would be thriving all around us!"

I had never thought of this: worshipers of taiga spirits would never destroy their gods.

Maria went on. "The end of the Soviet Union has worsened everything. The Soviets got us used to comforts. But now we have no comforts." For many here, she said, all that remained was the solace of vodka. "Nothing is left of our culture."

I thanked Maria for talking to me. Before leaving I asked if I might call the meteorological station. "Certainly!" she said.

The station's boss, Valery Velichko, was grim and succinct. "The weather's completely unpredictable now. This summer we've seen unprecedented windstorms and cold. There's been no rain up here. All the berries have been killed off, if they ever had a chance to grow."

"Can you give us an idea of what to expect up north?" I asked.

"In truth, no, except to say that for the next three days you can expect light wind and cool temperatures in our area. In any case, be careful out there."

The next afternoon I dropped into the green and blue municipal building, like many others in town a two-story wooden tenement, if a clean and freshly painted one, but distinguished by the Russian flag flying out front. I wanted to visit Yuri Shamayev, the Yakut mayor of Zhigansk. I had agreed to report to local authorities during my stay whenever possible — a matter less of surveillance than a courtesy that would let the Russian government know that my guide and I were alive and following our itinerary as planned.

Apparently most employees in the municipal building headed

home at lunchtime and stayed there, for I had trouble locating someone to show me to the mayor's office. But eventually I found Shamayev behind a plain wooden desk. He was youthful for someone in his early forties, dressed in loafers, a green wool sweater, and pressed chinos; he might have been pledging a conservative fraternity at an Ivy League university. He had intelligent if wary eyes — I thought of Stanislav back in Yakutsk, and Viktor's warning to me that Yakuts had ample reason to distrust white people.

After a handshake, I told him I was traveling from Ust'-Kut to Tiksi and wanted to learn about life in Zhigansk. There being nowhere to go in town to sit and talk and have coffee, Yuri invited me home, and we walked outside to his driver and Niva jeep. First we stopped at one of the many local liquor shacks, where I bought a half-dozen beers with which to treat my host. Then we bounced down dirt roads through a wilderness of larch huts toward his two-story cement apartment building, probably the most upscale lodgings in town, though from the outside it looked like a condemnable hovel. His apartment, however, turned out to be warm and clean, with a humming refrigerator, a Japanese television, and polished wood furniture. His wife, a shy, asthenic Yakut with her hair bundled into a pink scarf, made us a cucumber and tomato salad seasoned with sour cream and spread out sausage and salted fish for our delectation, but then disappeared with her mother to leave us men to eat and talk alone.

We sipped our beers. Yuri loosened up and warned me about the weather and the river. "This has been a bizarre year. The windstorm lasted a solid month, and it trapped fishermen in their cabins until their supplies ran out. Our Soviet boats can't take the waves and two or three people a year here die out on the water. [Vadim had been right; the beached cutters were dangerous tubs.] We've never had this kind of weather before in the summer. The cold has been terrible. Our local sages who usually make predictions have been confounded and now refuse to say more." He paused. "I fear going north of here, as do most of us. We don't have any way of knowing what you'll be up against."

That being the case, I would leave it to fate and change the subject. I told Yuri that as I traveled on the Lena, I was continually amazed by the sparseness of Russia's population. I wondered aloud how any sort of national feeling could arise among people so isolated and distant from one another.

"What patriotism we have is a holdover from Soviet days," he said, "and it's all that's holding our country together."

"But what could Yakuts and Muscovites have in common? Or Yakuts and people from the rest of Siberia? There seems to be no national feeling out here."

He livened up. "Sakha could easily feed and clothe itself if it weren't for Moscow, which takes our revenues. We aren't even a million people, and we have so much gold, so many diamonds. You know, a lot of people say they're sorry the Japanese didn't occupy us during World War II. That was a terrible time for us, with the Russians. The Soviets wouldn't draft us, because we're a minority people and were protected against the draft. But they resettled entire villages from the south of Sakha to the Lena, where they had to fish for the front and give up their entire catch. Our grandparents were boiling shoe leather for soup! If they killed their own cows to eat they were executed as 'enemies of the people!' So if the Japanese had occupied us, we'd be under their rule now, and we'd have a Japanese standard of living. We'd be *thriving*."

"Then why not try to separate?"

"Our mentality is Soviet. Our frosts hit minus sixty-five here. So many youths have gotten drunk and fallen down and frozen off their hands or feet and become invalids. Since we live in extreme conditions — just look at the black rings under people's eyes here, which are scars from frostbite — we expect the state to help us and give us privileges. The Soviet state *did*. We're no longer used to fending for ourselves. But there are too many incentives — educational institutes, high technology, and the like — available through Moscow alone, for Sakha-Yakutia to want out of Russia. Our patriotism is left over from Soviet days, and keeps us together."

This "patriotism" sounded like inertia. I told him, anyway, that I had heard more militant views, at least during previous trips to Sakha, and from Tatyana in Yakutsk.

"Okay," he said flatly, "ten years ago we wanted to separate, but not now. We're a strategically vital region of Russia. During Stalin's time we had separatists, but he got rid of them. We have too many diamonds, too much timber, coal, and even oil for them to let us go now." He estimated that Moscow returned 8 percent of the revenues it extracted from his republic, mostly through Alrosa, the Russian company with a monopoly on the country's $1.6-billion-a-year diamond business.

(Since 2001, shortly after Putin came to power, Alrosa has suffered repeated attempts by the federal government in Moscow to obtain a controlling share of its stock, practices that accord with the Kremlin's drive to recapture the resources in Russia's regions. The federal government now owns 37 percent of Alrosa; the government of Sakha, 32 percent; and diamond workers and the regions, the remaining shares. The struggle for Alrosa boils down to competition for a fifth of the world's diamonds. In any case, a glimpse of Sakha's poverty tells you that the people of the republic see precious little of their diamond wealth.)

"That sounds like robbery. Why not resist?"

"Even though we [Yakuts] are descended from Genghis Khan, we're not a hot-blooded mountain people like the Chechens, who love war. Besides, we're too few to fight like the Chechens. If we were three or five million, maybe we'd think differently."

I didn't expect secessionist declarations from a state official, but his last words conveyed the gist of what has, to a great extent, quelled separatist aspirations here and elsewhere in Russia: fear of annihilation, of suffering Chechnya's fate. A history of tragedy and oppression from the Kremlin and climatic hardships leave minority peoples weak and dependent on Moscow.

17

EARLY THE FOLLOWING afternoon we launched our craft into sparkling beryl blue waters, the taiga atop the granite, coal-creased defiles ahead towering in elegant repose. Thirty miles out of Zhigansk, the banks lowered and sandbars crept into the channel. Gone were the broad meanderings of the Lena's lower latitudes; now the river would max out at five miles wide, and often, for long stretches, shrink to half that or less, with a corresponding surge in current strength. Our next destination was the tiny settlement of Siktyakh, 250 miles north. Siktyakh was yet another notation on the map about which we knew nothing, except that its name meant, in Yakut, "wet place," presumably owing to the bogs around it — hardly distinguishing features here.

When the sun finally slipped through the silver-edged clouds down into the turquoise band of sky above the taiga, it bathed us in attenuated beams; the farther north we progressed, the more the world seemed to be shedding impurities, crystallizing. We trailed a widening wake, rippling white on panes of deep azure. Though northernmost Sakha is almost devoid of people, we were not always alone. Along sandbars near Kystatyyam (a village, like others, secluded by *sopki* from the river) we watched Yakut men fish in the traditional manner, in teams of two. Holding a weighted net some twenty feet long between them, one man walks along the bank and the other plods through thigh-deep shallows. This method sounds primitive, but it worked, yielding catches of sturgeon and taimen. Before the Yakuts arrived with their nets (made in bygone times out of entwined horsehair), the Evenks fished in a far clumsier way, building fenced enclosures of stakes near the shore and thrashing the water to drive fish into it, which they scooped out with their hands and tossed onto the bank. We chugged past the fishermen and shouted greetings, but they responded with only with blank stares — an unsettling reminder that out here Vadim and I were foreigners to be regarded with suspicion.

Around eight that evening we pitched camp on the high sandy bank of one of the inner Barannakh-Bereges Islands; as usual, we chose our site so as to sleep hidden from the view of passing villagers. Vadim set about frying nelma he had netted in Zhigansk, and I gazed out at the cold clear river. Not a bird sung, not a breeze stirred, and the currents slipped by quietly.

The hoarse, tinny roar of an old outboard motor broke the silence, sounding from somewhere downstream. From around a bend out raced a rusted tin tub of a speedboat with three men aboard. It bore down on us, high-bowed, and shot past our camp. But the captain cut hard to port, throwing out spray as he U-turned and slowed to a swishy stop, parallel with us. Three unsmiling Yakut men in their twenties fixed us with bleary eyes. One cast anchor. Their craft looked ready to disintegrate; its engine had long ago lost its hood; empty vodka bottles and trash and old fishing nets littered its concave floor.

So that they would see we were armed, I nonchalantly took out our shotgun and checked the shells loaded in its barrels, then placed it atop our bags.

Vadim and I climbed down the bank to greet them.

"*Zdorovo!*"

Stares.

Dressed in the usual fishermen's gear (patched hip boots, dirty canvas jackets and trousers), they wore soiled fishing caps yanked low over toggle ears and beady eyes; the face of the oldest one, the pilot, looked as if it were distorted by a funhouse mirror, so sharply did his nose curve to the left. He took off his fisherman's hat to reveal a head wrapped with a bloodied bandage. The second had dyed his hair piss yellow; the last had a mouthful of coal-shard teeth caked in crevices with shreds of his last meal. The Yakuts in towns had struck me as attractive people, tall and slender, with clear Asian features. These three looked inbred and menacing. Each bore minor or not-so-minor injuries that in urban Russia one would take as signs of alcoholic brawling.

Leaning forward to examine our gear, the pilot grunted, "Any smokes?"

His hunting knife hanging from his belt, Vadim apologized for not having anything to offer, employing the mix of jovial charm and brawny swagger that he had shown whenever strangers approached us on the river. "You fellows surprised us," he added. "We didn't see any villages around here."

"Oh, you never see where we live," the pilot replied. "We all Yakuts here. We live our own lives. Don't need anything from the government. Except gas for the boat."

"And where do you get that, if I might ask?" said Vadim.

"In Zhigansk. Where you go? Who that with you?"

"Just heading up to Dzhardzhan," Vadim said, "with this Muscovite." If he had disclosed our destination as Siktyakh, let alone Tiksi, they might conclude that we had money and supplies worth stealing. Just the gasoline in our jerry cans was worth several months' earnings out here. And of course he did not reveal who I was, for in Russia as in so many poor countries, "foreign" and especially "American" meant money and an easy target.

They stumbled over their words; they were uncomfortable speaking Russian. But our talk turned to how life was out here. They asked us what fish we had caught so far, what news there was from upriver, and, finally, what we had come to the Lena to do. (Vadim's response, to travel from Zhigansk to Dzhardzhan, didn't answer the question, but it satisfied them.) They told us about the recent bad winds that had cut into their fishing time and caused hunger; they lived close to the land and river, feeding from both, and had only a short summer during which to stock up on food. They were not hostile but surprised by our presence, if distrusting, as they had reason to be, given the history of Russians in Sakha. The wounds that gave them a threatening aspect reminded me how easy it is to hold victims responsible for their plights and lose track of the humanity we share. Still these observations took second place to caution and fear; we were two, they three, or many, many more, considering fellow villagers hidden in the taiga.

"Well, we've got to get back to our cooking," said Vadim. He sloshed into the water, hoisted their anchor, and dropped it into their tub. "Have a nice evening."

His farewell was abrupt, but all the same they wished us well. The passenger seated astern yanked the motor cord a few times. Finally it caught, and they swung around and sped away from whence they'd come.

Night, fleeting and pale though it was, left behind frigid air. Nevertheless, as was my habit, I got up at five in the morning (with temperatures in the thirties at that hour, no mosquitoes were out) and took a bucket bath. Then, benumbed and shivering, I dried off, put on my thermal suit, and climbed back into my sleeping bag. In a delirium of warmth, I turned on my shortwave and fiddled with the dial in search of news, now able to tune in to Voice of America in English. Almost every other day on the river I had followed this routine, and I had come to relish it as I would have a hot shower and silk sheets in a five-star hotel. The juxtaposition of pain and pleasure intensified my sense of both and was a pure product of circumstance; back in civilization, nothing could compel me to take a cold shower.

By noon we were cruising down a mile-wide river with currents that sped us beneath a five-hundred-foot-high wall of basalt and quartz on the eastern bank, eroded into escarpments handsomely crowned with taiga. Every mile or so a valley cut through the cliffs and funneled a steam-covered brook down to the Lena. We often slowed and peered into the hollows around them, where trees no taller than a man could shelter wolves, bears, and foxes. But we saw nothing alive.

"Look!" Vadim shouted, steering us toward the stony bank.

From the base of the cliff spread a purplish scree of pumiceous boulders covered with football-size carbuncles of what surely had been lava: only fierce heat and melting could have created the bubbles. Their bizarre shapes greatly excited Vadim.

"I've never seen anything like these boulders! Think what could have made them! Imagine how long they've been here!"

Maria Shchadrina had told me that in the Paleozoic era beginning 550 million years ago an ocean had covered the Zhigansk region. In the Jurassic period a few hundred million years later, a subtropical jungle of majestic sequoias had sheltered the dinosaurs. What had happened in geologic time seemed too remote to spark my interest, and I had hardly listened to her.

But then Vadim had pointed out the carbuncles. He clambered

among the boulders, shouting, "Oh, look!" each time he found a new specimen. Finally he made it to the base of the cliff. "Well, what do you know! A cave! Come here, quick!"

I climbed up to where he was. In the back of a cave fifteen feet deep and six feet high, snow covered the floor and ice mottled the walls. Sticks protruded from crevices. "Think," he said. "For centuries Yakut fishermen took shelter here, waiting out storms, marking the number of days. Maybe each stick means a day. Or a week. Or even a death on the river. Who will *ever* know?"

Once outside again, he held forth on the colors of the rocks, their shapes and combinations, finding more and more the closer he looked. He reminded me of Valle-Inclán's declaration, *"Toda expresión suprema de belleza es un divino centro que engendra infinitos círculos"* ("Every supreme expression of beauty is a divine center that engenders infinite circles"). I envied Vadim his enthusiasm, his eye for the comely in nature's craggy face. This discovery would buoy his mood for hours.

We climbed back down to the raft and lunched in the tepid sun. Vadim exulted, still expatiating on the beauty of the stones, the lost legends of the caves.

"You see," he concluded, "for some people, this land meant death and exile. For others, like me, it's a paradise. One stone can contain more beauty than all man's artwork."

We loaded up the boat and shoved off. As we were pulling out, he caught sight of a white cross — a grave marker — above the lava rubble at the base of the cliff. "Someone died here. In the north, behind beauty there's always tragedy."

The river flowed on, silent, swift, and deep. An autumnal melancholy came to reign. The larches yellowed. Among them not a squirrel stirred, not a songbird cheeped, although once a day a raven flapped out to perch on some unsteady branch and croak a requiem for the dying summer. A gold-tailed russet fox had emerged from the taiga to watch us eat one evening; unaccustomed to people, he didn't fear us and wandered to within twenty yards of camp, his ears perked, his tongue lolling. He reappeared the next morning to watch us pack. We left him eager and panting like a pet dog to await our return. But we wouldn't return.

Finally, on a clearing beneath where cliffs on the eastern bank parted to let the Dyardyan River pour into the Lena, Vadim spotted the settlement of Dzhardzhan. We had to stop here: the previous day Vadim had put one of his boots on the pontoon gunwale to dry and it had fallen into the water and sunk. Maybe we could find a replacement.

Vadim raised his binoculars. "Hmm. It's no Sangar, that's for sure. There seem to be all of three or four houses."

"Maybe other houses are up there somewhere behind the rise. Why would they put it on the map if that was all there was to it?"

"Don't know. But I see . . . I see a man in a tracksuit watching me through binoculars. He's . . . he's watching me watch him . . . he's on some sort of barge parked below the houses."

As we pulled toward the curving sandy bank beneath the village, the man began waving at us and jogging along the barge's deck. He leaped off the edge and flew five feet down, plopping into the sand, and recommenced running toward us, his untied boots beating the sand, his beer belly bouncing like a big untethered breast. He was Russian, and looked to be in his fifties.

We pulled up to the shore as he trotted over to us. Panting and shaking our hands warmly, he introduced himself as Viktor, tugboat captain. He was tanned and ruddy. His gold teeth flashed in the sun and his abundant white locks glinted clean and smooth; his nose was pug. He asked what we were doing out here. Vadim told him we needed a boot and inquired about what weather we could expect ahead.

"Well," he replied, "about the boot I don't know. Maybe you'll find one here, maybe not. But you've got about two more decent days ahead of you. That terrible windstorm will be back. I feel it in my *bones*." He clenched his teeth and his fists with a sort of relish. "This summer's been cold. It's got to be climate change: birds we've never seen are appearing up here, and trees are growing farther and farther north."

"Have you heard a forecast?" I asked.

"Don't need one. I feel it in my *bones*." He shivered audibly. "But you can ask at the weather station. Right up there. I'll show you."

Leaving Vadim at the boat, Viktor and I headed up a path to the houses, where all sorts of rusted junk littered tall grass amid a half-dozen dilapidated larch huts. On one was a post box nailed to the wall, so I knocked on that door.

No one answered but the door opened from my blows. I leaned in. "Hello! Anyone here?"

Victor leaned over my shoulder. "Come on out, Seryoga! This guy needs a boot and a weather forecast!"

We peeked further inside. A graying but fit man in his forties wearing a threadbare tracksuit sat up on his bed and rubbed his eyes. He looked hard at me and frowned. He walked over and stuck out his hand, and as he did so a big smile creased his face. "Well, how are you? Who are you? How'd you get here? Boots? Probably there were no extras, but why shouldn't we take a look?" Seryoga accompanied us to the next hut, where we found the Dzhardzhan weather station crew, all Russians, in their kitchen-cum-bedroom. A bare bulb on a gnarled wire cast jaundiced light over moldy green-blue walls; food pots on a stove emitted fetid odors; three messy cots stood in the corners. Each cot had an occupant: a young fellow in jeans, with trim dark hair and clear eyes; a hazy-eyed middle-aged man in a worn tracksuit; and a third fellow in a camouflage jacket and hat, his mouth full of gold teeth. Only the youngster looked fresh; the other two moved as if in pain — possibly they were hung-over. They kept their eyes down.

I felt as though I were walking in on a quarreling family. In fact, I might not have missed the mark by far: they told me that they left the station only once every two years for a two-month vacation and were cooped up together the rest of the time. They had the look of lost sailors. Along the Lena, they were marooned in their settlement like survivors of a shipwreck on a desert isle. Could they tell us the weather ahead? No, in fact, they couldn't. "Our job is to gather and report data, not to make predictions," said the young one, looking at his tattered tennis shoes.

Over tea, I told them about Vadim and the boot. No, they were sorry to say, they had no spares, and it would be a year before they could buy anything at all. No problem, I assured them, but I wondered how Vadim was going to handle Arctic temperatures in one boot and one sandal, albeit with a sock on.

Viktor and I walked back down to Vadim and our boat.

"I couldn't find you a boot," I told him.

"Oh?" he said. He unzipped the food bag and took out his bottle of spirits, then set out for the houses, his poncho flapping like a cape in the breeze.

Viktor let Vadim pass out of earshot. "So, he enjoys a little —" he flicked his forefinger against his jugular, making the Russian gesture for hard drinking.

"No. He really needs a boot."

"That's what they all say." It was pointless telling a Russian that one needed an excuse to drink. "You know," Viktor continued, "you guys could never have stopped here in the old days. This was a military outpost. You'd have been arrested right away! I should know. This is my forty-first trip up and down Lena."

"You must love it out here."

"Oh, I do. I've worked all over the north, on the Aldan, the Yana, the Kolyma" — rivers even bleaker than the Lena. "I'm from Yakutsk. I'll never leave the north, *never*. It's in my blood. Everything is better up here, *everything*. People follow the Law of the North — that is, they're true to their word and they help each other out. What would I want in Moscow or some other city? I *hate* civilization. All I need is this air, this taiga. Say, what do you guys eat on the river?" I told him. "Dog food!" he replied. "I have something for you on my boat, just the thing you need. Come on!"

We trudged down the sand. We hoisted ourselves up onto the deck of the adjacent barge, and from there jumped onto his tugboat.

"Sasha! Bring us a cut of reindeer!"

Down from the bridge jumped a smiling young blond fellow in a sailor's striped shirt. He disappeared through a door leading below deck and came up panting, lugging a fifty-pound chunk of frozen meat the size of a car engine. He dropped it on the deck. It rolled over, splattering ice, and almost crushed my foot.

"Oh, thanks so much," I said, "but we'd never be able to eat all this. It would spoil."

"Your appetites should be *northern* appetites out here, my son. But I understand. Sasha, cut him a few pounds' worth."

Sasha detached a small ax from his belt and started hacking away, chunks of ice, meat, and bone flying in every direction, until he had cut free a ten-pound chunk.

"You killed it yourself?" I asked.

"No, but I know people in the villages who hunt. They gave it to me. I myself have given up hunting. I just can't watch the animals suffer anymore. You know, when the Communists were in power, the government gave the Yakuts everything, so they stopped learning how to cure meat. Lost their traditions and techniques. Now they kill a reindeer and take only the heart and brain — that's all they eat. They don't even know what to do with the rest, or how to preserve it. A shame. Let me show you my boat."

Leaving the reindeer on deck, we went below and toured dirty bunks and crumb-covered tables ("We spend many an hour here during storms, waiting around this table, drinking our vodka!") and checked in at the map-strewn bridge. These cramped and crummy environs were his world, and it was clearly all he needed; like Vadim, he could expound at length on why river life suited him.

When we emerged, the wind was picking up ominously again. We hurried off the tug and jogged back to our boat. But Vadim wasn't there.

Viktor smiled. "Ah, he's up there with the fellows." He repeated the drinking gesture and winked. "What did I tell you? Out here you can drink yourself to death pretty easily."

"Vadim's not that kind of guy."

"Well, he needs a boot, doesn't he? Just wait and see."

As the wind rose and a chill set in, Viktor's face darkened.

"I buried my wife just a couple of months ago. . . . My company is offering me an apartment in Yakutsk and a desk job. My kids want me to take it; they say it's time now, it's time. I may do it, you know, since they're offering it free. Just as long as I'm up here, in the north, I'll be happy." He paused. "My wife, you know, she . . ." His voice shrank and he rubbed his eyes. "Say, you're really going to Tiksi in this little boat? Remember, the winds and waves out here can break a barge in two. Very dangerous. We pull over to the bank when a storm hits; we can't risk it. You'll have to get off the river if a storm hits, okay? Up where you're going, it gets pretty bad."

As if to lend credence to his warnings, volleys of wind barreled up the river from the south. We had to get going. I thanked Viktor for the meat and our chat, and I excused myself to go get Vadim.

Up among the houses, the tall grass now danced wildly in the wind, and doors banged here and there, windows creaked open and shut. In the weather station's foul kitchen I found Vadim pouring spirits, toasting, and picking at shreds of salted flesh with the men. I thought he might be working on his boot, so I slipped back down to the boat to wait.

A half-hour later, he sauntered down the bank carrying not one boot but two, and both were new. His bottle was half empty, his steps ranging and loose.

"You got boots."

"I'm Russian," he said archly. "You're not."

"So?"

"So, spirit is the hard currency of the north. All I did was offer to drink with them. They *gave* me the boots for a little booze. But you're not Russian. You don't think in terms of alcohol. And so you didn't get the boots."

We jumped in and shoved off, with the wind, mercifully, at our backs.

Evening found us camped on a giant arching bend in the river, facing west to get the last warming sun of the day. Our gift of reindeer had thawed, and Vadim, sober now, hacked apart the meat. The choicest bits he fried and decorated with onion; the rest he boiled. Our stock of lunchtime sausage was now running low, so the reindeer would come in handy as a replacement.

Just as we were about to dig in, the gagging choke of an ancient outboard announced the approach of visitors — two Yakuts from white tents we had seen a couple of miles upriver. Wanting no one around our camp at night, Vadim had purposely driven well past them.

The boat turned out to be an unpainted tin-can wreck with a lidless motor and no glass in its windshield frame. A glum, possibly retarded unshaved young man was turning the wheel; a grandma in a white scarf sat beside him. Through the river now awash with reds and yellows from the sinking sun they cut a frothy swath, then shot past and turned sharply toward us, slowing as they approached. He cut the motor and she dropped the anchor. She greeted us in bad Russian, her voice singsong and chirpy.

"Would you like to buy fish?"

Her lack of teeth hindered correct pronunciation, turning the word *ryba* (fish) into *byba*. She pointed to the catch strewn over the boat's bottom: three man-size sturgeon, slimy, yellow-brown prehistoric creatures with spikes and ridges and fleshy whiskers on sharklike snouts. They seemed straight out of the Paleozoic era, and befit this ancient river. "Or how about this?"

She held out a bucket brimming with black caviar — tens of thousands of dollars' worth of roe, at Western prices.

"Oh, thanks so much," Vadim said. "We've got reindeer to eat."

"Why didn't you stay at our camp? We'd feed you and you'd be safe from bears there."

"We didn't want to bother you."

"It wouldn't bother us at all." She put the bucket down and gave me a once-over with her kind eyes. "Who is he?" she asked Vadim. "He doesn't look like he's from around here."

"He's from Moscow," Vadim answered.

"Oh! I knew it! He's not going to report on us to the government, is he? We're aborigines and have to eat whatever we can find, even this caviar! We have no choice! We're people too!"

"Of course I'm not going to report you!" I told her.

It must have been illegal to catch sturgeon during the spawning season. We thanked them anyway. Once they realized that they couldn't sell us anything, they revved up and drove off.

"Contact with aborigines of the north is fine," said Vadim, watching them depart. "In limited doses, of course. I admire them for their taiga survival skills."

Using round rocks as stools, we sat down, grabbed our plates, and bit into the reindeer. It was tangy and rich, if tough.

The air chilled and the wind faded. Set amid the orange-yellow ridges of a magnificent cloud-spread, the sun bled red into the river and a crescent moon silvered the larches' golden boughs, silvered the eddies in the molten currents.

Blowing down from the top of the world, the polar wind scoured the sandy cliffs and ransacked the river, raising spray. Fording breaker after swell, rise upon trough, we progressed so slowly that we seemed to be moving backwards; for us, soaked and shivering, time stood still. Finally the waters spread from one mile across to two and their course curved east. Above the spray, atop a bluff at the bend, stood a hodgepodge of derelict cabins; beneath them spread a broad beach strewn with wrecked wooden and steel boats. Siktyakh, forty-five days and 1,963 miles from Ust'-Kut!

"You don't seriously want to stop here?" shouted Vadim, clutching the flaps of his poncho beneath his throat. This was his usual refrain, of course, but this time I was almost inclined to answer no. "It looks like it's been abandoned for years!"

Just then, three dark supine lumps on the ground by one of the cabins lengthened vertically into youths standing in khaki coats and black boots. They began loping down the bank, bumping into one another, their gait loose with booze. We reached the beach when they did. They were Evenks or Yakuts. They grabbed our bow rope and yanked us ashore, and then lost their balance and tumbled back onto the sand.

"*Otkuda?*" (Where from?) one shouted above the wind, raising his head groggily.

"*Izdaleka!*" (From a long way off!) I replied.

I jumped ashore, and they clambered to their feet. They shook our hands, making loud inebriated queries as to where we were going (far), what we were carrying (just the essentials), and why we had stopped in their village (to visit the store). As usual, Vadim deployed his half-menacing jocularity to deal with them. And, just in case, the shotgun's double barrels poked up from the pile of gear near the stern, where he sat.

I slogged up the bank through the soft sand. Up at the clearing, dead grass covered dried earth in scraggly patches, as thinning hair does an aging scalp; but at least the bluff lessened the wind. By the smashed-up cabin where the youths had been crouching, a toothless Yakut in his thirties sat slumped on a stool, sand-caked spittle drooling from his chin. He smiled at me as I passed, and I waved to him; he grinned and looked away bashfully. A ways on, a teen with the eyes and plumpness of Down's syndrome smiled and rose from a bench to shake my hand; his fingers were sticky.

"Welcome!" he said in Russian, his tongue too big for his mouth.

Beyond him spread Siktyakh: a smattering of izbas, many old but others new; in contrast to those overlooking the river, none had been abandoned. If the exteriors were of weatherworn larch, in most homes brightly colored curtains hung behind clean windows; intact fences crisscrossed between houses, and plank walkways led hither and yon beyond the "center" — the dirt square formed by the post office and a couple of other semiofficial-looking buildings. Impressions from afar had deceived me; people here took care of their village, and Nyuya with its German exiles came to mind. Did exiles live here too? I wondered.

I needed to find a store, so I stopped a Yakut grandmother ambling past. In accented Russian, she directed me to an unmarked hut on the square. Feeling as if I were entering someone's home, I cracked the door and peeked inside, into a dim green room outfitted with wall shelves stacked with cans and unmarked tins; on the floor lay sacks of flour and grain. In the corner, two women were talking in Yakut to a cashier in a white smock and chef's hat, their language singsong and dainty. All had lustrous black or henna-tinted hair, high cheeks, and prominent chins. Yet their eyes were tiny slits, their noses buttons — characteristics that set them apart from most Yakuts I had met.

They paused in their conversation and regarded me with curiosity. The younger of the two customers, who looked to be in her forties, addressed me in delicate Russian. "You accept fish, don't you?"

"Accept fish?" I wasn't sure what she meant. Remembering how fast word of our arrival got around elsewhere, I took her query to be an offer of hospitality. "Thanks very much, but we have about twenty kilos of reindeer to eat."

The other two turned their brown eyes on me and gave me a puzzled look.

"Are you Ignatenko?" the first one asked.

"Who?"

It turned out that they had mistaken me for a Ukrainian merchant whose barge visits Siktyakh once a year and was in fact here now. They told me that he parks by the shore across the river and trades with villagers, bringing Siktyakh manufactured goods, medicines, schoolbooks, and vegetables in exchange for fresh fish — nelma, chir, and omul — and caviar.

She introduced herself as Anna; her pudgy older friend was Galina. Galina wore reading glasses, Anna earrings, accessories I realized I hadn't seen since Yakutsk. Both were dressed in neatly pressed pantsuits, the modern and tailored likes of which I hadn't encountered anywhere on the river. With me they spoke Russian (correctly and succinctly) but reverted to Yakut when addressing one another.

"All our men are over there now, at Ignatenko's," said Anna. "They're really partying. You see, we've had so much trouble with alcohol here that we've proclaimed a dry law in Siktyakh. So many men were dying out on the river, and here in the village, getting drunk and having accidents and fights. Also, in our cold, during the winter, you fall down or lose your way home drunk, fall asleep, and bang, you're dead. But across the river, once a year, they can have all the booze they like. At least with the dry law it's peaceful in the village."

The drunken youths who met us at the beach had no doubt just arrived from a spot of partying chez Ignatenko, I surmised. I told them about my trip down the Lena.

"Really?" they answered in unison. They shook their heads with evident misgiving.

"So, you fish for a living?" I asked.

"Our husbands do," said Anna. "We're the schoolteachers here. Say, would you like to see our school? Come! We've never had an American in our school before!"

We set out across the village. Though there were a few *Sakhalyary* here, most of Siktyakh's three hundred people were Evenks or a mix of Evenk and Yakut blood — hence the distinct features. Anna herself was an Evenk, Galina half Evenk, half Yakut. After each of my answers, they chattered in birdlike diction to each other, stifling chuckles, apparently as nervous as they were pleased at meeting a foreigner.

"You must not have had many foreigners here?" I ventured.

"Oh, no. We *have* had foreigners here," said Anna.

Galina elaborated. "Pan Gromadki. He was Polish. Exiled out here. You see, during World War II he fled to the Soviet Union from Poland. As far as we know, the Soviets caught him and banished him here. He was so noble and kind. He did everything for us: he built us an electric power station and taught us to farm potatoes; he even managed to grow flowers here! He married a Yakut girl. Nothing grew here before him, and nothing has grown since he died!" We passed the ruins of his house. "The Soviets never let him return to Poland, though he tried. He passed away in 1985. He was so cultured and intelligent, and we still miss him and talk about him. He had a daughter here. In 1992 she returned to Poland, and we never heard from her again."

"We miss them both," said Anna wistfully.

"He wasn't the only foreigner out here," said Galina. "We had a Chinese guy, a merchant. But he didn't last too long."

"Well, I'm not surprised," I replied. "After all, it would be tough to adjust. You're so far away from everything."

"Oh, he adjusted all right. But during the polar nights we have these blizzards, with snow as thick as milk. The snow blows so hard you can't go outside or you lose your way, even going from one house to the next. The snow covers the walkways and even the fences. He didn't listen to our warnings. He went out and got lost in the middle of the village and froze to death, a few feet from someone's house."

Anna asked if I had children. No. "Oh, at twenty-four or so everyone here marries and has children. If they don't, there's something wrong with them."

"So you have children?"

"Of course. I have three."

"So do I," said Galina.

"The collapse of the Soviet Union hasn't discouraged people from having kids here?"

Galina answered. "We're having so many children up here that the government is building a middle school for us. A hundred of our three hundred villagers are children, in fact. Their lives will be more advanced than ours. You see, I grew up in the tundra to the north and lived there until 1969. Out there we had quite a life and a lot of fun! We migrated to new places every week with our reindeer herds. I was practically born riding a reindeer! We had everything back then, in our yurt. We slept under nets to keep off the mosquitoes; we were clean and burned our garbage. We left no litter out there in the tundra, and we were one with nature. The government forced us to settle, but our parents returned to live in yurts for the summer. I'm sorry our kids won't grow up on the tundra, even if their lives will be more civilized."

Galina was the first "pure" Evenk I had met. I reflected on what little I knew, or is known, about them. A tribal people of animists, Evenks in Neolithic times had lived mostly around Lake Baikal, hunting and herding cattle. Conflicts with the Yakuts and Buryats pushed many of them north; others apparently assimilated with Yakuts or Russians and worked for them as hired hands. The Cossacks' arrival brought the Evenks smallpox, and vast numbers of those in the far north, maybe as many as four-fifths, perished. The Evenk language has largely died out in favor of Yakut, but they, like the Yakuts, had no way to write until they adopted the Latin alphabet in 1931; six or seven years later, at the height of Stalin's terror, they switched to Russian letters. Today they number about thirty thousand, and most are settled. Like many peoples of the north, they have abandoned their traditional garb of furs and sealskins for Russian clothes, and some have even adopted Orthodox Christianity.

The school occupied a half-dozen rooms in a new single-story building; it was clean and cheerful and had been painted recently. Children studied in Yakut and also learned Russian. Anna and Galina showed me large dolls dressed in traditional Yakut and Evenk clothing that they had sewn themselves; they had also fashioned tiny traditional sleds for them.

"We want our children to remember their roots and see how we used to dress," they told me.

After the tour, Anna invited us home. Her house was typically battered larch on the outside, with a heavy red steel door, but inside, with its white walls, clean tile floor, and glistening appliances and picture windows, it looked more cheerful and Western than the cabins of Russians I had visited. Her teenage son bounded past us on his way out, his hair dyed orange and nappy with gel; her beautiful young teenage daughter came out to say hello and then returned to her books. A grand wood-burning stove took up the center of the living room; opposite it stood a new refrigerator and a freezer.

"I traded fish for that refrigerator in Yakutsk," Anna said. "I'm proud of it!"

We took seats around her kitchen table, by a picture window.

"So, the government forced you to settle?" I asked.

"The Soviets came along and told us, 'Your reindeer are all sick and must be put down.' We said *no!* We knew they were fine. But they insisted. They slaughtered them all. We knew it was a lie. They knew that without our herds we couldn't live in the tundra. You see, they wanted to close down so-called unprofitable small settlements and get everyone living like Russians do, in cities and villages. They even tried to close down Siktyakh and make us all move to Kyusyur [a hundred miles downriver], where they built two-story houses for us. Some left, but not the old, and then even the young began returning. Now we're doing just fine here. Look at our children and how healthy they are! All over the north, school is called off when it hits fifty-five below, but not here. Our children are very hardy. And they go on to become doctors and lawyers!"

Siktyakh looked better than any Russian village I had seen since Korshunovo. The difference had to be the dry law in combination with the self-respect and pride that minority peoples in Russia often display.

Soon Anna's ancient scarved mother hobbled out, step by slow step, from an adjacent room, and Anna guided her to a seat by the table. She was almost completely blind and deaf. Anna placed a plate of fish soup in front of her, which she slurped loudly and messily. The elderly here as in much of rural Russia live with the children until death. She then set out tea, biscuits, and a plate of salted taimen for me. The taimen was succulent.

"Mother's a 'veteran of labor'" — a grandiloquent but essentially meaningless title the Soviets bestowed on millions to show that the Marxist state favored the working class. However, a minority veteran was something special. "She was a reindeer herder and a milkmaid and a boiler operator. Now she gets her pension — thirty-five hundred rubles [about $125] a month. The state gave her this house as a reward. The state in Soviet times used to do *so* much for us. In those times we had five or six propeller planes a day landing on the ice in the winter, taking our fish — one hundred and fifty tons a year! — and travelers back to the *materik*."

"And now?"

"We have a helipad, so if someone gets sick we radio Tiksi and have him evacuated. But that's it."

Anna told me that Siktyakh was about to develop and grow: the middle school would bring new teachers from outside, whom they would be happy to meet, and encourage others to stay; at the moment, after elementary school, children had to study in Kyusyur.

"We're very proud of our village," Anna said. *Pride,* it occurred to me, was a word I had heard nowhere else on the Lena. "The vice president of Sakha visited and commended us, saying we don't ask for money like all the other villages, or like Zhigansk. In Soviet days the government ignored us, but not now."

Galina said, "I bought an apartment in Tiksi, but I just can't live there. Since I grew up on the tundra, I need the earth under my feet, not concrete, so I prefer Siktyakh. I get headaches living in a cement building."

It was getting late. By now, Vadim would have understood that I had met people here, and set up camp down the bank; such was our usual agreement. Galina offered to walk me to the river, but Anna refrained. ("My husband would be jealous if he found out," she said, giggling.) So Anna and I said goodbye, and I set out for the shore with Galina.

"Say," Galina said, "have you been sacrificing to the fire spirit out there?"

"I'm afraid not."

"Bad, bad. From now on, each time you eat a meal, toss some food into the fire. I'm amazed you got this far with no sacrifices. And ahead, well, ahead . . ."

"Yes?"

"There are evil spirits downriver. Abandoned cabins. With bad histories. Drop some food in the river if you pass one, but on no account look inside. And steer clear of cemeteries. Our ancestors don't like people poking around their graves, stepping all over them."

"We'll remember that."

We spotted Vadim a mile down the bank on a sandy spot, stoking a fire he had made behind two rocks to keep out the wind.

"*That's* your boat?" Galina asked.

"Yes."

"Oh my God — we don't go to Tiksi in little boats like that! Oh, *please* pray to the spirits! There are evil spirits and bad *bad* places ahead! They won't let you pass!"

I introduced Galina to Vadim. She repeated her warnings to him. He chuckled but listened graciously, and then told her not to worry; we'd certainly do all the sacrificing it took to get to Tiksi. But the more she went on about the dangerous winds and waves ahead, the more upset she became. She finally told us that it would be impossible to enter the Laptev Sea in a boat as small as ours.

"Really, to have any chance, you *must* pay your respects to the spirits. There are no Christians up here, and our spirits run things. Here we all *must* respect them, okay? You too. Or they're not going to let you pass."

She looked at her watch; the late sunshine had caused her to lose track of time, and she had to get back to Siktyakh to make dinner. She was close to tearing up as she wished us farewell.

As she walked off, unsteady on the sand, we looked at the river, now gilt with the low sun, foaming and vast and violent, as angry as a slighted spirit.

18

THROUGHOUT THE PALE MIDNIGHT hours winds thrashed the Lena, but at dawn they ceased and a chilly sun rose over calm waters. We enjoyed ten hours of idyllic cruising from Siktyakh, gliding down the icy blue river between cinder gray mountains sprinkled with the last trees of dwarf taiga. Beyond the slopes the tundra began.

With our load decreasing as we consumed fuel and food, our speed was picking up, and we moved north, our spirits high, toward Kyusyur, the last real settlement before the Arctic Ocean. After my uplifting sojourn in Siktyakh, I was eager to see Kyusyur. The one English-language guidebook I could find that mentioned Kyusyur described it as "a regional cultural centre boasting schools, libraries, shops, hospitals and kindergartens," and all sorts of questions came to mind about how people lived so far above the Arctic Circle. I knew Kyusyur's history. It owes its origins to Soviet planners, who built it in the 1930s to lure Evenks off the tundra and into kolkhozes. My Russian reference book noted, "Reindeer herders settled into the warm, well-lit houses, became acquainted with Russian stoves, baths, hot water, steam, and the electric lamp. . . . The move from crowded, cold, and smoky yurts took time, and occurred gradually, and was a part of the struggle between the Old and the New. . . . Kyusyur is a cultural center for a large region." Both books gave us to believe that it was a unique outpost of civilization for such a latitude. We decided we would spend a couple of nights there resting up in advance of our final push north, through the notorious *Truba* and out into the Laptev Sea.

Late in the evening we rounded a bend and entered a wide glassy bay. Ahead, set against the barren summits and slopes of the Kharaulakhsky massif, Kyusyur appeared to rest on a bumpy band of flint floating between matching infinities of flawless azure. As we approached, the windows of its huts and hovels glinted amber and orange with the late sun. Beneath the settlement, boulders of blackened ice jutted up along the shores — remnants of the spring thaw, when floes eight feet thick from the Lena and hundreds of its tributaries surge, grind, and crush their way down the river (less than a mile wide here) toward the Arctic Ocean. In front of the floes pairs of teenage boys bathed, frolicking in the glacial water, impervious to the 45-degree air.

Vadim and I pitched camp a half-mile beyond the last huts, on a sandy cape separated from the settlement by a stream. We would have to visit the sites alternately, so as not to leave our gear unattended. While Vadim started a fire, I set out to do the town, hiking back along the shore past the ice boulders and bathers. I was energized by the thought that, once again, I was about to actually visit a point on the map that had seemed, ever since I developed a passion for Russia, impossibly remote, lost amid Siberia's terra incognita.

Yet once in Kyusyur I felt like fleeing. Under low clouds of smoke from coal-burning stoves, amid a warren of filthy gray-brown shacks luminous with light from the lavender sky, Evenk and Yakut men dressed in parkas and boots teetered drunk and reeking of urine along wobbly plank walkways running over black muck and tangles of uncut grass. As I passed them, these fellows blurted out greetings to me in mangled Russian; it seemed that in Kyusyur, everyone said hello to everyone else when outside. "'Dasst'yi! 'Dorov'! 'Dasst'yi!" the slurred chorus went. Yakutian horses snorted and grazed under the watchful eyes of child herders, who tossed stones at them to keep them together. A pair of Siberian huskies growled and fell in behind me, trailing me like hyenas waiting for me to drop dead. In the "center," two-story tenements, gimcrack and dark and dirty, revived memories of roach-infested lodgings I had known twelve years before, during my first trans-Russian odyssey. A Russian flag hung soiled and limp by a municipal shack, which was closed. Only the sunlight on the windows was clean.

Perhaps there was a "cultural centre" somewhere in Kyusyur, but all at once I felt fatigued with the expedition, fearful of the *Truba*, and anxious to move on. Was it worth spending two days here? At least we could buy bread and jam, I hoped.

I turned and headed back to the center. Down the planks strolled a young Evenk woman, shapely and scarved, leading a bundled-up toddler.

"*Zdrasst'ye!*" I said. "Is there a store open, by any chance?"

"*Zdrasst'ye!*"

She stopped, and, with sympathetic brown eyes, told me that no, in fact, the shopkeeper was away these days. There was no café and "of course" no restaurant. She interrupted herself to issue an order in Yakut to an approaching drunk. She shoved him (her husband? her brother? her father? His face was so swollen that I couldn't tell his age) in the direction of her hovel-house, and then asked me what I was doing here. I told her we were on our way to Tiksi. There was no point in hiding anything now.

"Oh, my!" she answered, shaking her head. "We fear the river. So many die out there. You need a big boat or you'll never make it through the *Truba!*"

The Pipe! Suddenly a hell of narrowing rock walls, churning waters, and Arctic storms flashed before my eyes. Her words decided me: we would not spend two days here, tempting fate by risking bad weather, but pull out at dawn. I thanked her and hurried back over the walkways, down to the river and past the ice boulders, and set out along the shore to camp.

Long before I reached camp I heard multiple male voices, peals of mad drunken laughter, bad Russian, and shouted expletives. Across the stream from camp I halted. A tin boat was pulled up beneath our tents, and three Yakut lads, who could have been no older than twenty or twenty-two, in khakis and boots were sitting with Vadim around our fire. Their oaths and stupid hollering echoed off the rocky slopes of the mountain opposite. They were passing around a gallon-size bottle of brown beer and taking sloppy guzzles. Vadim drank from it too and occasionally laughed with them, but mostly he tended a pot bubbling over the fire and glanced at his watch.

As I walked into camp, one of the youths jumped up and stumbled toward me, his arms outstretched. He gave me a bear hug; he stank of sweat, and his buck teeth scratched my cheek.

"*Mein name ist* Vova! I shpreakin' English! You shrpeaken *eet to-zhe?*"

Vova doubled over with laughter at his "English," as did his cohorts, corpulent Eduard and muscular Sanya. All three were bigger than I was, though smaller than Vadim. But, reflecting on warnings from people we had met in Sakha, I thought, *Under jackets as bulky as theirs they could easily conceal a hunting knife or even a gun.* Sakha was notorious for drunken knife fights and shootings, which often began over trifles and took place among friends.

All laughed and guzzled more beer from the bottle and laughed again, this time maniacally, in long hoots dwindling into giggles. How could one get so high off beer? Their drunkenness seemed almost willful, and I thought of the inebriated kids in the Yakutsk café with their nutty dancing.

I longed to climb into my tent and go to sleep. But Vadim hinted with a glance that we should not relax. Vova repeated his garbled "English" banter and asked me something I could not understand. He got angry when I apologized and asked him to say it in Russian. He grabbed my collar and shoved his face in mine.

"You come with us to hunt and fish down the river! We'll sell you a bearskin! You need a bearskin!"

"I'd love one. But it's illegal to take bearskins out of Sakha, isn't it?"

"Bullshit! I sell you a bearskin! Here, let's drink on it!"

He shoved the beer bottle into my hands. I raised the opening to my lips and tasted something foul; I made as if drinking but in fact blocked the opening with my tongue.

"You put vodka in this?" I asked afterward.

"No!" answered Vova. "Vodka *bad!* Bearskin! *Mein name ist . . .* One hunred tousand miyon KILL! One hunred tousand miyon KILL! KILL KILL KILL!"

He seized the bottle from me and gulped beer, then thrust it into Vadim's hands. Vadim, to my surprise, drank several hefty drafts from it. And, judging from his eyes, they weren't his first.

"Okay, guys," he said, "the meal's ready."

He had prepared two pots, one filled with buckwheat and reindeer for me, and the other, for them, of macaroni. He served them and they gobbled it off their plates, belching and drinking more beer and gobbling and belching, and laughing.

The air turned almost frigid; "KILL KILL KILL miyon KILL!" shouted Vova, done with his meal, ever hugging me and laughing and reeking, the bottled emptied. Would we ever get rid of them?

Across the north, alcohol has been the bane of indigenous peoples; introduced by the Russians, it has destroyed communities, ruined health, and wrecked families. I don't know what the stats are for Yakuts and Evenks, but certainly they consume more than the average Russian (almost five gallons of *pure* alcohol per year) and die even earlier (male life expectancy is fifty-eight, against seventy-five in the States, and dropping).

Vadim jumped to his feet. "Okay, guys, thanks for the visit! Now leave us in peace!"

Vova objected, but Vadim pulled him to his feet. The other two clambered up and began lurching down the bank, undone by their brew, angry at their own intoxicated clumsiness. Vadim walked Vova down to their tin tub and steadied it while Eduard and Sanya tumbled aboard. Free of Vadim's grip, Vova splashed into the water, leaned over the gunwale, and fell over into the boat. Vadim shoved them off. They fumbled with their motor for a minute but got it started and sped away, not looking back. Their wake sloshed against the shore, and the echoing of their motor against the rock walls finally faded.

"You handled them really well," I said.

Vadim had a funny look in his eyes. He doubled over and grabbed his gut. "Oh, I . . . I think I've been poisoned." He staggered off behind a nearby hill. Ten minutes later he returned, pale and sweaty from retching and more. He unzipped his tent and fell inside.

"Eat your dinner," he croaked. "Eat."

They had probably spiked the beer with pure spirits. I gave him tablets for his vomiting, then sat down by the fire to dine.

Alone on the riverbank for possibly the first time since Ust'-Kut, I looked around. As the air chilled further and midnight drew on, I pulled the folds of my jacket tight and experienced an almost indomitable desire to run, to escape these dead Arctic mountains, this cold river, the gloom and abandon that hung over these rocks now glowing preternaturally with reflected skylight; I might as well have been lost on Mars or Uranus. The *Truba* and the Laptev Sea separated us from Tiksi, but I longed to quit the expedition now, to free myself of the endless light that never let me sleep deeply. I washed down the last of my meal with doses of Vadim's honey-flavored spirits, which warmed me and lent flavor to my food.

Vadim snored. The air chilled more and the damp bit harder. I threw on another sweater. His honeyed spirits now coursed through my veins, expanding them, and my mood swung from desperate to inspired. I suddenly could picture the Ganges at noon, the Sahara at dawn, the

Ponte Vecchio of Florence, and, of all things, China, with its teeming millions, to the south. Mallarmé's lines *"La chaire est triste . . . fuir, fuir la-bas!"* ("The flesh is weary . . . oh, to flee, flee far away!") rang in my ears. Escape! "Anywhere out of this world" sounded Baudelaire's cry, but he was writing of Paris. Paris! As I savored this near-hallucinatory élan, my annoyance with the youths disappeared, and in its place came empathy. I thought of growing up in this bleak outpost. Up here, without radio or television, what was there to do but drink? A violent drunken spell might produce a catharsis, but even a glass or two of alcohol loosed the spirit to escape this pitiless domain of stone and ice, where man so clearly was never meant to be.

I stood up, unsteady, took a look at the violet sky, and turned in for the night.

Dawn came and went, the day aged and died, and violet returned to the sky. I would sleep for the next twenty-eight hours, with only minor intervals of wakefulness.

Two days later, thoroughly rested, we set sail early, launching our craft onto still waters, floating past more boulders of black ice. The mountains now shed the last remnants of taiga and became green-gray humps of bald stone, snow-capped and riveted with ice, that funneled the river north. As it had on the way to Kyusyur, the Lena once again unfolded a shimmering turquoise waterway of hope.

"It looks like we're in luck," said Vadim. "If ever we needed calm weather, it's now. Somewhere up ahead we'll enter the *Truba*."

"Maybe someone is drinking to us back on the mainland."

"Maybe."

Abruptly, an hour later, the river narrowed from two miles across to less than one, and the mountains closed in and steepened, rising bleak and charcoal-colored against radiant azure heavens, their slopes mottled with snow, the Chekanovsky range forming the western bank, the Kharaulakhsky, the east. The *Truba*. Yet the air remained still, the currents, now surging, smooth, and dark, well over a hundred feet deep. Vadim said nothing now, forgoing his usual prolix tales of northern adventure in favor of careful and constant perusals of the map and sky.

Free of the fear of storms, I sat and faced the stern. I shut my eyes and dreamed of arrival in Tiksi. I was soon asleep.

· · ·

I awoke with my head resting sideways on my forearm, facing a thousand-foot rock wall. My eyes focused on a white stone pillar on a shelf at its base. It quickly receded from view as the currents carried us faster and faster toward the delta, the Arctic Ocean.

"Someone drowned here," said Vadim quietly. "The pillar's a memorial."

I looked ahead, down the dark winding chasm leading us north; the hulks of the Kharaulakhsky resembled tombstones stretching away into infinity. Pillar after pillar came into view, white against iron gray, announcing tragedy and death.

Vadim fidgeted in his seat. "We've got to press on and make Tiksi, and fast. God knows what weather awaits us."

I turned to answer. Behind him the southern sky had blackened. A low mass of storm clouds was gaining on us, advancing like an airborne tsunami subsuming mountain and river, and the winds pushing them transformed the Lena's smooth turquoise waters into ridges of pewter.

"Vadim, look!"

He swiveled around and raised his binoculars. "I don't believe it! A *southern* storm, *here?* How can this be? The cold air should be pushing weather down from the *north*." He rifled through the pages of our map, ordering them so that no paper protruded from its plastic case. He threw on his camouflage poncho and tied a dark camouflage bandana around his head. "Get ready!"

I barely had time to throw on my rain gear. Within minutes the wind struck, ripping past, roiling the waters, raising swells that powered us forward in great foamy sweeps over olive green depths. From clouds so low that they shrouded the summits rain battered down, frigid and soaking, drawing around us thrashing veils of silver-gray. The sky and river melded into a froth, through which waves, five-feet high and then six, propelled us in lurching bounds; in the troughs I felt a queasiness in the pit of my stomach. Water crashed at times over our stern and I bailed, noting the absence of a saving shoreline.

For six hours the storm assaulted us. Then the clouds and rain rolled north toward the North Pole, past us, leaving us drenched and dazed with fatigue, numbed in the deepening cold, but beyond the *Truba.* The winds kept on.

· · ·

Early that evening (too early, I thought), as the winds sped our advance, Vadim steered us toward the western shore, a rock beach marked with screes tumbling down along the base of tundra-covered mountains.

"Why are we stopping so early?" I asked, needing to shout above the wind but finding my voice breaking; I almost lacked the strength to speak. "Don't we need to move as quickly as possible now?"

"Look," he said, his own voice weak. "Just look." He pointed ahead to the north, to where the delta should have been. There was no horizon, only a wide expanse of crashing waves, a bizarre fusion of sand and spray overhung by the dark summits of empty stone mountains. "We've got a long open stretch, and we can't risk it in this wind. We'll be stuck here as long as it blows this way."

He showed me the map. A bay five miles wide preceded the delta. To the east, across the river, spread tundra, green and yellow, but just to the north hunkered more mountains, more black cliffs, in the lower reaches sodden from rain and mantled in snow atop the summits. The last of the Verkhoyansk. Seeing this, shivering and wearied, I felt I had reached, or neared, a breaking point of sorts. I lacked the desire to ask about the puzzling maelstrom ahead.

As our pontoons hit the beach, Vadim and I stumbled out and dragged the craft ashore. The cliffs here would shelter us from the wind.

An eagle — a turkey-size ball of brown and white feathers — sat atop the lichen-covered cliff a few hundred feet above us, screaming.

"That's a young bird," said Vadim. "He wants his mother."

I could see why.

I put on warm, dry clothes from the bottom of my pack. Later, finding conversation with Vadim difficult owing to our depressed moods and the cacophony of waves, I climbed up the natural stone staircase of a streambed, where water trickled toward the river beneath ice shards from the cliff. I reached down and cupped a drink. Could any liquid on earth have tasted purer? I climbed and climbed, now and again imbibing this glacial ambrosia. Forty minutes later I reached the top, four hundred feet above camp, and surveyed the tundra carpeting the massif beyond, a lumpy prairie bound in the north by the sullen ridges of Mount Chekanovsky (on the Arctic Ocean), swept by gales howling out of the south with such velocity that I had to sit on my haunches or risk being blown over. Squatting, I examined the lichen-carpeted plateau of tiny purple and yellow wildflowers. My readings told me the tundra, which covered a third of Sakha, should be a more colorful mat of red polar poppies, crimson moss, rosy ivan-chai. But the unseasonable cold had killed all except daisies. I started back down.

Vadim had laid out a feast of cold smoked reindeer and sturgeon, with warm buckwheat and hot tea. As usual, he had made the most of an unpromising spot, building his fire next to a rock wall that protected it from the wind, and setting out round stones on which we could sit in relative comfort. The shelter also allowed us peace of mind. He talked about what we had seen since departure: the temperate paradise near Ust'-Kut; the Lena Pillars north of Sinsk; the island-studded wandering waterway around Yakutsk. And what of all the people I met? When would I ever return to see Luka and his grandfather in Verkhnemarkovo? Irina and the teens in Korshunovo? Tatyana in Yakutsk? About these variegated lives I could draw no general conclusion, arrive at no answer to the grand question, Whither Russia? As Russia decayed, these Siberians soldiered on, finding ways to live and enjoy life — that much I knew, and it was enough. As Vadim talked, I kept their memories to myself, knowing he would care little to hear of them.

He poked at his food and stirred the fire's embers. He pensively rubbed his forehead, now brown with dirt and sun. "Soon it's back to the city. We've lived an entirely separate life out on this river. We've risked our lives. And yet at home, it will be as if we never left. We'll never be able to explain what we saw, never be able to pass it on."

I had not grown close to him. Surely he disdained me, believing that I valued less the wonders of nature, more the traumas that made up the history of his people, the unworthy "herd" for which he had almost died in war. But now, fatigued with the expedition, at the edge of this raging river, I said nothing more than "da," and turned in for the night.

The wind hollered on, casting up a surf that crashed over the banks; now and then eagles screamed. The Pipe was behind us, the Arctic Ocean ahead. I was, all in all, thankful to have Vadim at my side.

"Davay, sobirrraysya!" (Come on, get ready to leave!) Vadim shouted the next morning, above the gales. They had not lessened, and I was surprised to hear his call. I had suspected that we would wait out the storm. But no, we got going early and launched into heavy surf.

Through weak sunlight, newly cold tail winds roared down upon our raft in gusts that propelled us from one six-to-seven-foot swell to another, from each wave's crest down into the yawning trough ahead, passing us in relay fashion over angry brackish depths. Along the eastern bank, across three miles of foam and spray, stood the last vestiges of the Verkhoyansk, the Kharaulakhsky; their moss-mottled escarpments of black stone and sheer walls offered us no hope of refuge. To the north, across a six-mile-wide sea of swells, sands swirled beneath black stony mountains — the same maelstrom that had blocked our view the previous day.

"What is that?" I shouted, pointing to the sands.

Vadim had been eyeing the swirling haze through his binoculars. "The sandbanks of the delta!"

The delta, finally! A hundred and twenty-five miles wide, sixty-five miles long, covering nineteen thousand square miles and embracing fifteen hundred islands and sixty thousand lakes, the Lena's delta is exceeded in size only by the Mississippi panhandle. It is nothing short of an ecology apart, the preserve of 30 species of rare plants, 32 kinds of mammals, and 118 species of birds, for which it serves as a summer breeding ground.

But out on the waves we had no time to ponder these features. The waves rose higher. I gripped the crossbeam, facing astern, soaked and shivering from the constant wash of spray. With his camouflage poncho ballooning with the wind, his turquoise eyes set deep in bronzed, begrimed sockets, Vadim kept his gaze set ahead and gripped the outboard's lurching handle.

"We've got to get ashore," he shouted. "These waves'll do us in!"

With each swell pushing from behind, our craft dove nose-first into the preceding trough and we risked being swamped. We could not cross the waves and turn to head ashore — there was no shore on which to land, only rock wall. We could only keep on, hold tight, and bear the waves as they hit. Two hours later we penetrated the sand-and-spray maelstrom and came within sight of crooked tombstones and crosses of driftwood on a low sandy bluff, and, beyond, boxy cabins crouching against the wind, near shipwrecked tubs. Tit-Ary, the last and remotest village of the Lena.

Waves hurled us ashore beneath it. We stumbled out onto the soft sand, dragged the raft up, and collapsed. We lay and rested, too fatigued and relieved to budge, with the sand hissing against our ponchos.

After a while, Vadim rolled over onto his stomach and examined Tit-Ary through his binoculars. "It must have been abandoned. No sign of life."

The driving sand stung my face. I rose and walked down the beach toward the shacks, my feet slipping on the soft dunes, passing three or four rusted cutters. At the top of the bank I took the measure of Tit-Ary — twenty or thirty tumbledown cabins of salt-ravaged larch, most with collapsed walls, caved-in roofs, and glassless windows, scattered over a patch of tundra set against a moil of whirling sand and spray extending beyond the delta to infinity. But the village had not been abandoned, at least not entirely: here and there smoke issued from chimneys. I noticed fish, scaled, cleaned, and headless, caked in sand and swinging in the wind, hanging like laundry on a cord in front of the nearest cabin. I started walking toward it. When I was a few yards away the door swung open and a Yakut woman, short and stout, trudged out of the dark with a bucket.

"*Zdrasst'ye!*" I said, my words lost to the wind. Her eyes down, she trudged past me. A moment later she returned from behind the house, her bucket slopping fresh water. This time she looked up: the sight of me startled her into a spasmodic step backwards, and she dropped her pail.

"Oh, I'm so sorry!" I said. "I didn't mean to scare you. I said hello but you walked by."

"Who are you?"

"I'm traveling to Tiksi. I'm an American."

"A what?"

"An American. From the United States."

"The United what?" She finally smiled and stepped up to me. "Come inside and meet the men."

She yanked me through the door into the cabin, which was illuminated by sepulchral light seeping through tiny, spray-spattered windows rattling with the gales. The room was blue-walled, cluttered with stacks of dried fish and canned goods and boxes of sugar and tea. A blubbery-lipped young fellow, apparently retarded, sat on a stool and stoked the embers in a wood stove. He smiled at me, his tongue half extended. By a wooden table sat a toothless ancient and a middle-aged fellow, their arms crossed against the chill. All were indigenous, all wore fishermen's caps, hip-high boots, parkas. Girlish giggles sounded from a doorway leading into another room; two teenage girls were sitting on a bed and playing some sort of board game. Their skin was as pale as the moon; their cheeks were much higher, their faces flatter than those of Yakuts and Evenks, their eyes elegant brown slits, their hair long and glistening and tied in ponytails.

The retarded fellow bashfully looked away when I extended my hand, so I shook hands with the men by the table. The younger introduced himself as Manchara, the elder, Ilzar. Their words sounded garbled, as if spoken through marbles — an accent like none I had heard before.

The woman addressed me in ungrammatical Russian. "Sit, please. May I make you some macaroni and sausage?"

"Thank you, yes." I pulled up a chair, and saliva squirted in my cheeks at the names of such exotic dishes. She lit a match and turned the nozzle on a gas canister fitted with prongs; a flame arose. Then she blew the dust off a box of macaroni and poured the pasta into a tin pot and added water; she hacked at a baton of meat with a rusty knife.

Ilzar stared at me, or stared through me. Blasts of wind shook the cabin. Manchara spoke as though talking in his sleep. "What you doing out here?"

I told them about my expedition. Their faces remained blank. To break the silence, I asked, "Are you Evenks?"

Manchara raised his eyebrows, surprised. "You know about Evenks?"

"I've met quite a few coming down the river."

"Ah. No, I'm Yakut. But these folks are Evens."

"Evens?"

"We're an obscure nationality," said Ilzar.

He was right. Numbering about seventeen thousand, the Evens live in the harshest corners of Russia: along the Arctic Ocean's shores, on the Kolyma River, in Chukotka and Kamchatka, and on the coast of the Sea of Okhotsk. Like the Yakuts and Evenks, their original home was far to the south, near Lake Baikal, but they hightailed it north in the Middle Ages to escape the Yakuts. More historical exiles.

They asked me about my origins. It took me several minutes to convince them that I was not Russian. That I was American seemed even tougher for them to grasp. As the news sunk in, Ilzar worked his tongue over his gums; Manchara's eyes widened but then went dull again. The fire-tender wagged his tongue and squinted. All sat in silence.

"Well, do you fish out here?" I asked.

Manchara responded, "We fish and herd reindeer. But the RevCom made all the Evens join the state reindeer cooperative."

"The RevCom?"

"The Revolutionary Committee. They abolished the cooperative, saying, 'Join the kolkhoz.' But they didn't want to. So they executed them all."

He had to be referring to events in the late 1920s, when the state set about collectivizing agriculture and forcing nomadic herders to surrender their animals to kolkhozes. He talked as though this had all just happened.

"Now we're free again and have formed a family cooperative. But maybe they'll just abolish it and execute us again. What do you think?"

His words came out flat. The old man rubbed his eyes with his knuckles.

"I doubt they will," I said. "Wasn't all that pretty much related to communism?"

Manchara shrugged.

The woman finished cooking my meal and placed it before me. I thanked her and dug in.

"Are you from Tit-Ary, Manchara?"

"Oh, no. I was born in Tiksi. Come here on my snowmobile when there's ice, to fish. Stalin exiled my father here from Churancha, in 1942. I was born in Tiksi after they released him. Poles and Lithuanians and Finns were here in Tit-Ary too, all exiles. Back then, this village was an armed camp. The guards forced everyone to fish. Couldn't eat the catch, had to give it to the state. People starved. A bullet in the head if you ate your own fish."

"Are there any Poles or Lithuanians left?"

"Dead. All died out here. Cold and no food. And bullets. Say, we've heard Putin wants to take away our republic."

"That's what I hear. So I suppose you don't support him."

"Sixty-four percent of Sakha voted for him."

"Do you support him?"

"Things would be different if we had moved from Gorbachev and perestroika to democracy. But instead, we . . . we . . . You have democracy in the U.S. A good democracy, a perfect democracy, right? People are happy there, right?"

All faces turned toward mine. "I wouldn't say that. Certainly not since the elections of 2000."

All dropped their gazes to the floor.

"We're a minority people and have a tiny number of votes," said Manchara. "Our voices are never heard. We never . . . no one ever . . . The RevCom . . ."

The wind whistled through cracks around the window. The slobbering guy tossed a log into the stove and a gush of steam and sparks poured out of the aperture. He stomped on the embers.

The old man stared at his feet. Manchara closed his eyes. Even the teens in the next room now looked morose. *Dead Souls* came to mind. Dead souls! Dead souls! All around me were dead souls! Questions about tyranny and repression that appeared to have been settled in 1991 were resurfacing. The people sitting around me — how far *gone* they were! Why was Russia always despairing, angry, riddled with disaster, reeking of death?

Looking at the eyes of my hosts, listening to their drugged-sounding speech and the gales outside, I felt like fleeing. What a calamity the Cossacks' voyage through these parts now seemed, for indigenous peoples and Russians too! As inevitable as the Cossacks' march eastward had been, their annexation of vast Siberia had conferred on Russian rulers an equally inevitable obsession with becoming a power as great as their landmass and wealth — the primum mobile of repression from Ivan the Terrible to Stalin and beyond, and one that constantly trumped their peoples' desire for a decent life. In attaching Siberia to Russia, the Cossacks had unwittingly sealed the fate of Russia's citizens, who would live forever after as servants of one power or another, be it the Kremlin, the Winter Palace in Saint Petersburg, the *mafiya*, or the current corrupt state, for only the threat of violence could forge unity and obedience among people inhabiting such daunting, isolating expanses to which no human really belonged, yet which contained riches no state could renounce. In short, everyone in these barrens was an exile, if an unfettered one — an important point. Most people I had met on the river were getting by, even the Evens, and, for the first time in recent history, living in relative freedom.

I began worrying about the weather and Vadim. "I've got to get going," I said. "Thank you so much for the meal and the talk."

The woman smiled. The teenagers gave me a sad look, as though sorry to give up my curious presence. The men grunted farewell.

I opened the door and walked out into the winds. As I turned toward the river, I caught sight of the crosses atop a sandy hillock, standing stark against the thunderhead-filled southern sky. To whom did they belong? I followed a path their way, and I was soon trudging through waist-high grass, passing from one wrecked rowboat to another — they must have been there for decades, beached by floodwaters.

Something rustled and thudded behind me. I turned around to face a black Caucasian sheepdog — the fiercest breed in Russia — with the height and meaty build of a wolf. I turned away and slowly resumed my steps, but then a rustling of trampled grass preceded a bruising bump against my rear.

The dog had butted me and was bearing its fangs and growling deep, its eyes ablaze. Yelps came from the grass just ahead: there sat two fat black puppies. Slowly I picked up a shard of rowboat hull and walked away from the puppies and eventually out of the sheepdog's sight.

The crosses, of crooked driftwood and much abraded by blasting sand, stood over graves at the edge of the bluff overlooking the stormy bay we had just crossed. Before them all was a giant steel cross, a monument to Stalin's victims — the exiled Finns and Lithuanians interred there. A plaque at its base read TORN BY VIOLENCE FROM THEIR NATIVE LAND, FALLEN, BUT NOT FORGOTTEN. To my horror I saw that the wind had blown away the sand to expose the coffins. Some of them had warped open.

I stared at the coffins. There was something telling in their exposure. Since 1991 the passage of time and disillusionment with "democratic reforms" and the mass impoverishment they generated, plus no small measure of political guile, have largely wiped clean the Soviet slate, once so clotted with blood. If the people along the Lena are any indication, the majority of Russians will not resist a return to authoritarian rule; they are now too fatigued, too disillusioned and misguided, too dispersed across a giant hinterland, and too *atomized* to resist. Here and there monuments have been erected to the crimes of the Soviet era, but they are ill tended, and what do they mean besides the poverty and neglect people in the outback endure? Their souls were not really dead; they could be roused if the right leader came along. But probably, I sensed, roused to revolts similar to the doomed mutinies launched by the Cossacks against the tsars.

Sunlight fell on my face. The wind slowly died. I raised my eyes: to the south, the sky was clearing! I turned to head back to the boat but at once saw that in the sky to the north, over the Arctic Ocean, black clouds were massing, trailing rain. The roaring rush of an oncoming freight train sounded: gales battered in from the north, bringing mists, and soon all was lost in blowing sand and spray.

I stumbled through the graveyard, reached the edge of the bluff, and slid down it toward the boat.

"Come on," shouted Vadim. "We've got to get a move on or we could be in trouble passing the cape!"

We shoved off and set out in pitching leaden waters, skirting the black bulk of Krest-Khaya Mountain, the vertical walls of which banished any thought of an emergency landing. Now the winds and waves whirled and skirled, leaving us rocking amid waves that again dumped water into our craft as fast as I could bail. One bad swell and we would find ourselves washed overboard, clawing at rock walls, killed by the blows of the sea.

Yet Vadim never wavered. He steered us east into Bykov Channel, which would lead us to the Laptev Sea, with a dark mass looming in the fog just to the north — Stolb Island, a 350-foot-high pillar of stone that guards the Lena's mouth. It signaled tragedy. In 1879, out at sea forty miles beyond it, ice floes had trapped the ship of the nineteenth-century American explorer George Washington De Long and held it captive for two years before crushing it to pieces. Despite a blizzard, De Long and eleven of his men escaped on sleds and in lifeboats to reach the outer delta. But there they starved to death. A year later, their remains were discovered and buried in the delta, on Khugel'-Khaya Mountain. An archipelago of islands bears his name to this day.

In the channel, waves and currents bouncing off Krest-Khaya

kicked up a *boltanka* without warning, imperiling us anew. Only the serendipitous appearance of the polar station Sokol, on a lichen-covered cove at a break in the rock walls, saved us.

We came ashore and set up camp, soaked and frozen and exhausted once again. I was surprised by my own reaction to danger. I found myself not in fear during moments of peril but more alive than ever, feeling the visceral rush of adrenaline. Surely at such times, when closest to death, one is more alive than all the living.

19

POLAR STATION SOKOL consisted of four or five homey shacks outfitted with meteorological measuring instruments scattered across the lower reaches of a tundra-carpeted valley ending in a pebbly cove by the sea. The seven-person crew welcomed us warmly in from the storm (which died soon thereafter), letting us camp on their shore and feeding us a dinner of black bread, boiled potatoes, and rich Siberian dumplings smothered in sour cream. As we sat in the dining room of the main shack, the station's chief scientist warned us that the weather here changed every three hours. Contrary to Vadim's expectations, one could not count on northern winds. For now, the barometric pressure had stabilized. Did that mean we would have smooth sailing to Tiksi tomorrow? Impossible to predict, given the brief cycles.

Soon after we finished eating, a tugboat pulled into the cove, spoiling the transcendental placidity with its cranky sputtering motor and tooting horn. One of the crew came huffing up the path from the cove and informed me that I had to take my passport and permits and present myself to the official from Tiksi aboard. Immediately.

With some foreboding, I grabbed my papers and jogged down the path to the boat. High gunwales marked it as a craft, like the Cossack *kochi*, that could handle all manner of sea and possibly ice. On the pointy prow stood a short mustachioed man in his forties with a Brillo pad of black hair. In his black suit, black shirt, and stiff polyester white tie, he resembled a pint-size Mafioso, if one dressed in off-the-rack garb from a discount clothing store in Norilsk rather than in fashions from Naples.

"You the American?" he asked, his gold teeth flashing, as I approached the boat.

"Yes. What's the problem?"

"Get up here at once." I climbed the wobbly gangplank leading up to the deck. "My name is Petrov. I'm from the Tiksi Department of the Ministry of the Protection of Nature. Come with me into my office. *Immediately.*"

I followed him into his "office" — a paper-strewn cubbyhole beneath the bridge.

"Take a look at these." From his breast pocket he produced a laminated identity card, and from a folder he extracted a plastic-wrapped official letter stamped with an ornate seal, the text of which affirmed, to whomever it may concern, his position with the said ministry. The documents appeared to be authentic. He cocked his head, raising his wiry eyebrows. "Are you aware that you're on the territory of a state preserve? Where's your permit from our ministry permitting you to be here?"

"I'm traveling under the auspices of Dmitry Shparo, holder of the Order of Lenin, and I have all the permits I need — from the FSB, the government of Sakha, and the Russian Border Guards."

"Ah-ha, ah, ah. Right, sure. Show them to me."

"With pleasure."

He wiggled his fingers. We would duel *à la russe,* playing "my documents are bigger than your documents." I handed him my sheath of papers, also plastic-wrapped, emblazoned with sundry seals, signatures, and Cyrillic initials. I tossed in, for good measure, lab results certifying (as the government of Sakha required of foreigners on its soil) that I was free of HIV, tuberculosis, the plague, and other communicable diseases.

I might as well have shown him the crayon doodlings of a preschooler. He licked his forefinger and turned each page, sniffling. "*This* paper here? It's *not* from *my* ministry. And what about this little paper? Not from *my* ministry either. And *neither* is this. No, no, no." He chuckled, arching his brows. "You are *illegal* here. Simply illegal."

"I'm sorry, but Shparo contacted everyone in Moscow and Yakutsk, including the republic's president, to arrange these permits. They suffice."

"Oh, they do, do they?" he answered. "Look here, I'm from the federal government, not some bureau in Yakutsk. You are in *big* trouble. You'll either have to come with me now, on this boat, to Tiksi, where my boss will decide what to do with you, or you can sign a statement admitting you've violated Russian law. The fine will be forty thousand rubles [about $1,400], and once you've made a statement, only a court of law can repeal the fine."

To be sure, he was angling for a bribe, the amount of which would be far less than the "fine" (if such was in fact provided for by law), and which I would pay him for the immediate dismissal of my "case." But I had come almost 2,200 miles down a dangerous river, and I wasn't in the mood to be intimidated.

"I'm sorry, but I suspect that a permit from the FSB" — which Putin once headed, and which has thoroughly reestablished itself as the key authority outside the Kremlin — "outweighs the Ministry of Nature." This Tiksi pencil pusher, I judged, would not dare confront the president's former fiefdom. Even juxtaposing, in one sentence, "Ministry of Nature" with the organization whose predecessor ran Stalin's death camps diminished him and discredited his "charge."

My words only rankled him further. "*Oh?* You can tell *that* to my boss in Tiksi." He straightened his plastic tie — he was a Big Man out here, a don in Russia's *mafiya* state. "Or you can sign a statement stating you've broken the law. And pay the fine."

"I'm sorry, but I'm not signing anything without a lawyer present, and I'll pay you no fine. And I emphatically refuse to abandon my trip in the very last stretch. My guide and I have covered more than two thousand miles and risked our lives to get this far. I won't quit now."

"Your guide? Where is this guide? Call him this instant."

I stepped outside to go get Vadim, but he was already mounting the gangplank. I quietly explained the situation to him. His eyes lit and his face reddened. He pushed passed me, coming face-to-face with the official as he stepped out of his cubbyhole.

"Show me your documents," Petrov ordered. Vadim complied. "Ah-ha, ah-ha, right, sure. As I just told this American, you're camped illegally on a state preserve." He grabbed his official letter of introduction off his desk and pushed it on Vadim. "As I told him, you have to either sign a statement or —"

Vadim wouldn't touch the letter. He cut him off and stepped into his space, towering over him, pushing him back into the cubbyhole. "We have all our permits," he said, his voice fraught with bridled anger, "and we haven't done anything wrong. You have no business interfering with our expedition."

Taken aback, Petrov nevertheless repeated his charge, adding,

"Please sit down quietly and do *not* raise your voice to me. I'm a government official, not a drunk in a bar."

Vadim jabbed his forefinger into his cheap tie, pushing his red face close to Petrov's paling mug. "I *have* to raise my voice to you. You're behaving like any stupid traffic cop in Moscow creating false pretenses and demanding a bribe!"

Petrov leaned away, his hands shaking enough to make his papers tremble. "I repeat, please, that I'm a state official and you must sit down and lower your voice when addressing me. You and the American have violated the law, and the American no doubt will tell you that in his country there would be consequences. Either you write out a statement or —"

Vadim took another step closer, and Petrov backed into the window, his body thudding against the glass. "You *dare* — YOU DARE — to call yourself a state official? You should *respect* your office, and *cherish* your duty, and not make false charges! You know perfectly well what you're after! We haven't violated *any* law by landing here!"

"Please, lower your —"

"You really want to bring a problem on yourself? You really want to see what happens if you press this?"

"Please, calm down, and — "

"Acting like this, you *disgrace* your office, you *disgrace* our government, you *disgrace* Russia!"

Petrov broke into a sweat and stammered, speechless. In all my years in Russia I had never seen the implicit threat of violence used against a bureaucrat, and neither had I heard such words of genuine outrage expressed at a venality most Russians would take for granted. They would try to strike a deal, pay up amicably, and be done with the matter. I remembered Solzhenitsyn's lamenting the passivity that only emboldened Stalin's executioners. If everyone forswears resistance and submits to injustices, only more injustices result, and each uncontested instance of abuse sparks more. Since almost everyone pays bribes, almost everyone is guilty; citizens thus forfeit the right to expect decency, honesty, or efficiency from their public servants, who in fact are so poorly paid that they often turn to graft to survive. Yet as much as Vadim threatened with his gestures and tone of voice, he addressed Petrov with the respectful *Vy* form, and his words contained nothing obscene.

Petrov finally wavered. "Then, well, okay, then you can write me an explanatory note. I mean, please write me such a note, and we can forget about this misunderstanding."

Vadim slowly backed off. Petrov straightened his tie and ran his fingers through his Brillo hair, then pulled out a blank sheet of paper.

"Give me a pen," Vadim said. Petrov scrambled to find one on his person.

Later, after the tugboat had raised anchor and left the cove, I asked Vadim what he had written.

"What do you think? I wrote that the storm forced us ashore."

I had been in Russia so long that I hadn't even thought of offering that saving excuse — the truth. But Petrov had validated Vadim's remarks about what he wanted most from his government — that it leave him alone.

The next morning, in dreamy sun-gilt doldrums, we packed up, said goodbye to the Sokol crew, and pulled out into Bykov Channel, again finding ourselves floating past black mountains capped with snow, their gloomy bulks stretching away down the coast. We hoped to reach Tiksi by late afternoon.

How relieved I was. The expedition had taken its toll, at least on me. I had lost ten pounds, found my skin cracked and chapped from the damp and cold, suffered constant cramps in my legs, and grown weary of the winds and waters, of the ceaseless vistas painted from the most somber of palettes.

Two hours out of Sokol the weather spoiled. In from the Arctic Ocean rolled dark mushroom clouds and cold storm winds pushing banks of fog. The temperature plummeted from the fifties into the mid-thirties, and rain dowsed down. We crashed anew through waves and spray; our speed slowed from ten miles per hour to six, and then to three. We hugged the shoreline, wanting to keep well away from the pewter wastes of sea roiling north out toward an infinitely harsher world of ice floes and polar bears. I tossed on everything I owned, and still I froze. In the middle of August it simply should not have been this cold.

Now and again the storm clouds parted to disclose a firmament of brilliant azure. The landscape, all snow dust and withered yellow lichen and wet rock mountains overrun by windblown mists, put me in mind of the Ice Age. I stared into the wastes and saw Russia as vast and frozen and underpopulated, under the stomping boot of history. I saw Russians, their character forged by these frigid wilds, seeking extremes as freezing men seek fire, their heroism in wartime — or, indeed, in peacetime under their own repressive regimes — flowing from strength acquired by resisting the blows of a punishing climate.

Shivering and soaked, I turned and faced Vadim at the stern. At times he had been truculent, and I impatient, and we had quarreled. But I had come to admire him. No matter how high the waves, he never lost his grip on our throttle, never took his eyes off the horizon, never slackened in spirit. He was resourceful in turning desolate stretches of bank into comfortable campsites. Nikolai Nikitin, a prominent Russian historian and the chronicler of Semyon Dezhnyov's exploits, might have been writing of Vadim when he described Siberia's Cossack explorers as "harsh, merciless, but always hardy, steadfast, and courageous, hesitating neither before the boundless Siberian expanses nor its inhospitable weather nor its thousand unknown but unavoidable dangers." Vadim carried the indomitable spirit that allowed Russia to expand across eleven time zones, turned the country into a superpower (if an erstwhile one), and kept Russians marching forward, through trauma and disaster that would have broken lesser peoples. Not surprisingly, Vadim insisted that he admired strength and strongmen most of all — whether good or evil — and had no faith in democracy taking hold in his country. His powerful presence reminded me that whichever path Russia chooses, the rest of the world will have to take notice.

In midafternoon a *boltanka* hit. Gales and whipping rain followed, and then snow flurries. Vadim began piloting the craft toward a rocky cove at the foot of an icebound mountain. "That's it!" he said. "We've had it for the day."

"But we're so close to the end! We risked it at other times, so why not now!"

"No way! It's too rough! With our map's big scale, and with these mountains all looking the same, I can't even determine our position. We're quitting now."

And so we came ashore. We were either ahead of or beyond Cape Taudakh, but that was as much we knew. Perhaps we had twenty-five miles left to Tiksi, perhaps more.

In the pounding rain coming off the Arctic Ocean, with the Laptev Sea's surf crashing at our stony bank, we pitched camp. I tried to dry out my clothes in my tent, but it was hopeless. Vadim used a tiny gas stove to cook our meal, there being no longer any driftwood for a fire.

Outside the world was gray and cold and wet; the sky gray and lowering; the rain falling in rippling sheets of lusterless gray, thrumming on my tent. Fog drifted through my ventilation flap, bringing the damp to me. I ended up crawling into my sleeping bag — which was dry — to warm up and, listening to the surf, thinking of nothing, I dozed off.

"Could it be? No. No. It *couldn't* be."

Out on the water the next morning, Vadim was sitting astern, squinting into his binoculars, trying to steady himself against the *boltanka* that was besieging us out in Neyelov Bay. We had broken camp just two hours ago and had covered only a few miles, hindered by waves and mounting headwinds, with yet another weather-imposed sojourn on shore looking likely.

I turned to face forward. On a distant ridge leading down to the sea hunkered cement barracks, dark against the stormy sky.

"A gift of fate!" Vadim shouted. "A gift of fate! That's Tiksi!" With his words rain began to fall again, driven by the wind in blinding torrents. "We must have camped just shy of it!"

An hour later we pulled up beneath abandoned warehouses, a blue shack, and a beached barge: the disused port of Neyelovo, which at one time received much of Tiksi's traffic. An army truck with oversize wheels stood by the shack on high lichen-covered ground.

We looked at each other. We jumped into the waters and stepped onto the gravel. In a strangely unexpressive way, tired and soaked, we shook hands and said congratulations, then began unloading in the cold drizzle.

A little while later, Vadim jogged up to the shack. A few minutes later he jogged back. "I got you a ride into Tiksi."

"Aren't you coming?" I asked.

"No way. I'd rather stay out here until you settle how we're getting back to Moscow. Whatever Tiksi's hotel is like, it can't be better than this shore and my tent. Just come get me the day before the flight."

"Suit yourself."

I grabbed my pack and took out my permits, which the military in this closed settlement would surely want to see. Vadim lugged his sack and tent down the bank.

Up at the truck, a portly young blond sergeant in a khaki parka and black boots stood smoking a cigarette. He looked glumly at me and exhaled. "So you need a ride?"

"Yes," I said, growing almost giddy with our arrival.

"Well, throw your gear in the back and climb in." He tossed away his cigarette, jumped in the driver's side, and started the truck.

From the shack emerged a crisp-looking lieutenant, dark-haired and trim.

"Where you headed?" he said, climbing in beside me.

"Tiksi. The hotel."

"You come from?"

"Ust'-Kut."

The sergeant pulled out and wrestled with the wheel, steering us onto a potholed gravel track leading toward the barracks. A golden eagle flapped away from the shoulder. Neither officer responded to my words; perhaps they had never heard of Ust'-Kut, thousands of miles and a republic away.

"I need to see the base commander," I added, naming the man. Both then politely asked who I was and what I was doing here.

I told them, and they enthusiastically offered to put me up at the Arktika military hotel, on their base, the barracks of which we had first seen from the water. I politely declined. I wanted the comforts of Tiksi town, hidden behind the ridge ahead, and fast.

20

Black raven, I'm all yours.

—RUSSIAN FOLK SONG

LIKE A VISION from a gulag survivor's nightmare, Tiksi's frost-ravaged tenements and half-ruined log cabins hugged the last, snow-sprinkled slopes of the Kharaulakhsky Mountains as they swept down to the stormy sea. As we roared into town, cutting through drifting banks of fog, stray dogs cringed and skittered out of sight, and pedestrians clad in dark soiled parkas, wandering in midroad, stumbled out of our way. The only vehicles about were trucks, grimy Soviet-era behemoths spewing fumes and rocking over potholes in cement-slab streets. Giant rusted heating pipes snaked across junk-strewn fields. Yet above this panorama of decay and decrepitude, slogans painted in ten-foot red letters (GLORY TO LABOR! CHILDREN ARE OUR FUTURE! BLOOM, MY BELOVED YAKUTIA! RUSSIA IS OUR HOLY COUNTRY!) covered the pockmarked façades of the hilly center, announcing that this town of five thousand people, mostly Russian military and state functionaries, but, increasingly, Evenks and Yakuts fleeing impoverished villages, used to be a quintessentially Soviet redoubt — that is, a settlement closed to outsiders (for security reasons, this being a border zone and military port) in a hellish corner of the planet that no sane person would want to visit anyway.

Cossacks sailing east in the 1630s were the first Russians to set foot on the then uninhabited shores on which Tiksi now sits. But none other than Dmitry Laptev himself (the eponym of the adjacent sea), a participant in the Second Kamchatka Expedition led by the Dane Vitus Bering, was the first, in 1739, to record the spot on the tsar's maps, calling it Guba Gorelaya ("burnt bay"). In 1932 the Soviet government established the settlement of Tiksi to service the country's Northern Maritime Route, which runs along the Arctic coast from Archangelsk to the Bering Strait. Icebound for nine or ten months of the year, the route nevertheless played a key role in Stalin's plan to exploit the region's resources. Tiksi's population — in Soviet times numbering almost twelve thousand — enjoyed high pay and privileges for enduring tours of duty that included 60 days of polar nights (nicknamed by locals the *Polyarka*) and 120 days of gale-force winds a year, plus January temperatures averaging −30 degrees. "The winds here can move a twenty-ton container, and the blizzards are so bad, you can't see the hand in front of your face," an officer posted in Tiksi later told me.

Delivering as a valedictory the usual warnings about predatory Yakuts ("They think this settlement is theirs to destroy, so be careful of them day and night"), my two officers dropped me off at Tiksi's hotel and roared away. The hotel, a four-story edifice slapped together out of prefab concrete blocks, occupied the third floor of the municipal building that, it turned out, also housed the local museum, the district attorney's office, a dozen ad hoc stores, and a café that sold cheap vodka in addition to food; hence, criminals, drunks, prosecutors, and shoppers ambled through the dim halls in one noisy stream. It didn't matter to me. All I wanted was a hot shower, a bed, and a meal cooked in something other than Vadim's pot.

I mounted a cement staircase and opened the hotel's spring-powered door, which slammed with a gunshot bang once released. I pushed through the crowd to the glass reception booth, in which sat a smiling female clerk with big dark eyes and high Evenk cheeks.

I leaned down to speak into the waist-high slot and asked for a room, ignoring the outstretched hand of a disheveled Yakut beggar dressed in a parka-and-boots ensemble that seemed to consist of two-thirds cloth and rubber and one-third congealed bodily fluids. The clerk took my passport through the slot and asked if, being an American, I'd like the "deluxe suite" for thirty dollars a night. The beggar leaned into me, his breath sour with vodka and rotting teeth, and squealed.

"I'll take it." The beggar started yanking my sleeve and reaching for my passport. "Say," I asked the clerk, "is it safe here?"

"Of course! Welcome to Tiksi!"

She handed me the key and I climbed the stairs, the beggar following me, moaning, down an unlit corridor.

I found my room and slipped inside, closing the door on my malodorous pursuer. I put down my gear and rushed straight to the bathroom and turned the red knob in the "shower" — a rubber tube hanging over a rusty bathtub. Out streamed ice water that grew colder the longer it ran; the cold knob produced no better. The "deluxe suite" had no hot water now, this being a "warm month," said the receptionist later, of "rain and snow, not just snow"; so the town had turned off the central heater.

I decided that I should be glad of even cold water, knowing what the first Soviet pioneer builders suffered through here in the 1930s. They had arrived on barges in early September, a grim, slushy month of storms and bad winds. There were no cranes. They manually unloaded their tools, construction supplies and equipment, provisions, and whatever else they needed to survive, including cows and pigs. Instead of the horse-drawn carts used elsewhere in rural Russia at the time, human-drawn carts here were the norm: three men strapped into harnesses dragged while four pushed from behind. Living in tents heated by wood-burning stoves — even these were luxuries and so were known by the nickname *burzhuyki,* from the French "bourgeois" — for two months, they labored in foul weather to build a meteorological station, as well as shacks and shanties in which to live, hurrying to beat the onset of winter. Thanks to their labors and the work of those who followed them, within a couple of years Tiksi boasted a port, a shipyard, and a construction base.

But now least of all I wanted to reflect on past hardships. I wanted to savor the unique sense of deliverance that comes with completing a grueling journey, and I had my traditions. As preparation for a thorough cleaning and ordering of everything with me, I took out all my gear and spread it about my cavernous two rooms, noting the gray patterned wallpaper and synthetic beige curtains that would keep out the white night and afford me sound sleep. I checked the mattress (no bedbugs) and found it firm. There were no roaches anywhere — also a plus. I shed my insulated arctic suit and boots and rain gear, and showered under a copious stream of ice water, nonetheless pleased at having no mosquitoes to shoo away, no rocks to slip on, no bucket to fill and refill. After toweling myself dry, I put on my city clothes (jeans, oxford shirt, sweater) and sat down on the couch. Rain was thrumming on the windows.

Now warm and dry, in fresh clothes, I surveyed my belongings, growing drowsy. My journal, a green-covered notebook I had bought in Nigeria two years earlier, lay on the table, battered and creased, open to the entry "Korshunovo, 1 July 2004." I picked it up and straightaway felt a pang of nostalgia, a surge of melancholy. Korshunovo! There, two thousand miles back and what seemed like years ago, I had met the teens at the village discotheque. Their welcoming smiles and baby-fat cheeks came to mind; they would encounter a foreigner for the first time only once, just as they would be teens only once, and only once would I ever walk into their lives unannounced.

I flipped ahead, landing on "Nyuya, 8 July 2004." Would Sophia and Jakob, the German exiles, last until I made another trip to their village? Probably not. Finally, I chanced upon my entry for Sangar. Vera was the eidolon of innocence and beauty, but how long would she remain untainted? And how long before heart disease and strokes would start to pick off my boozing partners there? If I felt lucky to have met these people, I also grieved for their passing — their passing from *me*, for time, distance, and circumstance would probably keep us from ever meeting again.

Putting down my journal, I leaned back on the sofa and stared through the window into the foggy sky. After leaving Ust'-Kut, which now shined in my mind's eye a luminous vision of lavender heavens and soughing poplars, of young mothers strolling along a spruce-lined river, of drunken teens hollering their youthful glee into the glowing night, I felt I had sailed through purgatory. But I thought again; the hardships and people of my last weeks on the river left this impression. In most villages I had come across at least *some* whose fates I had to regard as tolerable, and, in a few cases, enviable. Even the German exiles had found their peace. This I had not expected. Sometimes we have to see things for ourselves.

Though Russia's superpower status has passed, Russians along the Lena are finding ways to live free of national ambition, shorn of the messianic ideals that had imbued their history after Ivan the Terrible's rise. With the Muscovite elite it is another matter, but for most Russians of the outback, life is Mama in the muddy village, Papa in the crumbling city along the railway tracks — life is *family* in places that are *home*, before notions of "reforms" or "democracy" intrude. Now as ever, the Kremlin is profiting from the apathy and passivity of its populace to entrench its power, but, with a repetition of Stalinist excesses improbable now, no one I met really seemed to care.

Deciding I would take stock of my effects later, I put away my journal and went downstairs to the café. There I ordered two helpings of cutlets and mashed potatoes and ate a Mars bar for dessert — a feast for me now. Men in dripping rain gear slogged in, bought beer and vodka and cabbage pastries, and slogged back out. The café's sole employee was a Russian woman in her late thirties named Klara. Wearing a smock over her slender yet slack-fleshed figure, she had dyed her long hair a rusty shade of yellow, daubed her crow's-feet with rouge, and gobbed her lashes with mascara. Her husky voice, rasping from a lifetime of cigarettes and alcohol, endeared her to me immediately.

I went up to pay her for my meal. She took my rubles and smiled, and asked who I was. I told her about my expedition and wondered aloud where could I go in Tiksi to pass the evening. Not to worry, she said: she and her girlfriend would show me the town.

"Meet me outside at seven," she said, "once I'm done with work. Of course, this isn't my usual job. I'm really a sailor. I plan on leaving for the sea again very soon."

Klara emerged from the eternally slamming doors on time, and her friend Tamara (another Russian) soon showed up. Tamara was a manager at Tiksi's port; she had bobbed flaxen hair and love handles. We set off down muddy paths and ended up by an unmarked two-story yellow cement shack with boarded-up windows.

"This is our restaurant," they said.

Klara knocked. No answer. She knocked again.

The door swung open. "What the hell do you want?" shouted the middle-aged doorwoman, a snarling, hefty troll topped with a bristly mop of peroxided hair. "Why didn't you let us know ahead of time you were coming!"

"Is that any way to treat customers?" replied Klara. "Why not just save your breath and slop shit on us instead!"

"Yeah!" chimed in Tamara. "We don't have to patronize your establishment!"

"Then don't!" The troll slammed the door.

In fact we had no choice, so we forced our way in despite the troll's objections and climbed the stairs to the dark wood-paneled bar on the second floor. We sat down. Still muttering at us but now resigned, the troll flicked on red, green, and white Christmas lights strung with tinsel and hanging behind the bar — the only illumination. A glum aproned barwoman took our orders of beer, peanuts, and steak with fries.

During my first years in Russia, such rudeness shocked and angered me, and I would yell back or at least mull over potential remedies for it in future reforms, in the entrenchment of the free-market mentality, and so on. But now I knew that the lives of these employees (and of Russian women in general) were much harder than mine would ever be, and that "reforms" might not help. So I ignored their surliness and smiled, earning their puzzled glances, and savored my return to Russian civilization, enjoying the shelter and warmth I had lacked on the river, plus the company of my hosts. I chewed salted nuts and listened to them talk of their glorious Soviet past.

"We felt like such pioneers out here! ... The state used to supply us with only the priciest delicacies! ... We knew only luxury! ... Our husbands used to fly to Moscow just to have a beer!"

Tamara and Klara told me, without rancor or despair, that most Tiksians were stranded. They had nowhere to go on the *materik* and their lives were destined to decay, with the port in decline since the collapse of the Soviet Union and the death of most plans for Siberia's development. These were facts that they had to accept, the result of a national cataclysm over which they had no control; they weren't angry. Both had found their own ways to enjoy life.

(Not all in Tiksi had, of course. The next day, Tamara's daughter, a shy flower of a girl home from university in western Russia, took me on a tour of the Tiksi of her youth. Under rheumy mists and drizzle, we picked across the rusting junk fields of her old neighborhood.

"All my childhood memories from here are happy," she intoned. "But when I returned this time, I saw that Tiksi is dying. Everything is closed up or collapsing. There, see that ruined building? That's where we lived when I was a kid. Just beyond, there's a building with smashed-in windows and no roof: that was my school. And that club over there, it's still running. But Yakuts have taken it over, and they get drunk and have fights, so we Russians stopped going long ago."

"Where's your father?" I asked, with some trepidation.

"Papa's an alcoholic. He's dying. All his internal organs are failing.

He's only forty but he looks seventy. I saw him when I got home and started crying. My sister and I are trying to convince Mama to divorce him and save herself. When I finish college, I'm going to get a job and get my mother and sister out of here, to western Russia.")

As I talked with Klara and Tamara, the bar filled with a somber, rain-splattered crowd: delicate Evenk women and young men, Russians and Yakuts, mostly sloshed and stumbling. Both sexes wore black leather. One loud youth staggered in, holding his hand to his ear and shouting into a cell phone. But there were no cell phones in Tiksi, and his hand was empty.

"He's drunk himself out of his mind," said Tamara, looking at him. "He was such a good boy, and now he's killing himself with vodka." He lurched toward our table and extended his hand, wanting money for booze. "Get away from our table! Get away!" she said firmly, and shoved him toward the bar. Another man, in his middle years, babbling and slobbering, pulled up a chair, but Tamara pushed him away too. "March!" She watched him stagger off. "My former neighbor. Also drinking himself to death. Men!"

"If I might ask," I said, "if you don't drink in this bar, what is there to do in Tiksi?"

"Drink at home," Klara said. "There're no cinemas and no theaters. When we go out here, we drink. And when we stay in, we drink."

The troll soon showed up, grabbed the drunks by the collars, led them away and down the stairs, and ejected them into the drizzling white night outside. The cheerless barwoman brought us our entrées. Still remembering Vadim's pot and canned dishes, I tucked in with relish. The barwoman broke her set frown and smiled at me, as did the troll bouncer.

A couple of hours later the young and not so young, all decked out and made up, surged through the entrance, climbed the stairs, and massed around double doors just outside the bar.

"Oh, come on!" said Tamara and Klara. "It's disco night!" I paid and we joined the thronging crowd.

The double doors opened and Russian pop blared from speakers on the floor. Green and red lights flickered on a spinning disco ball, above a dance floor onto which the crowd poured, laughing, many stumbling. We joined them in dance. Drink has always been the Joy of Rus'; grief, the constant; and carpe diem, the only philosophy of escape.

Amid the jostling elbows and excited drunken smiles and hot bodies and loud, ever-*louder* music, the lonely wilds of the Lena receded from my consciousness and I felt delivered into the sweaty arms of humanity.

A few days later, as snow fell, Vadim and I boarded the plane for the weekly flight to Moscow. It would take us nine hours to fly six time zones back, across Siberia and over the Urals — terrain the Cossacks had adjoined to Russia over the course of a century. As we mounted the sky I turned and looked down on Tiksi through falling snow. Someone, someday, may find a "solution" for Russia's ills. It won't be me.

Acknowledgments

I would like to express my gratitude to the Russian polar adventurer Dmitry Shparo, whose assistance made possible the expedition recounted in this book, and to his staff at the Adventure Club in Moscow, who aided me in dealing with bureaucratic matters, historical research, and outfitting, among many other things. To Vadim Alekseyev, my stalwart and skilled guide, I owe the expedition's success. At the *Smithsonian*, which published my article describing the expedition, I owe thanks to Terence Monmaney, executive editor, and to Carey Winfrey, editor, for their editorial, moral, and financial support; and to Lucinda Moore, associate editor, for her diligent research, which finds reflection in the book as well. As always, I would like to thank my agent and friend, Sonia Land, for her faith in me and her vigor in promoting my work. Finally, my wife, Tatyana, gave me a reason to wish for homecoming and the strength to endure all the grueling, soaked, near-hopeless weeks of travel that preceded it. Here words of gratitude fail me. Her spirit, cheer, and love pervade every page of this book, and every hour of my life.